D1752882

Researching Literacy in a Foreign Language
among Primary School Learners

Forschung zum Schrifterwerb in der Fremdsprache
bei Grundschülern

INQUIRIES IN LANGUAGE LEARNING
Forschungen zu Psycholinguistik und Fremdsprachendidaktik
Edited by / Herausgegeben von Christiane Bongartz / Jutta Rymarczyk

Vol. / Band 1

PETER LANG
Frankfurt am Main · Berlin · Bern · Bruxelles · New York · Oxford · Wien

Bärbel Diehr / Jutta Rymarczyk
(eds. / Hrsg.)

Researching Literacy in a Foreign Language among Primary School Learners

Forschung zum Schrifterwerb in der Fremdsprache bei Grundschülern

PETER LANG
Internationaler Verlag der Wissenschaften

Bibliographic Information published by the Deutsche Nationalbibliothek
The Deutsche Nationalbibliothek lists this publication in the Deutsche Nationalbibliografie; detailed bibliographic data is available in the internet at http://dnb.d-nb.de.

Cover Design:
Olaf Gloeckler, Atelier Platen, Friedberg

ISSN 1868-386X
ISBN 978-3-631-59500-8
© Peter Lang GmbH
Internationaler Verlag der Wissenschaften
Frankfurt am Main 2010
All rights reserved.

All parts of this publication are protected by copyright. Any utilisation outside the strict limits of the copyright law, without the permission of the publisher, is forbidden and liable to prosecution. This applies in particular to reproductions, translations, microfilming, and storage and processing in electronic retrieval systems.

www.peterlang.de

Vorwort

Sprachenlernen/ *Language Learning* ist das Bindeglied, das die naturwissenschaftliche Forschung der Psycholinguistik und die anwendungsorientierte Forschung der Fremdsprachendidaktik zusammenführt. Lange Zeit wurden die Disziplinen getrennt voneinander behandelt und die Betonung lag auf den disparaten Anteilen der beiden Gebiete. Vergleichbar zur Annäherung der Begriffe „Spracherwerb" und „Sprachenlernen" (*language acquisition* und *language learning*) ist jedoch seit einigen Jahren eine Annäherung der Psycholinguistik und der Fremdsprachendidaktik zu beobachten. Während die Psycholinguistik den schulischen Kontext des Spracherwerbs stärker beachtet, ist aus der Fremdsprachendidaktik die empirische Forschung nicht mehr wegzudenken, die linguistische Phänomene der Interaktion im Klassenzimmer beleuchtet.

Mit der Reihe „*Inquiries in Language Learning*. Forschungen zu Psycholinguistik und Fremdsprachendidaktik" wollen wir dieser Entwicklung Rechnung tragen. Da die Schnittstelle der beiden Forschungsgebiete, die durch die Reihe bedient wird, naturgemäß eine hohe Interdisziplinarität aufweist, strahlt ihre Relevanz in unterschiedliche Richtungen aus: Einerseits braucht guter Fremdsprachenunterricht Lehrkräfte, deren methodisch-didaktische Entscheidungen auf detaillierter Kenntnis spracherwerbstheoretischer Aspekte beruhen. Das Schreiben von Lehrbüchern für den Fremdsprachenunterricht muss auf einer soliden empirischen Basis geschehen. Andererseits bedarf die Interpretation psycholinguistischer Daten der Vertrautheit mit Unterrichtsabläufen und den Ritualen, die Vermittlungsprozesse prägen. Das Entwerfen eines psycholinguistischen Forschungsdesigns muss unterrichtstechnische Aspekte einbeziehen, um letztlich authentische Ergebnisse abbilden zu können.

Mit der Gesamtschau unserer Arbeitsbereiche hoffen wir dem Ineinandergreifen und den Verschränkungen von psycholinguistischen Grundlagen und fachdidaktischen Weiterentwicklungen, von Theorien und Methoden sowie von Forschung und Praxis gerecht werden zu können.

Christiane Bongartz
Jutta Rymarczyk

Contents

Deslea Konza, Leanne Fried, Maureen Michael
Responding to the challenge of teaching English language skills 13

Thorsten Piske
Positive and negative effects of exposure to L2 orthographic input in the early phases of foreign language learning: a review 37

Bärbel Diehr
Research into reading in the primary school: a fresh look at the use of written English with young learners of English as a Foreign Language 51

Jutta Rymarczyk, Annika Musall
Reading skills of first graders who learn to read and write in German and English 69

Amparo Lázaro Ibarrola
English *phonics* for Spanish children: adapting to new English as a Foreign Language classrooms 89

Stefanie Frisch
Bewusstmachende Verfahren beim Umgang mit dem Schriftbild im Englischunterricht der Primarstufe – erste Ergebnisse der LiPs Studie 107

Petra Burmeister
Did you now that 15 difrent Fish arts in the Kiel Canal live? On foreign language writing in partial immersion primary school classrooms 131

Constanze Weth
„Wörter, Wendungen und Sätze so aus dem Gedächtnis schreiben, dass sie eindeutig erkennbar sind": Überlegungen zum Umgang mit Schrift im frühen Fremdsprachenunterricht 147

Dieter Mindt, Gudrun Wagner
Das Schriftbild im Englischunterricht der Klassen 1 und 2 167

Authors 197

Preface

The idea for this publication arose from the compelling papers presented at our symposium *Researching literacy in a foreign language among primary school learners* (*Die Schriftsprache im Fremdsprachenunterricht der Grundschule*) conducted at the 15. World Congress of Applied Linguistics (AILA) in Essen on 25 August 2008. The conviction that literacy among primary foreign language learners is essential was reinforced by certain curriculum decisions, but, importantly, it was also based on direct observation of many primary school English lessons.

In 2004, the two federal states of Baden-Wuerttemberg and Rhineland-Palatinate decided to introduce English as a foreign language in primary school from grade 1 onwards. What is surprising, however, is that both, the syllabi in Baden-Wuerttemberg and Rhineland-Palatinate strongly suggest that written English should not be used before grade 3. Yet, our observations in numerous classrooms showed that young learners explicitly ask for written forms. If the written language is kept away from the classroom, learners begin to invent their own spelling rules. We realized that research into the early use of written English from grade 1 onwards, was urgently needed, to avoid risking the fossilisation of inaccuracies. To a certain extent, the ministry of education in North Rhine-Westphalia caught up with us, publishing a new syllabus in 2008 requiring teachers to use the written form of English from the second half of grade 1 onwards, but to our knowledge that decision was not accompanied by empirical evidence of L2 literacy learning. So, the need for empirical research, justifying the early use of written language, still continues.

At the time of our symposium there were many questions still waiting for an empirical answer. The most pressing issues were, and still are, related to:

The starting point
- When is the best time to introduce the written form of the foreign language?
- Should the written form in L2 be introduced parallel to L1 or at a later stage?
- Is it necessary to wait until all learners have firmly established their L1 literacy?
- Is it necessary to wait until they have mastered L2 oral skills?

The groups of learners
- What effect does a parallel introduction have on different groups of learners, on poor learners, on struggling readers, on children from a multilingual or migrant background?
- Are the effects beneficial or detrimental to their language growth?

The teaching approaches
- Where can teachers find methodological support for their teaching?
- Should they resort more to the so-called top-down approach or to the bottom-up approach?

The symposium brought together a selection of groundbreaking research being conducted into some of these issues. With this publication the results of this research are now available to a wide range of readers, including researchers, teachers, graduate students and policy makers in this field. The authors in their various ways challenge assumptions held too long in this area: e. g. that primary school children need to be literate in their first language (L1) before they can confront written English.

Deslea *Konza*, Leanne *Fried*, Maureen *Michael's* chapter "Responding to the challenge of teaching English language skills" leads in the discussion of early literacy from a native speaker point of view. The Australian authors analyze the most effective methods of developing initial reading skills and relate them to the English as a Foreign Language (EFL) context with the complexity of the English language in mind. Paying due respect to the difficulties for foreign language learners, they invite the readers to consider the potential of the notion of "challenge" as an element of effective teaching and learning. This idea of posing challenges undoubtedly provides food for thought for everybody involved in the further development of foreign language classes for young and very young learners where – as it is the case e. g. in Germany – current efforts mainly aim at the protection of poor learners who are thought to be easily overtaxed.

In his paper "Positive and negative effects of exposure to L2 orthographic input in the early phases of foreign language learning: a review", Thorsten *Piske* explores the controversy when primary school students should start learning to read and write in a foreign/second language. He provides a concise review of both arguments for and against simultaneous first and second language literacy instruction. Against the strong objections of some researchers to the simultaneous introduction of foreign language reading and writing in the early grades Piske suggests that early exposure to two writing systems may be beneficial for learners' literacy skills.

It is Bärbel *Diehr's* aim to offer a lens for understanding of systematic approaches to reading in the EFL classroom at primary level. Her chapter "Research into reading in the primary school: a fresh look at the use of written English with young learners of English as a Foreign Language" introduces the LiPs scheme designed to foster early literacy and to support both students and teachers alike in their common endeavour. Diehr's innovative concept is empirically well founded as it is based on the results of a prior research study into early reading. Such a solid empirical basis is still hard to find in the relatively new area of research into the field of early foreign language literacy.

Jutta *Rymarczyk* and Annika *Musall* look at the "Reading skills of firstgraders who learn to read and write in German and English". The results of their research study prove the ability of even poor learners to cope with simultaneous literacy acquisition. No negative transfer from the children's English into their German writing could be found. More diverse results, however, were achieved with respect to the children's reading skills. On the background of the children's use of German phoneme-grapheme-correspondences in their reading English, their good reading comprehension takes us by surprise. Clearly, here, more empirical data is much asked for. Taking all results into account the authors advocate the integration of the written form from the very beginning of early EFL classes.

Amparo Lázaro *Ibarrola's* article "English phonics for Spanish children: adapting to new English as a Foreign Language classrooms" offers suggestions for using the phonics approach to engage very young Spanish children in the EFL classroom. She stresses that phonics laid a solid foundation for the further learning of the foreign language as reading skills are crucial for success. Here the author puts forward a new perspective since she is referring to the age group of three-year-olds. After all, up to now phonics has been regarded as a rather analytical way of dealing with language which is not commonly associated with very young children.

Stefanie *Frisch*'s contribution "Bewusstmachende Verfahren beim Umgang mit dem Schriftbild im Englischunterricht der Primarstufe – erste Ergebnisse der LiPs Studie" brings us up to speed on awareness raising approaches and explains that using phonics only with first language readers represents a missed opportunity for all EFL students. On the basis of a qualitative study Frisch provides educators with insights into how firstgraders learn English grapheme-phoneme-correspondences with the help of awareness raising activities. This first hand experience certainly belongs to the very few current accounts on actual classroom interaction.

In her chapter *"*Did you now that 15 difrent Fish arts in the Kiel Canal live?* on foreign language writing in partial immersion primary school classrooms" Petra *Burmeister* pursues the pressing question of whether early partial immersion students should obtain systematic reading and writing lessons in English or whether they are able to transfer their literacy skills as they go along in their literacy acquisition in German. Some learner texts show that the transfer actually works but the author still asks what support tailored to the needs of the young immersion students should look like.

With Constanze *Weth*'s article „Wörter, Wendungen und Sätze so aus dem Gedächtnis schreiben, dass sie eindeutig erkennbar sind": Überlegungen zum Umgang mit Schrift im frühen Fremdsprachenunterricht" the scope of this publication is extended to include French as a Foreign Language. Weth proposes an approach to a definition of 'recognisable' writings in order to make the requirement in the Baden-Wuerttemberg curriculum viable, which asks pupils to 'write short, known and often-repeated words and sentences in a recognisable way'. Her article, too, helps fulfil the need for empirical analyses as it scrutinises first the L1 writings of German and French children and then the writing of German pupils learning French as a foreign language.

Finally, Dieter *Mindt* and Gudrun *Wagner* start off their paper "Das Schriftbild im Englischunterricht der Klassen 1 und 2" by exploring L1 and L2 literacy to arrive at a new way to teach literacy. In their minute description of the single steps towards literacy they introduce the tool of so-called patchwords in order to guide students systematically to full graphic forms of words with ambiguous phoneme-grapheme-correspondences. It is the authors' aim to explain how insights into the relation of the written form and the grammar of English might scaffold the literacy acquisition process.

If there is one principle uniting the papers in this volume, it is the realization that educators have consistently underestimated what primary school learners can achieve, given the right stimulus, challenging materials and the creation of the right ambience in the classroom. Teachers have been struggling for too long with materials ill adapted to their purpose, e. g., written texts that were really designed for much younger children.

Recent compulsory introduction of English in German primary schools provides the ideal opportunity, and indeed the imperative, to re-evaluate these materials and techniques, scrapping those that are not fit for purpose and designing new ones more suitable. We hope that our book will contribute to this ongoing debate and be inspiring for many readers.

Jutta Rymarczyk
Bärbel Diehr

Heidelberg and Wuppertal, March 2010

Deslea Konza, Leanne Fried and Maureen Michael

Responding to the challenge of teaching English language skills

Der vorliegende Beitrag diskutiert zunächst die Komplexität der englischen Sprache, die gemeinhin als Weltsprache betrachtet wird. Zudem wird die wichtige Debatte über das Lehren des Lesens in englischsprachigen Ländern erörtert. Diese Diskussion ist auch für Länder wie Deutschland von Belang, in denen eine ähnliche Debatte über den besten Englischunterricht und den geeigneten Zeitpunkt für die Einführung der englischen Orthographie geführt wird. An diese Einführung schließen sich die Ergebnisse jüngster Untersuchungen zu den effektivsten Erstleselehrmethoden an. Es werden die fünf wesentlichen Bestandteile der effektivsten Erstleseprogramme dargestellt. Die Schwierigkeiten, die mit dem Erlernen einer komplexen Sprache verbunden sind, bilden den Ausgangspunkt für eine Erörterung des Faktors 'Herausforderung': der Beweis, dass Herausforderung tatsächlich ein Bestandteil des effektiven Lehrens und Lernens ist; zudem: wie ein angemessener pädagogischer Rahmen die notwendige Stütze bereitstellen kann, um der Herausforderung zu begegnen und Lernende zu motivieren, die möglicherweise die Relevanz einer Sprache nicht sehen, die sie nicht regelmäßig benutzen, und um die kognitive Beanspruchung zu reduzieren, die mit dem Lernen einer so komplexen Sprache verbunden sein kann. Der Beitrag schließt mit einer Diskussion darüber, wie expliziter und systematischer Englischunterricht Lernenden helfen kann, in den vollen Genuss der Vorzüge von Zweisprachigkeit zu gelangen, als da sind: ein besseres Verständnis der eigenen Sprache, die Entwicklung höherwertiger Sprachverarbeitungsfähigkeiten, flexiblere und verfeinerte Fertigkeiten der Aufmerksamkeitssteuerung, gesteigerte neuronale Aktivität und ein potenziell größeres Selbstvertrauen und Durchhaltevermögen.

Introduction

English is widely recognised as the global language. It is the official language of the United Nations, and many other international organisations. It is acknowledged as the international language of business, and as "the most useful language to know" (Eurobarometer, 2006). Because of this, many people whose first language is not English want to, or are required to, learn it, and thus it is currently the language most often taught as a foreign language around the world. Indeed, there are more speakers of English as a foreign language than there are for whom English is the first language (Crystal 2003).

In terms of learning English as a second language, the difficulty of that task will be determined to some extent by how closely the structures of the first and the second language resemble each other. Even if the two languages are relatively similar, the English language presents some degree of complexity for learners across a number of domains The elements that contribute to this complexity range from pronunciation inconsistencies and grammatical intricacies, to enormous spelling variations, and difficulties related to the very large English lexicon.

Pronunciation challenges arise partially from the fact that some new speakers need to learn how to articulate sounds that do not exist in their first languages. The syllabic structure of English is also extremely complex, with up to three consonants before (for example, *str-, spl-*) and up to four consonants after the vowel (*gli-mpsed*). Speakers of languages that alternate vowels and consonants tend to insert vowels after every consonant in English, resulting in, at times, incomprehensible attempts at pronunciation.

Grammatical difficulties arise from the high level of idiomatic usage of common verbs such as *make* and *do* (for example, we "make a promise", but "do a favour") which adds to the lack of transparency around the structures of the English language. The use of definite and indefinite articles is also problematic for speakers of languages that do not include any articles.

Spelling difficulties relate essentially to the number of grapheme variations that represent the English phonemes. Whereas languages such as Spanish and German involve almost a one-to-one correspondence between sounds and the letter patterns that represent them, the English orthography is much more complex. It represents more than 40 phonemes with an alphabet of only 26 letters, and no accents. The following table demonstrates the degree of consistency of phoneme and spelling representations in different alphabetic languages. Spanish, German and Italian are relatively consistent, whereas English, at least at the individual phoneme level, has many variations.

Table 1. Phonemes and spelling representations in alphabetic languages

Language	Number of Phonemes	Representations (Spelling variations)
Spanish	23	28
German	34	39
Italian	25	33
French	32	250
English	44	1200

(Landerl, Wimmer and Frith, 1997)

English spelling often incorporates morphemic and/or grammatical information and this is often done at the expense of phonological consistency. For example, the *-ed* indicator of the past tense is maintained in the spelling of words, even if the pronunciation is /d/ as in "failed", /əd/ as in "wanted", or /t/ as in "shopped". English has incorporated words from other languages, including Latin, Classical Greek and Anglo-Saxon in its early written tradition, but it continues to borrow from other languages at a great rate. Usually, the spelling of the original language is maintained, bringing yet more variety to the orthography of English.

English has one of the largest *vocabularies* of any language, due partly to its amalgamation of words from so many other languages. The sheer size of the vocabulary presents problems for many learners. In some cases, words take on radically new meanings, often initiated by adolescents or marginalized groups that want to differentiate themselves from mainstream society. Thus "sick" and "deadly" have been given quite different meanings by today's generation of young people.

There is also a lack of consistency in the ways in which many linguistic functions operate. Because of the range of prefixes that are used to negate adjectives (*in-, un-, dis,* and *a-* to identify just four), many negated adjectives must be rote learnt. The fact that some words can have an identical meaning both with and without a prefix, as in *flammable* and *inflammable,* can also cause great confusion to learners of English.

Children who, from the moment of birth, hear the English language all around them learn the vocabulary and oral structures easily. It provides for them the means by which their needs and wants are met, and so motivation is high. Even so, a significant proportion (around 20%) of native English speakers has some difficulty learning to read English. It is even more difficult for those children who must learn it in a foreign language context – motivation is not as high and the cognitive load is greatly increased. Reading and writing this difficult and complex language represents a considerable challenge, and has been the topic of significant debate for both native English speakers and those learning it as an additional language. Before exploring issues more directly relevant to EFL[1] learners, the background to the longstanding difference of opinion around the teaching of reading in English-speaking countries is presented, as it may inform the current discussion of how this should be managed from a foreign language perspective.

---

1   The terms English Language Learners (ELL) and English as a Foreign Language (EFL) are both used in this chapter, to reflect the terminology of the academic literature in different countries.

Approaches to teaching reading in English-speaking countries

The question of how best to teach the English language, particularly the skills of reading and writing, has been the focus of educational research, public debate and, one must say, considerable teacher confusion in English speaking countries for many decades. In very simplistic terms, reading an alphabetic language incorporates a decoding element and a comprehension element. Competing theoretical orientations focusing on each of these two broad components of reading have been at the centre of the decades-long debate concerning the most effective way to teach reading.

The decoding approach

Early decoding or "bottom-up" explanations of the reading process viewed reading as a structured hierarchy of sequenced and separate skills, which were built up to create meaning. Gough's (1972) model was typical of this approach. He proposed that reading occurred as a series of sequential steps, with the smallest units of language (letters) being blended together to form the next highest unit (words), which were in turn joined together to form sentences, paragraphs, and so on. Thus the low level processes, or decoding of the various components of words, were seen to occur before higher-level processes were engaged to integrate meaning.

Decoding approaches to teaching reading survived for a long time because they seemed to be a logical way to teach an alphabetic language. An approach that recommended decoding, rather than remembering each new word as a sight word (the "look-say" method), had an obvious appeal. Even cursory analysis of the reading process, however, identified a number of weaknesses in these early models of reading acquisition:

~ The assumption that if a reader can decode a word and actually say it, the word is therefore understood, is clearly false. Many early readers could decode "disconsolate" or "protracted" but still have no idea of their meaning – the important role of vocabulary knowledge is not acknowledged by a strict decoding approach:
~ Fluent readers can read hundreds of words a minute, a rate that is not explained by decoding alone as it takes from one quarter to a third of a second to recognise a letter and assign it the appropriate sound. At this rate readers could not read more quickly than about sixty words per minute.
~ Pronunciation and comprehension usually require context. It is often impossible to access all the necessary information about word pronunciation

and meaning by simply decoding. Because so many identically spelt English words have different pronunciations and in some cases multiple meanings (for example, ground, tear, read, does, bow, minute), readers often need to see the word in context to decide both pronunciation and meaning.

More recent conceptualisations of the role of decoding in the reading process acknowledge that readers do not simply proceed from letters to words and then to meaning. Reading involves simultaneous processing of information from many different sources. Information such as letter shape, and orthographic, syntactic and semantic knowledge interact within the short term or "working" memory to contribute to comprehension. "The efficient reader simultaneously uses background knowledge, facility with language, ongoing comprehension and decoding skills" (Gunning 2006: 9). This is not to downplay the role of decoding in comprehension of text – it is an essential component of the process, and one that all readers must master if they are to progress to independent reading.

The whole language approach

It was perhaps in response to the fact that some teachers focused on drilling of letter-sound relationships without enough opportunities to use these skills in engaging texts, that the whole language or "top down" approach originally gained favour in the late 1970s and 80s. In this approach, the development of reading is considered to be as natural a process as learning to speak. It contends that children will learn to read effortlessly and enjoyably if given the opportunity to read in a print-rich and engaging environment with teachers who hold high expectations of them (Goodman 1989). In this model, decoding individual words is considered much less important than the reader's expectations and knowledge of syntax, semantics and general knowledge to anticipate what may be ahead, indeed breaking words up into their component sounds is regarded as being an unnatural and unhelpful process. The contention is that letter-sound relationships will be learned incidentally, without explicit instruction, in the context of engaging reading of high quality literature.

    The whole language approach encouraged teachers to bring engaging and motivating books into the classroom to use as the basis of their teaching of reading. It had great intuitive appeal for many teachers who wanted to nurture a love of reading in their students. A phonic or decoding approach, by comparison, appeared to lack stimulation and motivation. This "real reading" approach was adopted widely in English-speaking countries. Academics promoted the whole language pedagogy in teacher education institutions, and the teaching of phonics, in addition to the explicit teaching of spelling and grammatical structures, was abandoned by many practising teachers.

This approach was, however, based on a number of misconceptions, and some discussion of the research that brought these weaknesses to light, is worthy of mention at this point.

Learning to read is not as easy as learning to speak

The whole language model does not acknowledge the different processes involved in learning to speak and learning to read (Foorman 1995). Speech is part of our biological destiny - the human brain has in place the systems to decipher oral language as the result of the evolutionary process, however there is no unique system for processing reading. Unlike other animals, our brain has evolved to facilitate the development of spoken language and as a species we have been using it for approximately 200,000 years (Liberman, 1997). The translation of these sounds onto a page, however, involves many additional skills, especially in a language like English.

There is no need to analyse the phonological structures of oral language in order to understand a spoken message. In order to learn to read, however, the system in the brain used for developing oral language must be accessed for use in reading development – the "symbols of print must be translated into identifiable spoken words that are readily accessible to the central processor" (Center 2005:11). Readers must be able to break sentences into words, words into separate sounds (phonemes) and then relate these sounds to quite random and meaningless symbols. This is not as straightforward a process as learning oral language (Gleitman 1985; Gough & Hillinger 1980; Liberman & Shankweiler 1985; Lyon 1998). This explains why written forms of alphabetic languages have been around for only about 4000 years. Reading and writing have developed as secondary responses to evolution.

Use of context requires about 90% word recognition skills

Whole language explanations posit that words can be read by using the surrounding context to derive their meaning. This fails to acknowledge that using context to identify unknown words is only possible when most of the text can be decoded by the reader. Beginning and poor readers cannot do this. They have difficulty with a great deal of the text, therefore they have no context to draw upon.

The first author has used the following example to illustrate this point (Konza 2006). Consider the different ways a skilled reader and a poor reader would approach the following sentence completion task.

The knight reined in his horse and drew his _____.

It is quite easy for a good reader to fill in *sword*. This is the logical answer if the reader has the relevant vocabulary knowledge and if the words *knight* and *reined* are easily read. If, however, those two quite difficult words cannot be read, then predicting the word *sword* becomes almost impossible. Using context is a very relevant and useful skill only if the reader can read 90% of the words, thus providing a context to use. Without word recognition, there is no context.

It is true that if the above sentence were accompanied by a picture of a mounted knight drawing a sword, then the chances of "reading" the words would be much higher. In fact, this is how many poor readers do access word meaning. They use the context provided by the pictures. Unfortunately, pictures do not accompany most of the text we will read in our lives, and cannot accurately portray the essence of most of the words in our language.

Fluent readers decode almost every word

Whole language theorists contend that fluent reading is not dependent upon decoding skills – the good readers merely dip into print occasionally to confirm their predictions before moving on. Eye movement technology, which developed rapidly in the 1980s, has revealed otherwise, by tracking eye movements as the eyes move along a line of print in a series of jumps (called *saccades*) between points of fixation. This technology has revealed that good readers actually decode, albeit extraordinarily rapidly, at approximately the 3–4 letter level (Balota, Pollatsek & Rayner 1985; Rayner & Pollatsek 1989; Sereno & Rayner 2000). Fluent reading relies extensively on highly automatised, and therefore very rapid, decoding.

Many children do not discover letter-sound correspondences without explicit instruction

While a small percentage of readers will store accurate orthographic representations of words after one or two exposures and generalise from those to other words, there is now overwhelming evidence that most beginning readers need explicit instruction in letter-sound relationships or their reading development will be affected (Adams, 1990; Castle, 1999; Chall, 1967; Henry, 1993; Rayner, Foorman, Perfetti, Pesetsky & Seidenberg, 2002; Share & Stanovich, 1995). The literature-based approach does not provide enough practice of new words or word parts for these to be stored in long-term memory for future reference. The vast array of letter patterns in English is too complex for such an opportunistic and random approach to meet the needs of most readers. It would not provide the amount of practice required for EFL learners.

Putting the debate to rest: evidence from empirical research

There have been a number of attempts to put the debate to rest. In 1984, the report commissioned by the US National Academy of Education, "Becoming a Nation of Readers" (Anderson et al. 1984), concluded that phonics instruction was required for most children to learn to read, and that such instruction should occur in conjunction with opportunities to read words in meaningful text. This did not stop the debate.

In 1990, Marilyn Jaegar Adams produced "Beginning to Read: Thinking and Learning about Print", another commissioned piece of research, which again supported the need for phonics instruction to teach children the alphabetic code, a "necessary but not sufficient" element of beginning reading instruction. This was an acknowledgement of the need to also include practice of the skills of reading in engaging text. While Adams was essentially saying that both decoding and context-based practice were required, neither side seemed satisfied and the debate continued.

In 1997, in an effort to make definitive recommendations about beginning reading instruction to an increasingly divided and confused teacher population, the National Reading Panel (NRP) was convened by the US Congress to assess the effectiveness of different approaches used to teach children to read. The NRP reviewed over 100,000 large-scale, peer-reviewed studies and identified the components of the most effective beginning reading programs. The NRP report, published in 2000, has been supported by Burns, Griffin and Snow 1999; Ehri, Nunes, Stahl & Willows 2001; Rose 2006, 2009a, 2009b; and research conducted in Australia (Rowe 2005, 2005a, 2005b; Louden et al. 2000; Louden, Rohl and Hopkins 2008). Five particular elements were identified by the NRP, and while research since that time has refined them somewhat, they remain the most strongly supported indicators of an effective reading program. These are presented below.

Essential elements of an effective reading program

1. Instruction in phonological skills

Instruction in phonological awareness, and in particular *phonemic awareness*, is required, particularly for those children who have not experienced rich literacy experiences prior to school. Phonemic awareness refers to an individual's understanding that words in the English language are made up of a series of separate sounds. Without this understanding, beginning readers cannot relate written symbols (graphemes) to the sounds in words. The compression of the sounds of spoken English disguises its segmental nature, rendering an awareness of those separate sounds very difficult for some. EFL learners, without long exposure to the sounds of oral English, may find words in the English language particularly impenetrable.

2. Instruction in letter-sound relationships

English is an alphabetic language, thus knowledge of the letters of the alphabet, and the various combinations in which they may appear, is the key to learning to read and spell. This requires explicit instruction in the "alphabetic principle" or letter-sound correspondences – often referred to as phonics which builds on phonemic awareness. A systematic, as well as an explicit approach to teaching these relationships, has been found to be consistently more effective than an embedded or analytic approach of pointing out letter-sound relationships in words read in context. This point will be expanded upon at a later point in this chapter.

3. Instruction in vocabulary

Readers find it far more difficult to read words that are not already part of their oral vocabulary, therefore building a wide vocabulary is an important component of a reading program (Biemiller 2001, 2003; Biemiller and Slonim 2001; Beck & McKeown 2007). Vocabulary has been found to contribute to as much as 80% of comprehension. If children are not immersed in a rich and diverse English vocabulary, this element of English must also be explicitly taught. While this is true of native English speakers, it is of perhaps even more importance for EFL learners who do not hear the English language around them at all.

4. Instruction in fluency

Extensive practice in combining word recognition with alphabetic knowledge develops the fluency required for comprehension. It is only when these early acquisition skills are developed to the *point of automaticity* that fluent reading can occur, and the reader can apply his or her full cognitive capacity to understanding the content. While a reader is still focussing on the decoding aspect of reading, there is no cognitive space available for concentrating on meaning. Automaticity develops fluency as readers combine visual, phonological, semantic and syntactic information in an integrated and flexible manner.

5. Instruction in comprehension

Explicit instruction in comprehension skills is required for most students to facilitate meaningful engagement with the text. The main comprehension strategy employed by some teachers is asking children to answer a series of questions after reading a passage. This practice *tests* comprehension, but does not *teach* it. Students need to be taught to understand the different purposes for reading so they can adapt their reading style (for example, scanning, skimming or reading closely); how to assimilate new material into current knowledge; to monitor their own reading so they are aware when meaning is lost; to ask and answer questions as they read; to distinguish major content from detail and to create mental images as they read. Different strategies for summarising, note-taking and structuring knowledge gained by their reading need to be explicitly taught to most children if they are to gain maximum benefit from their reading.

Fluent and meaningful reading requires mastery of all the above elements. It is important that teachers understand the critical importance of each of these factors, and the impact of any one not being included in programs of instruction. If beginning readers have difficulty with any one of these, overall achievement will be negatively affected because the cognitive demands of the reading tasks will outweigh the resources available for it. This brings us to a discussion of cognitive load, and how it can be managed.

The cognitive demands of learning English

For some first, and most second, language users, becoming a fluent speaker and reader of English presents a significant cognitive load. Cognitive load theory (CLT) posits that tasks requiring the processing of information result in cognitive

Responding to the challenge of teaching English language skills 23

load (CL) in the working memory. The capacity of the working memory is limited and tasks that exceed such capacity create problems for learners. Cognitive overload occurs when the total processing demands exceed available attentional resources (Sweller 1994) and this can occur when too many non-automatic processes are required to perform a skill or solve a problem. Cognitive load can be controlled, however, by attending to its various components (see Figure 1) and by using effective instructional design (Merrienboer & Sluijsmans 2009).

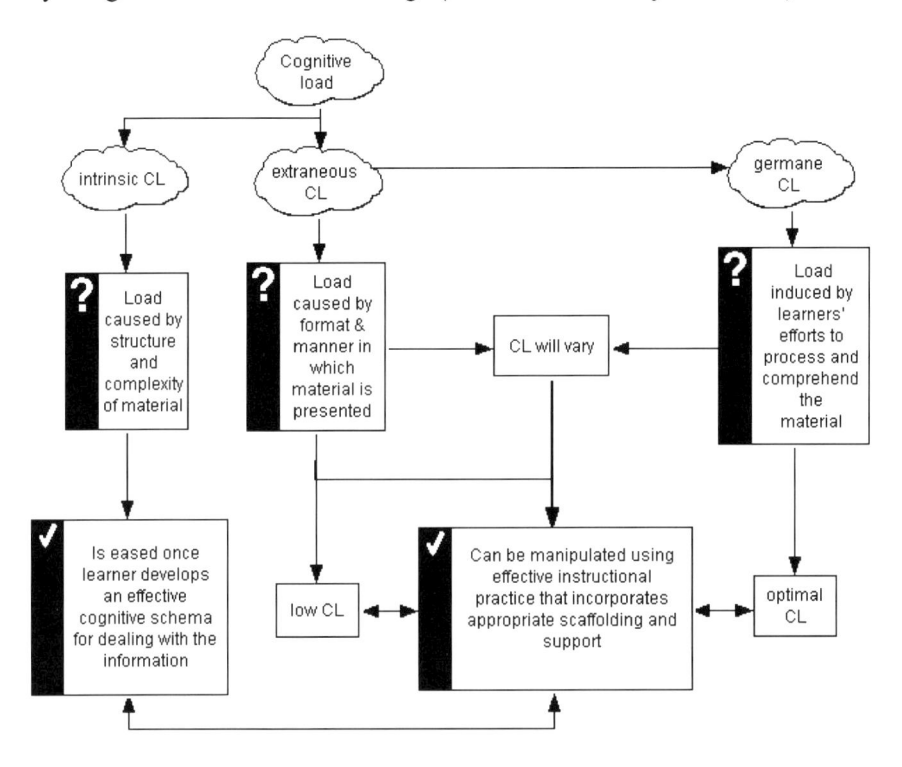

Figure 1. Components of cognitive load (Michael 2010, after Schunk 2008, and Snowman, Dobozy, Scevak, Bryer & Bartlett 2009)

The components of CL are interdependent. *Intrinsic CL* results from the demands created by the complexity of the materials to be learned. The manner in which the material is presented is the *extraneous CL*, and this can either intensify or reduce the cognitive demands of the material. Instructional practices can be designed to minimise *extraneous CL* by providing explicit targeted instruction and by using methods that gradually build autonomy for learners by providing ample opportunity to practise and work with new material with appropriate support (Merrienboer & Sluijsmans 2009). This, in turn, helps learners build the knowledge base they need to develop automaticity, and thus keep the cognitive load manageable. *Germane CL* is a function of the effort that learners need to expend to process and understand new material. This effort cannot exceed the level of motivation or skill if learning is to occur. Supporting students with appropriate instructional practices is of paramount importance with EFL learners, particularly if motivation is affected by the learners not seeing the relevance of a language they are not using in their daily lives.

Instructional design that is mindful of the learners' *zone of proximal development* (Vygotsky 1978) and provides appropriate support can minimise CL and facilitate learning that demands high levels of cognition. Using effective practices that acknowledge the demands of the English language and help learners develop strategies to deal with its complexity reduces the potential for cognitive overload. Thus the teacher's role and the practices used are of critical importance.

Responding to the challenge of teaching English: implications for practice

Having established that English is a very complex language, and the potential for cognitive overload in students trying to come to terms with its complexity is high, how should teachers respond to this challenge? What particular expertise underpins exceptional teaching? How do the most exceptional teachers scaffold the learning of students so that the challenge is manageable, and students do not experience cognitive overload? The following section of this chapter explores these questions.

What do the most effective teachers of language and literacy do in the classroom?

In a nation-wide investigation of literacy teaching practices in Australia, the Classroom Literacy Observation Schedule (CLOS) (Louden & Rohl 2003) was designed to identify classroom practices that were associated with different levels of student achievement. Its formulation was based on analysis of an extensive body of literature that considered "effective teaching, effective teaching of literacy and early years literacy teaching" (Louden & Rohl 2008:106). The CLOS was initially constructed with two axes for observing the elements of classroom practice: the teaching practice axis included 33 literacy teaching practices that were grouped under six dimensions, and the activity axis listed 17 common teaching activities (see Appendix A). The tool was used to analyse classroom practice and identify the practices of teachers whose students were variously achieving above expected levels, at expected levels, or below expected levels in literacy (Louden et al. 2005). In a subsequent revision, the CLOS-R (Louden & Rohl 2008) consolidated the original literacy teaching practices and added others, for example those associated with oral language to meet the needs of early childhood literacy learning.

Analysis of classroom observation data revealed that the most effective literacy teachers, that is, those teachers whose students consistently achieved above expected levels, created safe learning environments that incorporated challenge and support for learning in ways that met the needs of their students, encouraged participation and fostered motivation. *Challenge* and *support* were the attributes of excellence possessed by those teachers who made the most difference to their students' learning. These elements were not evident in less effective teachers who tended to focus on low-level "busywork" activities designed to keep students quiet and occupied. Challenge and support mirror Vygosky's *Zone of Proximal Development* (1978), where the knowledgeable teacher provides learning opportunities that support students to extend beyond the point where they can reach themselves. Less effective teachers expect less of their students, and set less demanding tasks. If there is little challenge, there is little need to teach students how to meet the demands of such tasks, and less need for teachers to investigate the pedagogy they must employ to support students through highly demanding tasks.

Hattie (2005), when examining effective teaching more broadly, also identified challenge as one of three key factors that distinguish the learning environments created by "expert" teachers, from those created by their "experienced" (but less expert) colleagues. Hattie also highlighted a tendency amongst less effective teachers to design student learning experiences that were geared more towards lower level engagement in activities rather than deepening the component of challenge in learning tasks. Expert teachers are those who are able to enhance and maximise student learning through the manifestation of an effective repertoire of teaching practices that combine both the setting of challenging learning experiences and the provision of support. These highly effective teachers ensure that students are explicitly taught what they need to know in order to feel safe and thus be able to complete challenging tasks. If students are ill prepared for the challenge and feel like "someone in the wilderness" (Connell 2009:34) because they do not know what to do, the brain will respond in a particularly primitive manner:

> *If the amygdala, located inside our limbic system, perceives the learning environment as "unsafe," it will essentially shift the blood and oxygen in the brain into a "flight or fight" mode, making it impossible for a student to learn content.* (Connell 2009:34)

A poorly supported foreign language-learning environment would similarly detract from effective learning. According to Lombardi (2008), English language learners (ELLs), like all learners, thrive in a supportive but challenging learning environment:

Complex learning is enhanced by challenge and inhibited by threat. At what level should we teach our ELL students? Teaching at a slightly elevated level that is challenging but not impossible in a warm and inviting atmosphere encourages our students to strive. (Lombardi 2008:221)

It would appear that although English has some level of complexity, the demands alone should not, and do not, intimidate effective teachers. Indeed, challenge is fundamental to high-level learning and has become a consistent element of those practices deemed to be most effective in enhancing student achievement. Challenge is not a problem for students if their preparation is comprehensive and they have opportunities to learn and practise the essential elements they need to know, understand, and accomplish, to be successful.

Having acknowledged that English is a challenging language to teach, but also that providing challenge in an appropriately supportive and scaffolded manner leads to higher learning gains, we must then address the question of how this is best achieved. What are the most effective teaching strategies to accomplish this? The next section explores the teaching of English in EFL contexts, particularly the orthography of the English alphabet, in order to help students learn to read this most complex of alphabetic languages.

Implications for teaching English in the EFL context

There is some debate around the most appropriate time to introduce English orthography to English language learners. Much of the division relates to the same arguments that have polarised researchers and practitioners in native English-speaking countries about how best to teach reading. Diehr (this volume) points out an inherent contradiction in some German curricula – while specifically excluded from instruction in English orthography in Years 1 and 2, students are expected from Year 3 to be interacting with printed forms of the language and developing their own portfolios. This optimistic expectation appears to be based on the notion that, once oral language is mastered, mastery of the complex written form of the English language will also emerge without any systematic or explicit instruction in English grapheme-phoneme correspondence. As explained earlier, this notion does not acknowledge the very real differences between the development of oral and literate English skills, nor is it consistent with the findings of successive reports in different countries about how best to teach the reading of English (Adams 1990; NRP 2000; Rose 2006, 2009a; 2009b; Rowe 2005)

For some, the belief is that the early introduction of a complex code such as that of the English alphabetic system would place too great a burden on young learners. We have already argued that learners respond well to challenging material if they are appropriately scaffolded, thus ensuring that the learning context is both stimulating and safe. Rymarczyk's research with young children (this volume) further supports this position. Her studies found that early exposure to English orthography had no detrimental effect on any learners, even the lower achieving students. In fact, not teaching the orthography of the English language along with the oral skills extended learning time unnecessarily, and affected student motivation.

Another aspect of the "how to teach reading" debate in English-speaking countries is also of relevance to the debate about teaching English orthography in EFL contexts. While most researchers and teachers (some only reluctantly) now acknowledge the vast research evidence pointing to the need for phonic instruction for beginning readers, just how explicit and systematic this needs to be has transpired into an entirely new battleground. This issue is explored in the next section.

Recommended practices for teaching English orthography

Before discussing the relative merits of two current approaches to teaching phonics, some discussion of the terms *systematic* and *explicit* is required. These terms have so often been placed together when referring to phonics instruction that many regard them as synonymous, but there are important differences.

Systematic language teaching employs a sequential approach, one that recognises that particular skills or concepts need to be taught before others. Such an approach also acknowledges the importance of repeated practise of learned concepts and skills. *Explicit* instruction refers to lesson delivery wherein the teacher clearly demonstrates for the students what he or she is teaching in a particular lesson, and makes the necessary connections for the student. Although some children may be able to learn to read without such explicit instruction, Snow and Juel (2005) concluded that explicit teaching of alphabetic coding skills in early reading instruction is helpful to all students for a variety of reasons, harmful to none, and, importantly, crucial for some. Explicit instruction of concepts of phonological and phonemic awareness provides the support for students to not only make the connection between the sounds of speech and the written language but also enables second language learners to use valuable information related to the structure of their native language.

Synthetic versus analytic approaches

Of the approaches to teaching phonics, it is *synthetic* programs that are characterised by explicit, systematic teaching methods, with the term *synthetic* referring to the emphasis on synthesising or blending sounds. Within a synthetic phonics approach, students are first taught the alphabet in an order that promotes blending of consonants and vowels into common CVC words. This early emphasis on the process of blending sounds together reflects the importance of this skill for independent reading; it not only enables students to make the connection between oral language and written, it also provides them with self-teaching strategies.

The synthetic approach may be seen in contrast to an *embedded* or *analytic* approach, which is connected to the whole-language model of reading acquisition. Whole language advocates contend that if phonic instruction is required, such instruction should be conducted in an embedded manner, that is, by drawing words from connected text for analysis. Students are encouraged to compare and contrast whole words, generally presented in context, in order to decipher the sounds that go with the letters. Children's attention is directed to patterns within words only as they arise in class reading. While the notion of moving from meaningful words to their component parts has strong intuitive appeal, especially when one considers that reading is essentially about making meaning and is not just a decoding exercise, strong evidence has emerged that an embedded or analytic approach is not as effective as a synthetic approach.

A significant portion of students exposed to the whole language method of literacy development struggle to make progress as they suffer under the cognitive load of trying to remember large numbers of words by sight. The conclusion drawn from a case study reported by Diehr (this volume) supported the view that sight words may be useful for the first few months of learning English, but this does not prepare children for the task of reading connected text. In order to learn how to approach the increasing number of words young readers will encounter, they need to know the English letter-sound relationships and how sounds are blended together.

With regard to teaching letter-sound correspondences, it has been found that systematic exposure to a reduced set of overlapping words consisting of a few letters makes it easier for beginning readers to understand the alphabetic principle, rather than exposure to a large amount of words (de Graaff et al. 2009). Reading engaging material to the class is still important and is done simultaneously, and as taught patterns and relationships appear in text, these are noted and discussed, but in the early stages, the teaching of the letters and their accompanying sounds is done in isolation.

The National Reading Panel's review of many hundreds of studies highlighted the superiority of this approach over an embedded approach in the 2000 report, and these findings have been supported in England (Rose 2006, 2009b), and in Australia (Rowe 2005). The conclusion was that the array of letter-sound patterns represented in English is too vast and complex to be adequately covered by the random analysis of words that may appear in a literature-based approach to phonic instruction. Beginning readers do not have enough exposures to the various patterns for them to be internalised. They need the often-slight differences between patterns pointed out in a highly explicit manner. A systematic approach is required to ensure that all the patterns are taught, and this is particularly important for beginning readers who do not have the benefit of rich oral language and extended exposure to print material before school. Five year follow-up studies have revealed that the superior effects of the synthetic approach do not wash out. Astonishingly, the enhanced performance of girls over boys in early reading development, a factor that many of us took for granted, appears to disappear when a synthetic approach is used – little boys do equally as well as little girls!

It would appear logical that this approach would also benefit EFL learners – the teaching of the patterns of English in a systematic and explicit manner would provide the necessary support for new learners to overcome the challenge that learning English represents. An explicit and systematic approach will assist young learners to discriminate not only the differences between English patterns, but also the differences between English and the patterns in their own language. This is particularly important when one considers the enormous differences between relatively transparent language like Spanish, Italian and German, and the opaque orthography of English.

Developing automaticity

A systematic approach also provides opportunities to practise explicitly taught concepts and skills, enabling automaticity to develop. Automaticity occurs when little or no conscious effort is required to process information or perform a task (Artino 2008), and is crucial for fluency in a complex skill such as reading. The characteristics of a skill learned to the point of automaticity are that it (a) occurs without intention; (b) is not subject to conscious monitoring; (c) utilizes few attentional resources; and (d) happens rapidly (Moors & De Houwer 2007). Automaticity frees the processing space in working memory for higher order thinking such as comprehension. The differences in comprehension between strong and weak readers can usually be attributed to automaticity of decoding skills (Hudsen, Lane & Pullen 2005). Because the reading process requires information from different sources to be held in working memory, the greater the amount of attention required to decode or predict the words, the less attention will be available to integrate the information in order for comprehension to take place. Without automaticity, too much attention is focused on the decoding part of reading, leaving too little attention available for determining meaning. Using appropriate classroom practices to promote automaticity at the letter-sound level, the word level and phrase and text level, can prevent cognitive overload when students learn English as a first or second language, and facilitate comprehension. This is best achieved by a systematic approach to the teaching of these skills from the early stages of reading acquisition.

Conclusion

Systematic and explicit instruction has been confirmed by overwhelming empirical evidence as the most effective way to teach English orthography. Many English-speaking education systems were persuaded for decades to implement an approach that denies the importance of the explicit teaching of letter-sound knowledge, grammatical structures or spelling of this most complex alphabetic language. The result is that these countries have generations of citizens who do not understand English language structures, who struggle to express themselves in an articulate or even grammatically correct manner, who cannot spell accurately, and who feel badly let down by an education system that did not teach them how their own language works. Many of these citizens are now teachers themselves, putting at risk the English language skills of new generations of children.

As English is the global language, an increasing number of education systems now face the challenges associated with teaching English in foreign language contexts. It is to be hoped that lessons can be learned from the experiences described above. The key to student learning and achievement is simple: it is reliant on effective practice. Volumes of reading research are now available that identify the reading acquisition skills we should be teaching, and how we should be teaching them (Hattie 2005; Louden et al. 2005; Louden, Rohl & Hopkins 2008; Lombardi 2008; NRP 2000; Rose 2006, 2009a, 2009b; Rowe 2005).

While English is challenging, using supportive teaching practices can engage students in meaningful learning while preventing cognitive overload. This will allow students to reap the many benefits of bilingualism: the development of higher processing skills, more complex attending skills, and the ability to ignore misleading information (Bialystok 2007), increased neural capacity (Ellis 2008) and more sophisticated use of executive processes and metacognitive activity (Schunk 2008). Students who are given appropriate support can thrive in challenging learning environments. Mastering complex material builds universal transferable skills, confidence and resilience. In Lombardi's (2008) words:

The brain's complex, adaptive nature means ELLs are not stuck on a one-way street but can happily navigate a twelve-lane highway of choices and opportunities (2008: 222).

References

Adams, M. J. (1990). Beginning to read: Thinking and learning about print. Cambridge, MA: MIT Press.
Anderson, R. C.; Hiebert, E. H.; Scott, J. A. & Wilkinson, I. A. G. (1984). *Becoming a Nation of Readers: The report of the Commission on Reading.* Washington, DC: The National Institute of Education.
Artino, A. R., Jr. (2008). Cognitive load theory and the role of learner experience: An abbreviated review for educational practitioners. *AACE Journal, 16*(4), 425–439.
Balota, D. A.; Pollatsek, A. & Rayner, K. (1985). The interaction of contextual constraints and parafoveal visual information in reading. *Cognitive Psychology*, 17, 364–390.
Beck, I. L. & McKeown, M. G., (2007). Increasing young low income children's oral vocabulary repertoires through rich and focused instruction. *Elementary School Journal*, 107 (3), 251–271.
Bialystok, E. (2007). Cognitive effects of bilingualism: How linguistic experience leads to cognitive change. *International Journal of Bilingual Education and Bilingualism, 10* (3), 210–223.
Biemiller, A. (2001). Teaching vocabulary: Early, direct, and sequential. *The American Educator*, 25 (1), 24–28.
Biemiller, A. (2003). Vocabulary: needed if more children are to read well. *Reading Psychology*, 24, 323–335.
Biemiller, A. & Slonim, N. (2001). Estimating root word vocabulary growth in normative and advantaged populations: Evidence for a common sequence of vocabulary acquisition. *Journal of Educational Psychology*, 93, 498–520.
Burns, M.; Griffin, P. & Snow, C. (1999). Starting out right: A guide to promoting children's reading success. Washington, DC: National Academy Press.
Castle, M. J. (1999). Learning and teaching phonological awareness. In G. B. Thompson & T. Nicholson (eds.), *Learning to read: Beyond phonics and whole language* (pp.55–73). New York: Teachers College Press.

Chall, J. (1967). *The great debate.* New York: McGraw Hill.
Connell, J. D. (2009). The global aspects of brain-based learning. [Feature Article]. *Educational Horizons, 88* (1), 28–39.
Crystal, D. (2003). *English as a global language.* Cambridge: Cambridge University Press.
de Graaff, S.; Bosman, A.M.T.; Hasselman, F. & Verhoeven, L. (2009). Benefits of systematic phonics instruction. *Scientific Studies of Reading,* 13(4) 318–333.
Ehri, L C.; Nunes, S. R.; Stahl, S. A. & Willows, D. M. (2001). Systematic phonics instruction helps students learn to read: Evidence from the National Reading Panel's Meta-analysis. *Review of Educational Research,* 71(3), 393–447.
Ellis, R. (2008). *The study of second language aquisition* (2nd edn.). Oxford: Oxford University Press.
Eurobarometer. (2006). *Europeans and languages.* Retrieved January 2010 from the European Commission website: http://ec.europa.eu/education/languages/pdf/doc631_en.pdf
Field, J. (2003). Promoting perception: Lexical segmentation in second language listening. *ELT Journal* 57(4), 325–33.
Foorman, B. R. (1995). Research on the great debate: Code-oriented versus whole language approaches to reading instruction. *School Psychology Review,* 24, 376–392.
Gleitman, L. R. (1985). Orthographic resources affect reading acquisition – if they are used. *Remedial and Special Education,* 6, 24–36.
Goodman, K. (1989). The Whole Language approach: A conversation with Kenneth Goodman. The Writing Teacher, 3(1), 5–8.
Gough, P. (1972). One second of reading. In J. Kavanagh & I. Mattingly (eds.), Language by ear and eye. Cambridge, MA: MIT Press, 331–358.
Gough, P. & Hillinger, M. L. (1980). Learning to read: An unnatural act. *Bulletin of the Orton Society,* 30, 171–176.
Gunning, T. G. (2006). Closing the literacy gap. Boston: Pearson.
Hattie, J. (2003). *Teachers make a difference: What is the research evidence?* Retrieved 4/12/2006, from http://www.acer.edu.au/workshops/documents/Teachers_Make_a_Difference_Hattie.pdf
Hattie, J. (2005). *What is the nature of evidence that makes a difference to learning?* Retrieved 14/2/2010, from http://www.acer.edu.au/workshops/documents/Hattie.pdf
Henry, M. K. (1993). The role of decoding in reading research and instruction. *Reading and Writing Interdisciplinary Journal,* 15, 105–12.
Hudson, R. F.; Lane, H. B. & Pullen, P. C. (2005). Reading fluency assessment and instruction: What, why, and how? *The Reading Teacher,* 58, 702–714.
Konza, D. (2006). *Teaching children with reading difficulties.* Melbourne: Thompson Social Science Press.

Landerl, K., Wimmer, H. & Frith, U. (1997). The impact of orthographic consistency on dyslexia: A German-English comparison. *Cognition*, 63, 315–334.

Liberman, A. M. (1997). How theories of speech affect research in reading and writing. In B. Blachman (ed.), *Foundations of reading acquisition and dyslexia* Maywah, NJ: Laurence Erlbaum Associates. 3–19.

Liberman, A. M. & Shankweiler, D. (1985). Phonology and the problems of learning to read and write. *Remedial and Special Education*, 6, 686–700.

Lombardi, J. (2008). Beyond learning styles: Brain-based research and English language learners. [Feature Article]. *The Clearing House, 81*(5), 219–222.

Louden, W.; Chan, L.; Elkins, J.; Greaves, D.; House, H.; Milton, M. et al. (2000). *Mapping the Territory: Primary students with learning difficulties.* Vol.2, (pp. 256–264). Retrieved 14/02/2010, from
http://www.dest.gov.au/NR/rdonlyres/259888FA-B5CB-4030-9E0A-7C9BD3ACCEC6/4102/v2.PDF

Louden, W. & Rohl, M. (2003). *Classroom Literacy Observation Schedule (CLOS).* Perth: Edith Cowan University.

Louden, W. & Rohl, M. (2008). *Classroom Observation Schedule - Revised (CLOS-R).* Perth: The University of Western Australia.

Louden, W.; Rohl, M.; Barratt Pugh, C.; Brown, C.; Cairney, T.; Elderfield, J., et al. (2005). *In Teachers' Hands: Effective literacy teaching practices in the early years of schooling.* Retrieved 14/02/2010, from http://ith.education.ecu.edu.au/index.php?page=43

Louden, W.; Rohl, M. & Hopkins, S. (2008). *Teaching for growth: Effective teaching of literacy and numeracy.* Perth: Graduate School of Education, University of Western Australia.

Lyon, R. (1998). *Overview of reading and literacy initiatives.* Retrieved 14/02/2010 from http://www.dys-add.com/ReidLyonJeffords.pdf

Merrienboer, J. J. G. & Sluijsmans, D. M. A. (2009). Toward a synthesis of Cognitive Load Theory, four-component instructional design, and self-directed learning. [Feature Article]. *Educational Psychology Review, 21*(1), 55–66.

Michael, M. (2010). Components of cognitive load: A schematic representation. Unpublished document, Edith Cowan University.

Moors, A. & De Houwer, J. (2007). What is automaticity? An analysis of its component features and their interrelations. In J. A. Bargh (ed.), *Automatic processes in social thinking and behavior.* Hove, England: Psychology Press. 11–50.

National Reading Panel (2000). Report of the National Reading Panel. *Teaching children to read: An evidence-based assessment of the scientific research literature on reading ad its implications for reading instruction.* Retrieved 14/02/2010 from http://www.nichd.nih.gov/publications/nrp/smallbook.cfm

Rayner, K.; Foorman, B. R.; Perfetti, C. A.; Pesetsky, D. & Seidenberg, M. S. (2002). How should reading be taught? *Scientific American*, March, 71–7.

Rayner, K. & Pollatsek, A. (1989). *The psychology of reading.* Hillsdale, NJ: Erlbaum.

Rose, J. (2006). *Independent review of the teaching of early reading.* Retrieved 14/02/2010, from http://www.standards.dfes.gov.uk/rosereview/report.pdf

Rose, J. (2009a). *Independent review of the Primary Curriculum.* Retrieved 14/02/2010 from http://www.dcsf.gov.uk/primarycurriculumreview/downloads/primary_curriculum_execs_summary.pdf

Rose, J. (2009b). *Identifying and teaching children and young people with dyslexia and literacy difficulties.* Retrieved 14/02/2010, from http://publications.dcsf.gov.uk/default.aspx?PageFunction=productdetails&PageMode=publications&ProductId=DCSF-00659-2009

Rowe, K. (2005). *Teaching Reading: Literature Review.* Canberra: AGPS

Rowe, K. (2005a). *Teaching Reading: Report and Recommendations.* Canberra: AGPS.

Rowe, K. (2005b). *Teaching Reading: Executive Summary.* Retrieved 14/02/2010 from http://www.dest.gov.au/nitl/documents/executive_summary.pdf

Schunk, D. H. (2008). *Learning theories: An educational perspective.* Upper Saddle River: Pearson: Merrill Prentice Hall.

Sereno, S. & Rayner, K. (2000). The when and where of reading in the brain. *Brain and Cognition*, 42(1), 78–81.

Share, D. & Stanovich, K. (1995). Cognitive processes in early reading development: Accommodating individual differences into a model of acquisition. *Issues in Education*, 1, 1–57.

Snow, C.; Cancino, H.; De Temple, J. & Schley, S. (1991). Giving formal definitions: A linguistic or metalinguistic skill? In E. Bialystok (ed.), *Language processing in bilingual children.* New York: Cambridge University Press. 90–112.

Snow, C. E. & Juel, C. (2005). Teaching children to read: What do we know about how to do it? In M. J. Snowling & C. Hulme (eds.), *The science of reading: A handbook..* Oxford, UK: Blackwell. 501–520.

Snowman, J.; Dobozy, E.; Scevak, J.; Bryer, F. & Bartlett, B. (2009). *Psychology applied to teaching* (1st edn.). Milton, Qld: John Wiley and Sons, Australia.

Sweller, J. (1994). Cognitive load theory, learning difficulty, and instructional design. *Learning and Instruction*, 4, 295–312.

Vygotsky, L. S. (1978). *Mind in society, the development of higher psychological processes.* Cambridge, Massachusetts: Harvard University Press.

Appendix A   **Classroom Literacy Observation Survey – Revised (CLOS-R)**

Respect	1	Rapport	The teacher creates a warm, positive and inviting class-room where relationships with children encourage literacy learning
	2	Credibility	Children's respect for the teacher enables her to maintain order and lesson flow
	3	Citizenship	The teacher promotes equality, tolerance, inclusivity and awareness of the needs of others
Knowledge	4	Purpose	Children's responses indicate tacit or explicit understanding of the purpose of the literacy task
	5	Substance	The teacher provides a lesson/task that leads to substantial literacy engagement, not busy-work
	6	Explanation Word	The teacher clearly explains specific word, letter or sound strategies or concepts
	7	Explanation Sentence	The teacher clearly explains specific grammatical strategies or concepts
	8	Explanation Text	The teacher clearly explains specific textual strategies or concepts
	9	Metalanguage	The teacher provides children with language for talking about and exemplifying literacy concepts
	10	Oral Language	The teacher focuses on the development of children's oral language
	11	Oral/Written Language	The teacher makes logical connections between oral and written language
	12	Awareness	The teacher has a high level of awareness of literacy activities and participation by children
	13	Environment	The teacher uses the literate physical environment as a resource
	14	Structure	The teacher manages a predictable environment in which children understand consistent literacy routines

Orchestration	15	Independence	Children take some responsibility for their own literacy learning
	16	Pace	The teacher provides strong forward momentum in literacy lessons
	17	Transition	The teacher spends minimal time changing activities or uses this time productively
	18	Attention	The teacher ensures that children are focused on the literacy task
	19	Stimulation	The teacher motivates interest in literacy through the creation of a pleasurable, enthusiastic and energetic classroom.
Support	20	Assessment	The teacher uses fine-grained knowledge of children's literacy performance in planning and teaching
	21	Scaffolding	The teacher extends literacy learning through reinforcement, modification or modelling
	22	Feedback	The teacher intervenes in timely, focused, tactful and explicit ways that support children's literacy learning
	23	Responsiveness	The teacher is flexible in sharing and building on children's literacy contributions
	24	Persistence	The teacher provides many opportunities to practise and master new literacy learning
Differentiation	25	Challenge	The teacher extends and promotes higher levels of thinking in literacy learning
	26	Inclusion	The teacher differentiates literacy instruction to recognize individual needs
	27	Connection	The teacher makes connections between class or community literacy-related knowledge for individuals or groups

From Louden, W.; Rohl, M. & Hopkins, S. (2008). *Teaching for growth: Effective teaching of literacy and numeracy*. Perth: Graduate School of Education, The University of Western Australia

Thorsten Piske

Positive and negative effects of exposure to L2 orthographic input in the early phases of foreign language learning: a review

In Ländern wie Deutschland, in denen Schülerinnen und Schüler bereits in der Grundschule damit beginnen, ihre erste Fremdsprache zu erlernen, wird nach wie vor darüber diskutiert, ab wann Grundschulkinder mit dem Lesen und Schreiben in der Fremdsprache beginnen sollten. Nach Einschätzung einiger Wissenschaftlerinnen und Wissenschaftler sprechen verschiedene Argumente gegen die Einführung des Schriftbildes der Fremdsprache in der ersten und zweiten Klasse, d. h. in Klassenstufen, in denen Grundschulkinder noch intensiv damit beschäftigt sind, das Lesen und Schreiben in der Erstsprache zu erlernen. Unter Berücksichtigung verschiedener Forschungsergebnisse werden im vorliegenden Beitrag einige der Argumente gegen die simultane Alphabetisierung in zwei Sprachen diskutiert. Die Ergebnisse dieser Diskussion legen die Schlussfolgerung nahe, dass sich der frühe gleichzeitige Kontakt zu zwei Schriftbildern auf längere Sicht eher positiv als negativ auf die (schrift)sprachliche Entwicklung von Fremdsprachenlernern auswirkt.

1. Introduction

In the literature on second or foreign language (L2) learning, different suggestions have been made with regard to the point in time when primary school students should start to read and write in the L2. According to some researchers, the L2 writing system should not be introduced before the writing system of the students' first language (L1) is well established. Other authors emphasize that there are good reasons why primary school students should be introduced to the writing systems of both their L1 and their L2 at the same time. In this paper, we will first discuss some of the arguments that have been put forward by researchers who have suggested that the introduction of an L2 writing system should be delayed until the L1 writing system is well established. Then, we will describe the results of research examining how early exposure to two writing systems affects primary school students' reading and writing abilities in both their L1 and the L2. The chapter ends with a brief summary and conclusions regarding the effects of early exposure to two writing systems on the development of L2 learners' literacy skills.

2. A discussion of arguments against simultaneous first and second language literacy instruction

Different concerns have been raised in the literature against the simultaneous introduction of two writing systems in the primary school classroom. Some researchers have suggested that foreign language learners should exclusively concentrate on listening to and speaking the L2 in the first one or two years of primary school. Reading and writing in the L2 should, on the other hand, at first be excluded from the early foreign language classroom. These researchers have repeatedly emphasized the primacy of spoken language over written language. This primacy is reflected by the fact that spoken language existed before written language and that children generally learn to listen and speak before they learn to read and write (see, e. g., Bleyhl 2007; Wolf 2007). Consequently, this order in the development of different linguistic abilities should also be followed in the early foreign language classroom. It is, of course, true that children learn to listen and speak before they learn to read and write. However, as research on bilingualism has often shown, many children learn to *speak* two or more languages well if they are exposed to these languages from an early age onwards (e. g., Flege, MacKay & Piske 2002; for reviews, see Baker & Prys Jones 1998; Baker 2006). Thus, it may well be possible that children can also learn to *read and write* in more than one language if they are exposed to more than one writing system at the same time.

Researchers who are skeptical about the simultaneous introduction of two writing systems in primary school have also pointed out that the L2 writing system is likely to interfere with that of the students' L1 if it is introduced too early. According to these researchers, interferences between the L1 and L2 writing systems might have detrimental effects especially on those students who suffer from reading and writing disabilities (e. g., Bleyhl 2000; Füssenich 2006). Other authors have pointed out that most primary school students will – at least in the long run – be more successful in learning to read and write in both their L1 and their L2 if they are given the opportunity to get used to the differences between the two writing systems as early as possible. This would be particularly true in those cases in which the two writing systems differ considerably in terms of phonological transparency, that is in those cases in which the writing system of one language, for example Finnish, is characterized by a highly regular correspondence between the written symbols and the sounds of the language, whereas the writing system of the other language, for example English, is characterized by much less regular correspondences between orthography and phonology (e. g., Zaunbauer 2007; Rymarczyk 2008a, b; see also Bassetti 2009). Rymarczyk (2008a, b), for example, examined German primary school students who had been exposed to the L2 English for two years but who had not received any systematic instruction in English reading and writing. One of the results obtained by Rymarczyk (2008a, b) was that many of the errors made by the students were based on the orthographic rules of German. For example, just like in German, nouns were capitalized (e. g., *Dog* instead of *dog* or *Milk* instead of *milk*). English phonemes were spelt as they are spelt in German (see, e. g., the long vowel /iː/ in *bee* spelt *Bie*). As it is often the case in German, <h> was added to mark a long vowel (e. g., *bluh* instead of *blue*), and consonants were doubled after short vowels (e. g., *mepp* instead of *map*). According to Rymarczyk (2008a, b), such incorrect spellings are much more likely to be used for only a rather short period of time if systematic reading and writing in the L2 English is introduced as early as possible. If, on the other hand, reading and writing in English is delayed, foreign language students will find it difficult to overcome the incorrect spellings established in their minds. Grabe (2009) discusses the results of research examining the role of L1-L2 differences in reading development. On the basis of his literature review he infers different more general implications for L2 reading instruction including the following ones: a) Automatic processing skills developed for reading in the L1 can produce strong interference effects and L2 learners need *explicit* L2 reading instruction so that associative processing can be reset to L2 input. b) It is important for L2 reading instruction to explore ways as to how L1 reading skills can support L2 reading development. c) Reading curricula have to consistently implement some form of extensive reading, i. e. L2 learners should be given the opportunity to read longer texts for extended periods of time.

As far as learners with reading and writing disabilities are concerned, it is interesting to note that some learners with reading disabilities only have difficulties in reading in one of their two languages. Rickard Liow (1999), for example, describes a Chinese learner of English who is dyslexic in English, but not in Chinese. Similarly, Wydell & Butterworth (1999) describe the case of a Japanese learner of English who is dyslexic only in English but not in Japanese. According to Sasaki (2005), the incidence of dyslexia is lower in phonologically transparent writing systems characterized by consistent relationships between letters and sounds than in writing systems with less systematic relationships between letters and sounds. This assumption is supported by a study by Paulesu, Demonet, Fazio, McCrory, Chanonine, Brunswick, Crappa, Cossu, Habib, Frith & Frith (2001) that has shown that dyslexics are half as numerous in Italy as in Britain. As Cook & Bassetti (2005: 8) point out, "English is less phonologically transparent than Italian in that more effort is required to make the connections between letters and sounds in terms both of correspondence rules and orthographic regularities". Finally, Sasaki (2005) reports that in countries using meaning-based writing systems such as Japan or China an awareness of dyslexia is still not widespread.

Meaning-based writing systems may not produce such a high incidence of developmental dyslexia because in these writing systems reading and spelling rely more on visual-orthographic information than on phonological coding. On the whole, the observations just reported suggest that the difficulties learners may experience when learning to read and write in a specific language are always dependent on the specific characteristics of the writing system of this language and in particular on whether the writing system is phonologically more or less transparent or on whether it is meaning-based or sound-based.

A third reason why several authors are skeptical about simultaneous L1 and L2 literacy instruction is based on the observation that primary school students are likely to mispronounce new words if they encounter them in their written forms first. It has repeatedly been reported that learners may pronounce the letters in a new L2 word as they are pronounced in their L1 if the learners are exposed to the spelling of the new word before they have learnt to pronounce it well (e. g., Kahl & Knebler 1996; Young-Scholten 2002; Bleyhl 2007; Bassetti 2009). Young-Scholten (2002), for example, reported that native speakers of American English who spent a year as exchange students in Germany pronounced German words such as *rund* (round) and *Bund* (federation) as [ʁʊnd] and [bʊnd]. This means that they produced final voiced obstruents in these words although German obstruents are usually devoiced in final position. According to Young-Scholten (2002), these learners apparently realized the grapheme <d> as a voiced obstruent because graphemes such as <b, d, g> are usually pronounced as voiced stops in their native language English. The more some of these learners were exposed to aural input from native speakers of German, the more they started to devoice German obstruents in final position.

A study by Piske, Flege, MacKay & Meador (2002) indicates in which way the writing system of a learner's L1 may influence his pronunciation of words in the L2 even if the learner has already been exposed to the L2 for many years. In this study, which examined L2 vowel production accuracy, native speakers of Italian who had immigrated to Canada were asked to pronounce English vowels in real English words and in non-words, i. e. in words such as *bido* that do not exist in the English language. The words the participants of the study were asked to produce were presented to them over loudspeakers and in written form (e. g., <bido>). It was found that a group of native speakers of Italian who had started to learn their L2 English as children and who had already been living in Canada for about 40 years when they were tested did not show any difficulties in accurately pronouncing English vowels such as /ɪ/ and /ɛ/ in a target-like way when these vowels occurred in real English words. However, in many cases, in which the same native speakers of Italian were asked to pronounce the English vowels /ɪ/ and /ɛ/ in non-words, their pronunciation appears to have been influenced by the letters representing the vowels. In the non-word *bido*, which just like the word *bid* was written with the letter <i> in the orthographic representation presented to the participants, the vowel /ɪ/ was, for example, pronounced as an [iː]-quality vowel, reflecting the way the letter <i> is pronounced in Italian. Similarly, in the non-word *bedo*, which just like the word *bed* was written with the letter <e> in the orthographic representation presented to the participants the vowel /ɛ/ was realized as /e/, which reflects the way the letter <e> is often pronounced in Italian. Findings like these suggest that even after many years of exposure to a second or a foreign language, the grapheme-phoneme correspondence rules of a learner's L1 may still have an influence on his pronunciation of an L2 if the learner is asked to read out unfamiliar words or non-words in an L2. However, if the learner is asked to read out familiar words in the L2, the lexical information provided by the spelling of the whole word appears to help him to pronounce these words correctly (see also Ehri, 1999). In other words, if a foreign language student is able to recognize a word because of its spelling as a whole, he will probably be able to pronounce this word in a rather target-like way. If the student, on the other hand, is not able to recognize a word on the basis of its spelling, he appears to be likely to focus on individual letters in this word and may pronounce these letters as they are pronounced in his L1.

Bassetti (2009: 192–193) describes evidence which appears to suggest that L2 learners may even find it easier in some cases to pronounce a familiar word correctly if they see it in its written form. She refers to the observation that Japanese learners of English as an L2 usually show great difficulties in perceiving the difference between English /l/ and /r/ in pairs such as *lip* vs. *rip* or *clown* vs. *crown*. However, as reported, for example, by Brown (1998) and Eckman (2004), Japanese learners of English are much more likely to be able to pronounce /l/ and /r/ if they know whether an English word is spelled with an <l> or an <r>. According to Bassetti (2009), these observations suggest that orthographic input can in some cases be used to complement L2 learners' defective perception of certain L2 sounds and that orthographic input may thus help learners to produce L2 contrasts they do not easily perceive.

On the whole, then, it appears that there are often counterexamples to the arguments presented in the literature to explain why literacy instruction should at first be excluded from the primary school foreign language classroom. Moreover, it has been suggested that children may also benefit from L2 orthographic input in ways other than those discussed so far. As, for example, pointed out by Schmid-Schönbein (2001: 70), written input appears to help children identify word boundaries. Children who have only heard expressions such as *That's right!* may think that these expressions consist of only one word. Only when they see such expressions in their written form, will they often understand that they consist of more than one word. According to Schmid-Schönbein (2001), it also appears to be easier for some L2 learners to remember words or phrases if they have seen them in their orthographic form.

Finally, some authors (e. g. Lüdtke 1969, 1982, 1983) have suggested that only when children learn to read and write alphabetic symbols, will they start to develop an awareness of individual sound segments such as consonants and vowels. Other authors have questioned this assumption. According to these authors, children will not be able to learn to read and write alphabetic symbols unless they have already developed a certain degree of phonological awareness (e. g. Studdert-Kennedy 1987; Piske 2001; Piske 2008). This latter assumption is supported by studies showing that humans are indeed able to segment speech into phonemic units before they learn to read and write (e. g., Smith & Tager-Flusberg 1980; Thompson, Fletcher-Flinn & Cotrell 1999). One thing that appears to happen when humans start to read and write in an alphabetic system is that their ability to segment speech into phonemic units is in most cases noticeably enhanced (e. g. Sendlmeier 1987). According to Studdert-Kennedy (1987), there are different sources of evidence confirming that humans mentally organize speech on the basis of phonemic units. Apart from humans' ability to learn to read and write in an alphabetic system, these sources of evidence include errors of perception and production, backward talking and aphasic deficit. Studdert-Kennedy (1987) also points out that the alphabet not only serves to notate but to control human behavior. Most humans could not write and read with such ease if alphabetic symbols did not correspond to units of perceptuomotor control. He concludes that lexical items are stored in the brain as sequences of abstract perceptuomotor units for which the letters of an alphabet are symbols and that alphabetic writing systems could not have developed unless the mental organization of speech was based on segmental units such as phonemes:

> Historically, the possibility of the alphabet was discovered, not invented. Just as the bicycle was a discovery of locomotor possibilities implicit in the cyclical motions of walking and running, so the alphabet was a discovery of linguistic possibilities implicit in patterns of speaking. (Studdert-Kennedy, 1987: 46)

To summarize the discussion in this section, it appears that the concerns that have been expressed by different researchers about an early introduction of reading and writing in the primary school foreign language classroom are not well founded. Of course, interferences between the L1 and L2 writing systems are likely to occur when L2 learners, and in particular young L2 learners, are exposed to two writing systems at the same time. However, only rarely and only under specific circumstances do these interferences appear to have any longer lasting negative effects on L2 learners' literacy development. This assumption is also supported by the results of studies that have examined primary school students who were exposed to two writing systems from the beginning of primary school. Findings of studies examining such students will be described in the following section.

3. Effects of simultaneous L1 and L2 literacy instruction on primary school students' L1 literacy skills

The previous section mainly concentrated on discussing how early exposure to two writing systems may generally affect L2 learners' linguistic skills. This section will review the results of a few studies that have examined how early exposure to two writing systems affects primary school students' literacy skills in both their L1 and the L2. Some of these studies were carried out in Northern Germany and compared the L1 reading and writing skills of students enrolled in a German-English immersion program to the L1 reading and writing skills of students who received most of their instruction in German and only single lessons in English.

The primary schools students enrolled in the German-English immersion program received their instruction in all subjects, except for German language arts, in the L2 English from the first day of grade 1 onwards. Just like their peers in non-immersion classes, the students in the partial immersion program received their literacy training in German in daily 45-minute German lessons (for more details regarding the characteristics of immersion programs, see e. g., Johnson & Swain 1997; Wesche 2002; Piske & Burmeister 2008; Wode 2009). In the L2 English, on the other hand, they were not systematically taught to read and write during their time at primary school. However, this does not mean that the English writing system was excluded from the classroom. From the start their teachers created a "literacy-rich environment" (e. g., Peregoy & Boyle 2005: 183) by providing written input in English in books, on worksheets, labels, posters, wall dictionaries, etc. This means that although the children received systematic literacy instruction only in German, they had the opportunity to get used to both the German and English writing systems from the beginning (for more details regarding the students' literacy instruction and their ability to read and write in English, see Burmeister & Piske 2008 and Burmeister, this volume). The immersion students' peers in non-immersion classrooms were taught English only once a week in 'regular' 45-minute English lessons, and they were, thus exposed to both aural and written L2 input much less frequently than the students in the immersion classes.

Several studies have compared the immersion students' reading and writing skills in German to the German reading and writing skills displayed by primary school students in non-immersion classes from the same school and different schools by using the following standardized tests of reading and writing: a) *Würzburger Leise Leseprobe* (e. g., Küspert & Schneider 1998). When participating in this test children have to select one out of four pictures corresponding to a certain word. This test was used by Zaunbauer & Möller (2006, 2007) to examine first, second and third graders' reading abilities at word level. b) Reading comprehension test from PIRLS (Progress in International Reading Literacy Study). Zaunbauer, Bonerad & Möller (2005) and Zaunbauer & Möller (2006) used this test to examine third and fourth graders' reading comprehension abilities in German. The students had to read one or two German texts and answer open and closed questions (for further details regarding this test, see Bos, Lankes, Prenzel, Schwippert, Valtin & Walther 2004). c) *Hamburger Lesetest für Klassen 3 und 4* (Lehmann, Peek & Poerschke 1997). This test was developed to determine reading speed and comprehension and was used by Bachem (2004) to examine fourth graders' reading abilities. d) *Hamburger Schreib-Probe* (May 2002). By measuring the number of correctly written words as well as the number of correctly written letters and combinations of letters, this test can be used to examine primary schools students' writing skills. It was employed by Zaunbauer & Möller (2006, 2007) with first, second and third grade primary school students. One of the major findings of the studies examining primary school students from immersion and non-immersion classes in Northern Germany was that the scores obtained by the immersion students in the different tests examining their reading and writing skills in German were not significantly different from those of students who had received their instruction almost exclusively in German. This finding suggests that the high amount of L2 orthographic input the immersion students are exposed to does not have any negative effects on their literacy skills in German. Moreover, in an L1 literacy study by Turnbull, Lapkin & Hart (2001), immersion students in grade 6 received test scores that were notably better than the scores obtained by monolingually educated peers. This means that over time the exposure to two writing systems might even have increasingly positive effects on immersion students' literacy skills in both the L2 and the L1.

The assumption that young foreign language learners benefit from an early introduction to reading and writing in the L2 is also supported by research examining primary school students exposed to the foreign language for only fairly brief periods of time per week. Schaer & Bader (2003) and Bader & Schaer (2006, for a summary of these two studies, see Husfeldt & Bader-Lehmann 2009), for example, examined primary schools students in Switzerland, who started to learn English in grade 3. Among other things, they examined the students' reading comprehension skills in English at the end of grades 4 and 6[1] and their skills in writing a letter in English. According to the authors, the students achieved very good results at the end of grades 4 and 6 in tasks examining their reading comprehension abilities. At the end of grade 6, i. e. after four years of exposure to English in primary school, all students were able to write comprehensible English letters consisting of an average of 9 sentences within 15 minutes.

One of the major goals of a study by Edelenbos, Johnstone & Kubanek (2006, for a summary of this study, see also Edelenbos & Kubanek 2009) conducted for the European Commission was to provide a review of research carried out in Europe in the field of early foreign language learning and teaching. The authors point out that only a few studies have systematically examined how primary school students' reading and writing skills develop if they learn to read and write in two languages from an early age onwards. One of the studies cited by the authors is Dlugosz (2000), who found that the simultaneous introduction of reading in the L1 and the L2 in grade 1 helped children to develop more fluent speaking skills in the foreign language. Mertens (2003) is another study the authors refer to. He found that children who learnt French in Grade 1 in primary schools in Germany benefitted from being introduced to written French immediately. Based on the results of the studies by Dlugosz (2000), Mertens (2003) and others, Edelenbos, Johnstone & Kubanek (2006: 148) conclude that foreign language teachers should not only focus on listening and speaking in the early primary grades, but that reading and writing in the L2 should be introduced at an early stage, too:

> The evidence suggests that young children can benefit in a number of ways if their initial experience is not restricted to 'listening', 'speaking' and 'doing' but includes a gradual and systematic introduction to reading and writing from an early point. The reading and writing ought desirably to fit into a broader school approach to literacy development and equally may focus on local community languages as well as on the particular language the children are learning.

4. Conclusions

The review presented in this paper has shown that the concerns about simultaneous L1 and L2 literacy instruction that have sometimes been expressed in the literature have usually not been supported by the results of studies examining primary school immersion students and students from non-immersion classes who were exposed to two writing systems from the beginning or from a relatively early point onwards. On the contrary, according to the results of several studies cited in this paper, it appears to be the case that students who are exposed to two

---

1 In Switzerland, primary school covers grades 1 to 6.

writing systems immediately may – at least in the long run – even obtain better results in tests examining their literacy skills than primary school students who are exposed to only one writing system. Moreover, if arguments against simultaneous L1 and L2 literacy instruction in the early grades are explored in more detail, it becomes obvious that these arguments are usually not well founded, because long-lasting negative effects of early exposure to two writing systems on L2 learners' literacy skills have only been observed under rather specific circumstances. All of this suggests that researchers should not focus on the question *when* literacy instruction in an L2 should be introduced in primary schools but that they should rather examine *how* primary school children should systematically be taught to read and write in two languages at the same time.

5. References

Bachem, Jessica (2004), *Lesefähigkeiten deutscher Kinder im frühen englischen Immersionsunterricht*. Unpublished master's thesis. University of Kiel.

Bader, Ursula & Schaer, Ursula (2006), Evaluation Englisch in den 6. Klassen Appenzell Innerrhoden 2005. Bericht. Fachochoschule Nordwestschweiz und Pädagogische Hochschule Bern. Available at: http://www.ai.ch/dl.php/de/0cqlr-ovtpgv/Evaluationsbericht_Englisch_an_der_Primarschule_6._Klasse.pdf. Accessed 17.01.10.

Baker, Colin (2006), *Foundations of Bilingual Education and Bilingualism* (4th edition). Clevedon: Multilingual Matters.

Baker, Colin & Prys Jones, Sylvia (1998), *Encyclopedia of Bilingualism and Bilingual Education*. Clevedon: Multilingual Matters.

Bassetti, Benedetta (2009), Orthographic input and second language phonology. In: Piske, Thorsten & Young-Scholten, Martha (eds.) (2009), *Input Matters in SLA*. Bristol: Multilingual Matters, 191–206.

Bleyhl, Werner (2000), Empfehlungen zur Verwendung des Schriftlichen im Fremdspracherwerb der Grundschule. In: Bleyhl, Werner (ed.) (2000), *Fremdsprachen in der Grundschule. Grundlagen und Praxisbeispiele*. Hannover: Schroedel, 84–91.

Bleyhl, Werner (2007), Schrift im fremdsprachlichen Anfangsunterricht – ein zweischneidiges Schwert. *Take off! Zeitschrift für frühes Englischlernen* 1/2007, 47.

Bos, Wilfried, Lankes, Eva-Maria, Prenzel, Manfred, Schwippert, Knut, Valtin, Renate & Walther, Gerd (eds.), (2004), *IGLU. Einige Länder der Bundesrepublik Deuschland im nationalen und internationalen Vergleich*. Münster: Waxmann.

Brown, Cynthia A. (1998), The role of L1 grammar in the L2 acquisition of segmental structure. *Second Language Research* 14, 136–193.

Burmeister, P. & Piske, T. (2008). Schriftlichkeit im fremdsprachlichen Sachfachunterricht an der Grundschule. In: Böttger, Heiner (ed.) (2008), *Fortschritte im Frühen Fremdsprachenlernen. Ausgewählte Tagungsbeiträge Nürnberg 2007.* München: Domino Verlag, 183–193.

Cook, Vivian & Bassetti, Benedetta (2005), An introduction to researching second language writing systems. In: Cook, Vivian & Bassetti, Benedetta (eds.) (2005), *Second Language Writing Systems.* Clevedon: Multilingual Matters, 1–67.

Dlugosz, D.W. (2000), Rethinking the role of reading in teaching a foreign language to young learners. *ELT Journal* 54, 284 - 290.

Eckman, Fred (2004), From phonemic differences to constraint rankings: Research on second language phonology. *Studies in Second Language Acquisition* 26, 371–385.

Edelenbos, Peter, Johnstone, Richard & Kubanek, Angelika (2006/07), *The Main Pedagogical Principles Underlying the Teaching of Languages to Very Young Learners. Languages for the Children of Europe. Published Research, Good Practice & Main Principles. Final Report of the EAC 89/04, Lot 1 study.* Brussels: European Commission, Education and Culture, Culture and Communication, Multilingualism Policy.

Edelenbos, Peter & Kubanek, Angelika (2009), Die EU-Schlüsselstudie über Frühbeginn – Forschung, gute Praxis und pädagogische Grundsätze. In: Engel, Gaby, Groot-Wilken, Bernd & Thürmann, Eike (eds.) (2009), *Englisch in der Primarstufe – Chancen und Herausforderungen. Evaluation und Erfahrungen aus der Praxis.* Berlin: Cornelsen, 23–34.

Ehri, Linnea (1999), Phases of development in learning to read words. In: Oakhill, Jane & Beard, Roger (eds.), *Reading Development and the Teaching of Reading: A Psychological Perspective.* Oxford: Blackwell, 79–108.

Flege, James E., MacKay, Ian R. A. & Piske, Thorsten (2002), Assessing bilingual dominance. *Applied Psycholinguistics* 23, 567–598.

Füssenich, Iris (2006), Frühes Fremdsprachenlernen – Herausforderung oder Überforderung für Kinder mit Förderbedarf? In: Hahn, Angelika & Klippel, Friederike (eds.), *Sprachen schaffen Chancen. Dokumentation zum 21. Kongress für Fremdsprachendidaktik der Deutschen Gesellschaft für Fremdsprachenforschung (DGFF) München, Oktober 2005.* München, Düsseldorf, Stuttgart: Oldenbourg, 111–126.

Grabe, William (2009), *Reading in a Second Language: Moving from Theory to Practice.* Cambridge: Cambridge University Press.

Husfeldt, Vera & Bader-Lehmann, Ursula (2009), Englisch in der Primarstufe – Erfahrungen aus der Schweiz. In: Engel, Gaby, Groot-Wilken, Bernd & Thürmann,

Eike (eds.) (2009), *Englisch in der Primarstufe – Chancen und Herausforderungen. Evaluation und Erfahrungen aus der Praxis.* Berlin: Cornelsen, 111–123.

Johnson, Robert K. & Swain, Merrill (eds.) (1997). *Immersion Education: International Perspectives.* New York: Cambridge University Press.

Kahl, Peter & Knebler, Ulrike (1996), *Englisch in der Grundschule – und dann? Evaluation des Hamburger Schulversuchs „Englisch ab Klasse 3".* Berlin: Cornelsen.

Küspert, Petra & Schneider, Wolfgang (1998). *Würzburger Leise Leseprobe (WLLP):* Ein Gruppenlesetest für die Grundschule. Göttingen: Hogrefe.

Lehmann, Rainer H., Peek, Rainer & Poerschke, Jan (1997). *HAMLET 3–4. Hamburger Lesetest für 3. und 4. Klassen. Beiheft mit Anleitung.* Weinheim und Basel: Beltz Verlag.

Lüdtke, H. (1969), Die Alphabetschrift und das Problem der Lautsegmentierung. *Phonetica* 20, 147–176.

Lüdtke, Helmut (1982), Die ‚sprachlichen Einheiten' als wissenschaftstheoretisches Problem. In: Detering, Klaus, Schmidt-Radefeldt, Jürgen & Sucharowski Wolfgang (eds.) (1982), *Sprache beschreiben und erklären: Akten des 16. linguistischen Kolloquiums. Kiel 1981, Band 1.* Tübingen: Niemeyer, 32–39.

Lüdtke, Helmut (1983), Sprache und Schrift: sieben Thesen. *Zeitschrift für Semiotik* 5, 353–361.

May, Peter (2002), *Hamburger Schreib-Probe. (6th updated and expanded edition).* Hamburg: vpm.

Mertens, Jürgen (2003). Rhythm, rhymes and rules. Vom Nutzen der Schrift (nicht nur) beim frühen Englischlernen. *Fremdsprachenunterricht*, 47 (56), 168–173.

Paulesu Eraldo, Demonet, Jean-François, Fazio, Ferruccio, McCrory, Eamon, Chanoine, Valérie, Brunswick, Nicola, Cappa, Stefano F., Cossu, Giuseppe, Habib, Michel, Frith, Christopher D. & Frith, Uta (2001), Dyslexia: Cultural diversity and biological unity. *Science* 291, 2165–2167.

Peregoy, Suzanne F. & Boyle, Owen F. (2005), *Reading, Writing, and Learning in ESL. A Resource Book for K-12 Teachers.* Boston: Pearson Education.

Piske, Thorsten (2001), *Artikulatorische Muster im frühen Laut- und Lexikonerwerb.* Tübingen: Narr.

Piske, Thorsten; Flege, James E., MacKay, Ian R. A. & Meador, Diane (2002), The production of English vowels by fluent early and late Italian-English bilinguals. *Phonetica* 59, 49–71.

Piske, Thorsten (2008), Phonetic awareness, phonetic sensitivity and the second language learner. In: Cenoz, Jasone & Hornberger, Nancy, H. (eds.) (2008), *Encyclopedia of Language and Education (2nd edition). Volume 6. Knowledge about Language.* New York: Springer, 155–166.

Piske, Thorsten & Burmeister, Petra (2008), Erfahrungen mit früher englischer Immersion an norddeutschen Grundschulen. In: Schlemminger, Gerald (ed.) (2008), *Erforschung des bilingualen Lehrens und Lernens: Forschungsarbeiten und Erprobungen von Unterrichtskonzepten und -materialien in der Grundschule*. Baltmannsweiler: Schneider Verlag Hohengehren, 131–151.

Rickard Liow, Susan J. (1999), Reading skill development in bilingual Singaporean children. In: Harris, Margaret & Hatano, Giyoo. (eds.) (1999), *Learning to Read and Write: A Cross-Linguistic Perspective*. Cambridge: Cambridge University Press, 196–213.

Rymarczyk, Jutta (2008a), Früher oder später? Zur Einführung des Schriftbildes in der Grundschule. In: Böttger, Heiner (ed.) (2008), *Fortschritte im Frühen Fremdsprachenlernen. Ausgewählte Tagungsbeiträge Nürnberg 2007*. München: Domino Verlag, 170–182.

Rymarczyk, Jutta (2008b), Mythos-Box: „Paralleler Schriftspracherwerb in Erst- und Fremdsprache ist unmöglich!" *Take off! Zeitschrift für frühes Englischlernen* 4/2008, 48.

Sasaki, Miho (2005), The effect of L1 reading processes on L2: A crosslinguistic comparison of Italian and Japanese users of English. In: Cook, Vivian & Bassetti, Benedetta (eds.) (2005), *Second Language Writing Systems*. Clevedon: Multilingual Matters, 289–308.

Schaer, Ursula & Bader, Ursula (2003), *Evaluation Englisch an der Primarschule Projekt 012. Appenzell Innerrhoden Mai bis November 2003*. Available at: http://www.ai.ch/dl.php/de/0cqlr-bux78p/Evaluationsbericht_Englisch_an_ der_Primarschule_3._4._Klasse.pdf. Accessed 17.01.10.

Smith, Carol & Tager-Flusberg, Helen (1980), The relationship between language comprehension and the development of metalinguistic awareness. *Paper presented at the Annual Boston University Conference on Language Development* (5th, Boston, MA, October 1980).

Schmid-Schönbein, Gisela (2001), *Didaktik. Grundschulenglisch*. Berlin: Cornelsen.

Sendlmeier, Walter F. (1987), Die psychologische Realität von Einzellauten bei Analphabeten. *Sprache und Kognition* 2, 64–71.

Studdert-Kennedy, Michael (1987), The phoneme as a perceptuomotor structure. *Haskins Laboratories Status Report on Speech Research* 1987, SR-91, 45–57.

Thompson, G. Brian, Fletcher-Flinn, Claire M. & Cottrell, David S. (1999), Learning correspondences between letters and phonemes without explicit instruction. *Applied Psycholinguistics* 20, 21–50.

Turnbull, Miles, Lapkin, Sharon & Hart, Doug (2001), Grade 3 Immersion students' performance in literacy and mathematics: province-wide results from Ontario (1998–99). *The Canadian Modern Language Review* 58, 9–26.

Wesche, Marjorie Bingham (2002), Early French immersion: How has the original Canadian model stood the test of time? In: Burmeister, Petra, Piske, Thorsten & Rohde, Andreas (eds.) (2002), *An Integrated View of Language Development. Papers in Honor of Henning Wode*. Trier: Wissenschaftlicher Verlag Trier, 357–379.

Wolf, Maryanne (2007). *Proust and the Squid. The Story and Science of the Reading Brain*. New York: HarperCollins Publishers.

Wode, Henning (2009), *Frühes Fremdsprachenlernen in Kindergärten und Grundschulen*. Braunschweig: Westermann.

Wydell, Taeko N. & Butterworth, Brian L. (1999), A case study of an English-Japanese bilingual with monolingual dyslexia. *Cognition* 70, 273–305.

Young-Scholten, Martha (2002), Orthographic input in L2 phonological development. In: Burmeister, Petra; Piske, Thorsten & Rohde, Andreas (eds.) (2002), *An Integrated View of Language Development: Papers in Honor of Henning Wode*. Trier: Wissenschaftlicher Verlag Trier, 264–279.

Zaunbauer, Anna C. M. (2007), Lesen und Schreiben in der Fremdsprache – von Anfang an. *Take off! Zeitschrift für frühes Englischlernen* 1/2007, 46.

Zaunbauer, Anna C. M. & Möller, Jens (2006), Ein Vergleich monolingual und teilimmersiv unterrichteter Kinder der zweiten und dritten Klassenstufe. *Zeitschrift für Fremdsprachenforschung* 17, 181–200.

Zaunbauer, Anna C. M. & Möller, Jens (2007), Schulleistungen monolingual und immersiv unterrichteter Kinder am Ende des ersten Schuljahres. *Zeitschrift für Entwicklungspsychologie und Pädagogische Psychologie* 39, 141–153.

Zaunbauer, Anna C. M., Bonerad, Eva-Marie & Möller, Jens (2005), Muttersprachliches Leseverständnis immersiv unterrichteter Kinder. *Zeitschrift für Pädagogische Psychologie* 19, 233–235.

Bärbel Diehr

Research into reading in the primary school: a fresh look at the use of written English with young learners of English as a Foreign Language

Nach etlichen Jahren des Erprobens verschiedener Konzepte und der lokalen und regionalen Schulversuche erfolgte die Einführung des regulären Fremdsprachenunterrichts an Grundschulen je nach Bundesland zwischen 1999 bis 2004. Im Laufe der Zeit etablierte sich eine Theorie des Lehrens und Lernens, die Lehrkräften und Forschern eine solide Grundlage bietet, auf der jungen Lernenden fremdsprachliche Kompetenzen vermittelt werden. Allerdings mangelt es bis heute an einem systematischen Ansatz zur Vermittlung der Schriftsprache im Fremdsprachenunterricht der Grundschule. Nach nunmehr fast einem Jahrzehnt des trial and error – und punktuellen Einzelstudien – steht der Erwerb von fremdsprachiger Lese- und Schreibfähigkeit erst jetzt im Mittelpunkt von Fremdsprachendidaktik und Bildungspolitik. Der vorliegende Beitrag stellt einer breiten akademischen und professionellen Leserschaft das innovative Konzept LiPs (Lesen im Englischunterricht der Primarstufe) vor. LiPs wurde konzipiert, um den oben skizzierten Mangel an systematischen Vorgehensweisen zu beheben. Die Ergebnisse der von 2005 bis 2007 durchgeführten Vorläuferstudie JuLE (Junge Lerner lesen Englisch) wurden sowohl bei der Entwicklung des hier vorgestellten Konzeptes als auch bei der Planung des aktuellen LiPs-Foschungsprojekts berücksichtigt. Abschließend wird der Bedarf an einer weiteren Erforschung des hier vorgestellten Ansatzes umrissen, der die Lösung einer Reihe von Schwierigkeiten verspricht, denen Grundschullerner und ihre Lehrer angesichts der Integration der englischen Schriftsprache in das Grundschulcurriculum begegnen.

1. Written English in the primary school and the need for a reading scheme

Despite the enormous impact on the German educational system of English as a Foreign Language (EFL) in primary school, its likely implications were at first not fully considered. Since the learners were 'just children', and since they were 'just picking up a new language', the hurried training of EFL primary teachers was provided in a rather slapdash manner. In addition, the primary EFL programmes in the different federal states of Germany differed widely in conception and projected outcome. No consensus on a systematic national scheme for teaching foreign languages to children aged 6 to 10 has so far been reached. Some federal states introduced foreign language learning earlier than others. Then, at the beginning of the 21st century, most German primary schools started teaching a foreign language in year 3; gradually some ministries brought the beginning forward to year 1. Yet there is still no consensus on the standards of achievement for the end of primary schooling.

This lack of consistency is also reflected in the attitudes of educationalists and researchers to the use of written English in primary classrooms: In the federal state of Baden-Wurttemberg, children start learning English in year 1, but the syllabus proposes that written forms are not to be introduced to learners before year 3 (cf. MKJS 2004: 70f.). In the federal state of North Rhine-Westphalia on the other hand, the ministry of education took a noticeably different course after having at first implemented English in year 3 in 2004: from 2008 onwards primary school children start learning English from year 1 onwards, with the written language being used right from the beginning (cf. MSW 2008: 73). These basically political decisions about written English were accompanied neither by empirical evidence of second language literacy learning nor by practical suggestions for practitioners who were required, despite insufficient training, to implement EFL in primary school. Regardless of the importance of reading, a carefully considered scheme for introducing written forms in primary school EFL classes has not so far been proposed, leaving teachers to find out by trial and error what approach best serves their learners in coping with written English. Due to the degree of disorganization and the randomness of the methods chosen, the children's potential has never been fully realized.

The educational approach adopted roughly between 1999 and 2007 gave exclusive priority to oral language during the first years of regular EFL teaching in primary school. It has led to the exclusion of English written forms in years 1 and 2 as well as a significant marginalisation of the written language in years 3 and 4. Thus the practice of teaching English as a foreign language in primary school has failed to give pupils a satisfactory exposure to the written language.

The scattergun approach to dealing with written English was exacerbated by certain curricular contradictions: despite the widespread exclusion of written forms, the syllabi nevertheless prescribe that from year 3 onwards learners should be able to use dictionaries and electronic media, and should document their own learning progress in portfolios – all of these skills requiring a secure command of the written language (cf. e. g. MKJS 2004: 77; MSW 2008: 75). Paradoxically, also, pupils at the end of year 4 are expected to be able to read and write English texts. The assumption in all this seems to be that the skill of reading English will emerge automatically, and that primary school children will effortlessly and independently develop the ability to read English writing and discover the rules of grapheme-phoneme correspondence in the foreign language. It is apparently presumed that learners who are familiar with the spoken form of words will recognise the written forms of those words and phrases with little or no tuition.

Between 2002 and 2007 a study was conducted to trial methods and tasks for the assessment of young learners' speaking skills in a foreign language (Diehr 2006; Diehr & Frisch 2008). An unexpected by-product of this study was the realisation of the degree of difficulty experienced by those learners who had to deal with a short written text in one specific assessment task. This led to the hypothesis that without help from the teacher and without a certain amount of explicit instruction the allegedly uncomplicated acquisition of literacy skills does not occur. Rather, learners in years 3 and 4 participating in the study initially exhibited considerable difficulty in reading aloud familiar texts. Familiarity with the phonological forms of words, and first experiences with written forms, did not guarantee the effortless recognition of familiar lexical items at all. Following these observations the JuLE project (*Junge Lerner lesen Englisch*, German for: Young Learners Read in English) was launched to explore further the question of how written English can successfully be used in the primary EFL class, and specifically what role oral reading may play in the acquisition of second language literacy.

The JuLE project (see section 3) consists of three case studies, conducted between 2005 and 2007, which have helped to develop the proposed second language reading scheme for primary school learners of English. The new scheme features two major innovations: first, the use of oral reading as a technique for raising language awareness, especially phonological awareness, and supporting the development of a second language inner voice (Vygotsky 1986), and second, the transfer of the based phonics method (e. g. Johnston & Watson 2007) to second language learning. These two features are placed at the centre of the recent follow-up LiPs study and are explained both here and in the paper by Frisch in this volume.

2. Towards a structured reading scheme for EFL in primary schools

This new reading scheme, LiPs, has been developed in response to classroom observations that children as early as in year 1 show a keen interest in written English. Although it proposes a structured approach to reading, this scheme does not question the primacy of oral communication in the primary EFL class. To assist children aged 6 to 10 to become confident speakers of English and express themselves in the spoken language remains the leading objective of primary school English. In contrast to the 'script-free' programmes for second language teaching, the key assumption here is that a carefully considered use of written English will actually improve teaching and learning EFL in primary school.

There is reason to assume that written English may be employed as early as in primary classes as an analytic tool that stimulates reflection on language (Reichart-Wallrabenstein 2004; Rymarczyk 2008). Thus, experience of English writing also focuses the learners' attention on differences between their mother tongue and the new language. For now, a short example may suffice: without recourse to the written version the utterance "I take a /peə(r)ː/" remains ambiguous. 'A pair' or 'a pear'? Even adult foreign language learners are known to struggle with the meaning of unfamiliar sequences of sounds, and, in their effort to make sense of what they have heard in actual fact, distort the meaning. Pinker lists a number of amusing oronyms, strings of sound that learners carved into words different from their original meaning, e. g. "They played the Bohemian Rap City" instead of "Bohemian Rhapsody" (Pinker 1994: 160 f.). The written language has the effect of clarifying meaning by separating the stream of sounds into negotiable lexical items. It can serve as a visual support – especially with young learners – helping them to come to terms with the segmentation of not yet habitualised sound sequences into words.

Further, there are those characteristics of human memory that should prompt us not to ignore written forms in primary school. Above all, our understanding of the way working memory operates leads to the conclusion that the parallel demonstration of phonological and visual symbols relieves the burden on working memory while processing language. Therefore, to exploit fully the mnemonic effect of written forms and to encourage beneficial interaction between sound and letter, oral reading plays an important role at certain stages within the proposed scheme (cf. Karcher 1994: 271; cf. Reichart-Wallrabenstein 2004: 145).

2.1 Guidelines for a structured reading scheme

The LiPs scheme accords with the latest primary English syllabus published by the federal government of North Rhine-Westphalia, which requires teachers to use the written language as an aid to learning English as a foreign language right from the beginning of year 1 (MSW 2008: 73). Yet, the proposed scheme expands the syllabus' approach to written English, insofar as it suggests that the written language fulfils functions beyond merely aiding oral learning. Written language constitutes a means of communication in its own right and thus requires clear objectives as well as explicit instruction.

Starting point

Ideally, then, the second language literacy learning process starts in year 1, with a quasi-simultaneous introduction of written forms in the first as well as in the second language, although explicit literacy instruction in the second language may be delayed by a few months to give children the chance to first familiarise themselves with the idea of a writing system in their first language.

Objectives

The competencies targeted by the scheme need to be laid down as clearly defined learning outcomes, quite similar to, yet more explicitly stated than in the standards used in the syllabus referred to (cf. MSW 2008: 78). These standards would then fulfil two functions, a destination for primary school teachers and a point of departure for secondary school teachers. My understanding of young learners' handling of written English suggests that pupils' potential exceeds the abilities described in the curricular standards. The syllabus regards written forms largely as an additional aid to learning a new language, while in the scheme proposed here written English is considered as a medium in its own right, deserving to be given its own place on the syllabus because it allows learners to express themselves and to access information and material that interests them. In particular, the ability to read authentic English texts is likely to boost learners' motivation and pride, and to increase their awareness of the progress they have made. Thus, expanding the ministerial standards, the LiPs scheme aims at enabling primary school EFL learners to read unfamiliar texts, enjoy new stories and use print and electronic material for gathering information by the end of year 4.

Teaching methods

The challenging goals set by the LiPs scheme require a carefully considered and structured teaching method that draws on both accepted theory and successful existing practices. It needs to give primary school learners space at first for implicit learning and discovery of patterns, but later on they also need well designed tasks and explicit instruction encouraging them to notice specific features of the written language. At present we are working to develop a comprehensive set of techniques, a typology, as it were, geared towards raising young learners' awareness of English writing. What follows is, by way of example, a brief explanation of three of these techniques.

1. Foregrounding English grapheme-phoneme correspondence (GPC) rules: In order to draw learners' attention to certain peculiarities of English GPC rules, techniques are required that help them notice detail. In this area it is important to note the fundamental differences that exist between the comparatively regular German GPC with its shallow orthography and English with its deep orthography and complex GPC rules (cf. e. g. Elbro 1999: 130ff.; cf. Grabe & Stoller 2002: 125ff.) Direct instruction helps learners notice differences: "There is a small animal that is called /maʊs/ in English and in German. But look, when we write the English word, we can see an <e> on the end of the word, but when we read it, we do not say it and we cannot hear it. It is a silent <e>." Also, without directly talking about the GPC rules teachers can point at particular instances, which at a later stage will be elaborated upon. "We write 'eyes', and we say it with a buzzing /z/. If we say /aɪs/ with a hissing /s/, we are saying something totally different: 'ice'."
2. Employing analogies: Faced with numerous grapheme-phoneme irregularities, the employment of analogies assists learning: "'Mouse' looks like 'house', four letters are the same, and we say it in the same way as we say 'house'." In the same way, rhymes such as 'nice/ice' or 'paw/saw' are useful in furthering learners' phonological awareness of the foreign language.
3. Adopting the phonics approach: At this point a third practice deserves special mention: the phonics approach, which in English speaking countries has recently been successfully adopted in the early stages of literacy teaching and whose usefulness to second language reading is being investigated (cf. Frisch in this volume; cf. Lázaro in this volume).

2.2 A roadmap to reading: phases in a structured reading scheme

At the present stage of the scheme's development, it is planned that reading is taught in approximately five major phases which are not to be misunderstood as rigid steps but rather as a model roadmap or programme ensuring that learners are given enough support and stimulation to achieve the goal of reading unfamiliar texts independently. Teachers can and must interpret and adapt this roadmap to reading to suit the needs of their particular groups of learners, taking into account conditions in their actual classrooms.

Phase one: Maintaining a strong emphasis on oral communication, frequently used content words are introduced with the help of flashcards and posters to build up a vocabulary of sight words and contribute to a print-rich environment. In this phase "reading" is practised in the form of choral reading and imitating the teacher while looking at the written word on a flashcard. Individual learners may be asked to "read" whole words that they recognize as units of meaning thanks to their visual shape, or conspicuous features of their shape e. g. the <ll> in yellow (cf. Ehri 1999: 99). This phase serves to support the rapid acquisition of a basic oral vocabulary that allows learners in year one to communicate in the foreign language. Learners come across a selection of written forms at the same time as they are introduced to the spoken items. Thus learners become aware of the two modes, in a way which complements their experience in their first tongue.

Phase two: Learners are encouraged to use the same techniques as in phase one, i.e. read with the teacher and then try to recognize written items by themselves, but now the word cards are replaced by strips of sentences, which can then be combined into short texts consisting of three or four sentences. This second phase should follow the first one quite quickly, possibly even after only a couple of weeks: after all, communicative language learning cannot be based on isolated lexical items, but requires the joining together of inflected forms to create sentences and the linking of sentences to produce extended text. From phase two onwards, the use of authentic children's books becomes possible without the teacher straining to hide the written text or to simplify phrases the learners are not yet familiar with.

Phase three: A significant step forward is taken when awareness-raising methods are employed and orthographic features are explicitly introduced, roughly around the beginning of year two depending on the readiness of the individual groups of learners (see 'Teaching methods' in 2.1 above). With very keen and able learners, teachers may decide to speak directly about written forms as early as in year one, whereas they may postpone explicit instruction with another group until the end of year two. The safest indicators of learners' readiness for explicit teaching are questions asked and assumptions made by the children themselves: "In English words are written differently" or "English spelling is harder (or funnier) than German spelling" or "This word sounds different in German from English" (cf. Reichart-Wallrabenstein 2004: 409 ff.) Then the time comes to speak specifically about the relation between written and spoken English, drawing the learners' attention to the difference in grapheme-phoneme correspondence (GPC) rules between their first language and English.

Phase four: Insights gleaned from literacy research in English speaking countries and observations made in British primary schools have reinforced my conviction that oral reading deserves more attention than it has received in the past (e. g. Gibson 2008; Opitz & Rasinski 1998). In phase four of the LiPs scheme individual oral reading commences in year 2 in order to practise and to check decoding skills and reading strategies. Furthermore, learners are encouraged to read through and make sense of children's books and stories with the help of semi-vocalisation (e. g. de Guerrero 2004; Kragler 1996;) and subvocalisation before they attempt silent reading for comprehension in the next phase.

Phase five: Now learners are exposed to a wider variety of reading materials and they build on skills already acquired to pursue reading for different purposes. This phase commences around the beginning of year 3 when learners habitualize silent reading strategies. Having mastered decoding skills they now read for pleasure and for information, focusing on comprehension skills. Oral reading still continues to be practised, but at this stage it fulfils a different function from phase four: the young learners read aloud to an audience, interpreting a written text for their listeners. This requires a very demanding set of skills similar to the ones demonstrated in the popular first language reading competitions. The following chapter will go more thoroughly into the matter of oral reading.

3. A case for oral reading in primary EFL

The JuLE project set out rigorously to question a dogma long held in the TEFL community, that reading is generally silent. Hermes (1998: 232) recommends that silent reading ought to be practised right from the beginning of EFL courses, and Nuttall issues a downright warning against oral reading "My instinct here [in the case of reading aloud. BD] is simply to repeat 'Don't'." (1996: 201). These assumptions are strongly challenged by everyday experience of reading in university, in church, and in school. Even skilled adult readers frequently and automatically resort to semi-vocalisation or even reading aloud in a variety of contexts, for example in a situation where the ambient noise is not conducive to silent reading (on a bus or train), or where the reading material contains complex thoughts and unfamiliar vocabulary. Since even the most experienced readers can benefit from the slowing down of the reading process together with an audible articulation of the written text, young learners who are still struggling with reading are sure to derive profit from oral reading. This is not to say that criticisms of reading aloud should not be taken seriously, but what the LiPs scheme proposes is a functional and focused use of oral reading within the overall context of primary EFL learning.

3.1 A theoretical perspective on oral reading

Reading in a foreign language calls for a highly complex operation of language processing, the success of which depends to a large extent on attending to phonological features, both in silent and in oral reading. Basically, there are three psycholinguistic arguments for oral reading.

The role of phonology in the subjective lexicon

Access to the mental lexicon – be it in listening or in reading – requires a form of phonological recoding (cf. Frost & Ziegler 2007: 108; cf. Marx 1997: 109). The subjective lexicon contains exclusively phonological representations of lexical items for the first years of life. This is to be explained by the ontogenetical priority of spoken language over written language (cf. Karcher 1994: 170). Graphematical entries into the lexicon are added at later stages depending on the child's first encounters with written language. When readers, in seeking to make sense of a printed text, retrieve items from their mental lexicon, the sounds of the stored words play a crucial role in finding the right entry.

Initially, the theory of the dual route posited that in processing written language readers could either take a direct path, called the lexical route, from an item's graphic form to its meaning, or a sub-lexical route that required the recoding of the graphemes into phonemes before obtaining the meaning (cf. e. g. Field 2003: 26f.). Researchers today, however, agree that bypassing the phonological components of language in reading is impossible (cf. Frost & Ziegler 2007: 108; cf. Marx 1997: 109). When working on a vocabulary of sight words with children of kindergarten age, Ehri noticed that the visual-phonological strategy accompanied the merely visual one (cf. Ehri 1992: 115). I am inclined to accept Ehri's view that even the lexical route taken by readers processing sight words involves the activation of an amalgam of phonological and semantic information.

Although it seems appropriate to distinguish between the manner in which skilled readers recode written language and the way unskilled readers transcode written language, it is safe to assume that the phonological features are of great importance to both the process of decoding and understanding. With accomplished readers, phonological recoding is thought to occur rapidly and post-lexically, i.e. almost at the same time or immediately after recognizing a word's meaning; whereas beginning readers carry out phonological transcoding slowly and pre-lexically, i.e. they sound out the word, only to establish its meaning when they have determined its sound shape (cf. Ehri 1992: 107; cf. Karcher 1994: 179). For this reason, beginning EFL readers need carefully administered support with oral reading that protects them against giving an English sequence of letters a German sequence of sounds, which would, in turn, prevent them from relating the printed item to the sound sequence they know. Advanced EFL learners have no trouble identifying a sequence of graphemes <t-e-a-c-h-e-r> as /tiːtʃə(r)/ and with it the meaning of 'a person whose job it is to induce learning in others especially young children and adolescents in a school'; they do not need to spend a long time visually analysing the shape of the letters and translating them into sounds. Beginning EFL readers whose first language is German cannot automatically retrieve the meaning assigned to the visual form of the word 'teacher', when they transcode the graphemes into phonemes following the GPC rules of their first language. They end up with the sound sequence /teʔaxə(r)/ for which they do not have an entry in their lexicon. They may be familiar with the oral form of the word 'teacher' from a very early stage of learning English, but they simply cannot map the written form onto this orally stored one. Oddly, the EFL primary syllabi seem to take it for granted that pupils at this age can automatically recognize the oral vocabulary they are familiar with when they encounter it in the written form (cf. e. g. MKJS 2004: 78; MSW 2008: 78). Due to the differences between English and German orthography this is not the case, or at least not to a degree that suggests that learners can be left to work out by themselves the differences and the particularities of English orthography. My research strongly indicates that learners need well-designed tuition to assist them in noticing the correspondence between specific graphemes and phonemes and associating the visual form of words with their phonological form. To support the learning process, an oral demonstration by the teacher together with oral practice by the learner is required.

The role of phonology in working memory

In accordance with Baddeley and Hitch's model of working memory (in: Gathercole & Baddeley 2003: 4), oral reading is seen as a precursor to subvocalisation, a mechanism enabling readers to process written material. Since the capacity of working memory is limited, the processing of written language requires a phonological loop, a rehearsal mechanism as it were, by which an inner voice vocalizes the written material generating a phonological version. This version is audible only to the inner ear (cf. de Guerrero 2004: 103) and thus allows the reader to access the phonological store. The main function at issue here is the retention of the visually presented information in a way which allows the individual to work out the semantic content and the syntactic structure of longer units. In this manner, subvocalisation enables readers to make sense of lengthy words, complex clauses and strings of related sentences. Skilled adult readers only ever become aware of subvocalisation when they are confronted with highly abstract texts or unfamiliar technical terms. With a lexical item such as 'chiropterogamy' they may consciously try to recode it phonologically letter by letter. Whether they can decode it, i.e. ascribe a meaning to it, depends on an entry in their personal lexicon, telling them that the item denotes 'the pollination of flowers by bats'. Another example of how much the working memory of even experienced readers relies on a phonological rehearsal mechanism can be drawn from the store of the so called garden path sentences, clauses that are syntactically ambiguous such as *The actor learnt the text amused the audience* (Field 2003: 124f.). To disambiguate a sentence like that the reader needs to hold it in his or her working memory until the meaningful syntactic structure has been assigned to it, most probably by also inaudibly inserting a 'that'. Of course, much simpler reading tasks than these remain daunting to primary EFL learners on account of their lack of acquaintance with English GPC rules, their restricted vocabulary and their unfamiliarity with English syntax. Oral reading therefore emerges as an indispensable precursor of subvocalisation.

The role of phonology in developing a second language inner voice

Following Vygotsky's idea of 'inner speech' as a cognitive tool, and the understanding that reading is an act of problem-solving, oral reading needs to be practised in order gradually to develop the habit of semi-vocalisation and then subvocalisation in a foreign language (Vygotsky 1986; for 'mumble reading' cf. Kragler 1996). Inner speech, which facilitates meaning making and problem solving, can be regarded as an instrument for carrying out mental operations (cf. de Guerrero 2004: 90; cf. Vygotsky 1986: 68ff.). After it has been shown to assist adolescent and adult learners in improving their reading skills, semi- and sub-vocalisation appear to be of even greater relevance to those readers just setting out to cope with texts in a foreign language. Repeated practices of oral reading and, later on, mumble reading are now thought to serve to habitualize and automatize young learners' use of a second language inner voice (cf. de Guerrero 2004: 103).

3.2 An empirical perspective on oral reading

Against the theoretical backdrop sketched above three qualitative, exploratory case studies of oral reading – forming the JuLE project – were carried out in German primary school EFL classes between 2005 and 2007. At the time there was neither practical experience nor research data available showing how young learners cope with reading EFL material. For that reason the study addressed the key question about an effective method of using oral reading with young learners. Initially, two different methods, one emulating the whole language approach (e. g. Smith 1997), the other strongly drawing on learning through imitating a model, were trialled, but led to unsatisfactory results. Therefore, shortly after the first two, a third case study was conducted to investigate the effects of a new method that relied on awareness-raising techniques prior to the oral reading. The corpus at the centre of the JuLE study consists of the pupils' oral reading of an episode from an authentic children's book. Beginning with a storytelling lesson, the learners had been introduced to one of three books from which they selected their favourite episode for reading aloud which was, after several rounds of practice, recorded on tape.

3.2.1 JuLE Case Study A

The first case study was carried out in a year 3. The class had been learning English for two and a half years, although the written language had not been used prior to this case study. Over a period of three lessons, learners were told the story *I Want a Cat* (Ross 1989). The main method of instruction followed the model of the whole word approach introducing the class to the core vocabulary of the story with the help of word cards. Having acquainted the young learners with those sight words, the teacher then put a couple of word cards together and added some functional words, so that from lesson four onwards the class could read strips of sentences from the story. In lesson five the whole story was presented in the written form and choral reading was practised. Finally, in lesson six, the children read the episode that they liked best.

Regarding the learners' motivation, the entire teaching unit was a great success, boosting the children's confidence in dealing with an authentic English book. However, listening to the recorded reading, the research team was shocked by the marked discrepancy between the pupils' excellent speaking performance and their extremely weak reading ability. Even though the children had pronounced for instance the bilabial semi-vowel /w/ correctly before, they mispronounced 'want', 'with' and 'when' producing the labiodental fricative /v/ when reading from the book. In some instances they struggled so hard with the reading of orally familiar words (e. g. teacher), that the sound sequences they produced became incomprehensible to anyone unfamiliar with the story, presumably even to themselves.

The JuLE case study A confirms what Karcher (1994: 177) has aptly named a first language phonation of second language lexical items. As English graphemes are visually identical with German ones, primary school learners take for granted the phonological quality experienced in their first language as a universal feature of the grapheme, no matter whether it occurs in an English or a German word (ibid.). With the whole word approach the meaning distinguishing differences, e. g. between /aɪz/ and /aɪs/, are not given the close attention they require and detailed features within one word are overlooked. The conclusion from case study A is that sight words may be useful for the first months of learning English, but the whole word approach cannot assist EFL beginning readers successfully to read coherent text.

3.2.2 JuLE Case Study B

The second case study was conducted in a year 4 class where children had been learning English for three and a half years, again following the oral approach which had kept written forms of English largely out of the lessons. The teacher and the research team had agreed on *A New Dog* (Hunt & Brychta 1986), a simple story from the Oxford Reading Tree series, level 2, to facilitate the learners' first encounter with print in English. Having heard an oral version of the story, the children were each presented with an audio-cassette recording by three different readers. The pupils listened to these recordings several times while they were following the printed text. Next, they read along with the recording and experimented with imitating the recorded readers' voices.

In terms of pronunciation the outcome of this study was astonishingly good: the children read expressively and with understanding; they made only very few predictable mistakes with sounds that are not phonemic in German such as /ð/ and /w/. By contrast, however, this case study demonstrated that in this particularly well motivated class the chosen method resulted in a marked dip in motivation. On the one hand, the method based on imitation and memory only succeeded in generating a mechanical, albeit phonetically correct reading performance; it did not offer enough scope for individuated response. On the other hand, linguistically simple children's books harbour the danger of infantilisation, because intellectually the contents are aimed at three-to-five-year olds. The results of this case study suggest the inadvisability of extensive use of this imitation-based approach. The observations made in this case study also lead one seriously to question the compromise by which EFL learners aged six to ten are given books intended for first language infants aged three to five.

3.2.3 JuLE Case Study C

The third case study was conducted in a year 3 class among children who had been learning English orally for two and a half years. The reading formed part of a 15-lesson teaching unit based on the approach known as content-and-language-integrated-learning (CLIL). The unit focused on creatures living in the river Rhine, among others seahorses, and also included a reading of the book *Mr Seahorse* (Carle 2004). The book was introduced according to the storyline method (Kocher 1999), and then the children were provided with the printed text. They were explicitly pointed towards a number of grapheme-phoneme correspondences that differ in English and German (for example in the word 'seahorse'), and they were further made aware of the weakening of vowels (for example in 'of course') and the linking of words (for example in 'You are doing a great job') in connected speech. One of the unforeseen outcomes of this study was the way in which the learners spontaneously annotated their printed copies of the text in a way that would assist their correct pronunciation when it came to reading aloud. Some readers, for instance, crossed out the silent <e> in 'have', or used a symbol in the shape of a tie employed by the teacher to indicate the linking of two words as in 'you are', or added the German umlaut to ensure that the indefinite article <a> would not be mispronounced as /a/ but correctly read as /eö/ or /ə/.

> Bŭt before long, Mr Seahorse met another fish.
> "How are you, Mr Bullhead?", said Mr Seahorse.
>
> "Tip-top", said Mr Bullhead. "No more eggs –
> we have babies now, I am babysitting!"
> "You are doing a great job!" said Mr Seahorse
> and swam on his way.

Example of a learner's attempt at transcribing an English written text (JuLE case study C)

In general terms, the method trialled here led to reading standards of a quality clearly superior to that achieved by learners in study A, and only slightly inferior to that attained by learners in study B. While preparing themselves for the oral reading, some highly stimulated learners went as far as transcribing the entire text, demonstrating a clear interest in the formal features of the foreign language.

The awareness-raising method led to a conscious use of German spelling: the children had shown themselves able to relate the oral forms of English correctly to the written ones; since they had become aware of the differences in the GPC patterns between their first language and their second language, they went on to take precautionary measures against mispronouncing the less familiar patterns of English by transcribing the sounds with the help of first language specific grapheme combinations. They had started inventing their own phonetic alphabet, or more precisely, using their first language orthography to mimic the second language phonology in very much the same way as adult learners, academics and linguists employ a phonetic alphabet.

The awareness-raising techniques applied in study C have proved to be appropriate and effective in helping EFL beginning readers to cope with unfamiliar

GPC patterns. The outcomes of study C also raise questions about the effects which the use of phonetic symbols may have on primary school learners, whether they might benefit from them as an additional support (Marschollek 2005), or whether a new set of symbols might jeopardize their motivation and learning process. As a phonetic alphabet would in fact enter as a third code, I would, for the time being, regard it cautiously as less of a help than a hindrance. Therefore the use of phonetic symbols will not be included in the upcoming LiPs project. Instead, we will take a more detailed look at a phonics approach that has been adjusted to suit the specific needs of German EFL learners.

4. Résumé

The conclusions to be drawn from the JuLE study are to be understood as provisional, yet they have already assisted in drawing up the new scheme for teaching EFL beginning readers. The main ingredients of this scheme may be summarized as follows: First, to familiarize young learners with the combination of spoken and written forms, lexical items are introduced as unsegmented sight words in year 1. It is important never to present the written forms without placing a strong emphasis on meaning and pronunciation. A pre-lexical phonological recoding is not yet aimed at in year 1. Second, from year 2 onwards, oral reading and awareness-raising techniques (noticing, contrasting the two languages, building on analogy, using phonics) are employed to enable learners to practise decoding skills on English words. These techniques are intended to ensure that young learners can go beyond recognizing memorized whole words and, by the end of year 4, can decipher text and make use of dictionaries without producing a disproportionately large number of inaccurate sound sequences. Third, later, in year 2 or early in year 3, learners begin to read stories and books individually, making the most of oral reading to the teacher or to a classmate, experimenting with semi-vocalisation and developing a second language inner voice through subvocalisation. Regular reading hours and reading competitions are intended to foster a reading culture among the children.

If it were to be objected that the proposed scheme is likely to overtax primary school learners, it is worth stressing that for children to find their place in the world fluent reading is fundamental. The enormous growth in the IT sector and the widespread increase in texts, whether in electronic form or in print, has in fact led to a greater rather than lesser demand on learners' reading competences, recently termed 'multiliteracies' (Cope & Kalantzis 2000). Assuming that all literacies are grounded in one common set of skills enabling us to decipher writing systems, I believe that learning to read is arguably the single most important precondition of educational success. It is the development of these reading competences in the primary EFL class that needs to take centre stage in future research projects, challenging us to reflect upon strategies to overcome difficulties likely to be faced by beginning readers.

References

Carle, Eric (2004), *Mister Seahorse*. London: Puffin Books.
Cope, Bill & Kalantzis, Mary (eds.) (2000), *Multiliteracies. Literacy Learning and the Design of Social Futures*. London: Routledge.
de Guerrero, María C.M. (2004), Early stages of L2 inner speech development: what verbal reports suggest. *International Journal of Applied Linguistics*. 14: 1, 90–112.
Diehr, Bärbel (2006), Reden und reden lassen. *Grundschule* 38: 9, 36–40.
Diehr, Bärbel & Frisch, Stefanie (2008), *Mark their words: Sprechleistungen im Englischunterricht der Grundschule fördern und beurteilen*. Braunschweig: Westermann.
Ehri, Linnea C. (1992), Reconceptualizing the Development of Sight Word Reading and its Relationship to Recoding. In: Gough, Philip B.; Ehri, Linnea C. & Treiman, Rebecca (eds.), *Reading Acquisition*. Hillsdale, NJ: Lawrence Erlbaum, 107–143.
Ehri, Linnea C. (1999), Phases of Development in Learning to Read Words. In: Oakhill, Jane & Beard, Roger (eds.) (1999), 79–108.
Elbro, Carsten (1999), Dyslexia: Core Difficulties, Variability and Causes. In: Oakhill, Jane & Beard, Roger (eds.) (1999), 131–156.
Field, John (2003), *Psycholinguistics. A resource book for students*. New York: Routledge.
Frost, Ram & Ziegler, Johannes C. (2007), Speech and spelling interaction: the interdependence of visual and auditory word recognition. In: Gaskell, M. Gareth (ed.) (2007), *The Oxford Handbook of Psycholinguistics*. Oxford: Oxford University Press, 107–118.
Gathercole, Susan E. & Baddeley, Alan D. (2003), *Working Memory and Language*. Hove: Psychology Press.
Gibson, Sally (2008), Reading aloud: a useful learning tool? *English Language Teaching Journal* 62: 1, 29–36.
Grabe, William & Stoller, Fredricka L. (2002), *Teaching and Researching Reading*. Harlow: Pearson Education.
Hermes, Liesel (1998), Leseverstehen. In: Timm, Johannes-P. (ed.) (1998), *Englisch lernen und lehren. Didaktik des Englischunterrichts*. Berlin: Cornelsen, 229–236.

Hunt, Roderick & Brychta, Alex (1986), *A New Dog. Oxford Reading Tree: Stage 2*. Oxford: Oxford University Press.

Johnston, Rhona & Watson, Joyce (2007), *Teaching Synthetic Phonics*. Exeter: Learning Matters.

Karcher, Günther L. (1994), *Das Lesen in der Erst- und Fremdsprache: Dimensionen und Aspekte einer Fremdsprachenlegetik*. Heidelberg: Groos.

Kocher, Doris (1999), *Das Klassenzimmer als Lernwerkstatt: Medien und Kommunikation im Englischunterricht nach der Storyline-Methode*. Hamburg: Verlag Dr. Kovač.

Kragler, Sherry (1996), Mumbling into Silent Reading. *Childhood Education* 72: 4, 206–209.

Marschollek, Andreas (2005), Phonetische Umschrift. Schon in der Grundschule? *Primary English* 2, 13–16.

Marx, Harald (1997), Kapitel IV. Erwerb des Lesen und des Rechtschreibens. Literaturüberblick. In: Weinert, Franz E. & Helmke, Andreas (eds.) (1997), *Entwicklung im Grundschulalter*. Weinheim: Beltz Psychologie Verlags Union, 85–112.

MKJS (Ministerium für Kultus, Jugend und Sport Baden-Württemberg) (2004), *Bildungsplan 2004 Grundschule*. Stuttgart: Neckar-Verlag.

MSW (Ministerium für Schule und Weiterbildung des Landes Nordrhein-Westfalen) (2008), *Richtlinien und Lehrpläne für die Grundschule in Nordrhein-Westfalen*. Frechen: Ritterbach.

Nuttall, Christine (1996), *Teaching Reading Skills in a Foreign Language*. Oxford: Macmillan.

Oakhill, Jane & Beard, Roger (eds.) (1999), *Reading Development and the Teaching of Reading*. Oxford: Blackwell.

Opitz, Michael F. & Rasinski, Timothy V. (1998), *Good-Bye Round Robin: Twenty-Five Effective Oral Reading Strategies*. Portsmouth: Heinemann.

Pinker, Steven (1994), *The Language Instinct. The New Science of Language and Mind*. London: Penguin Books.

Reichart-Wallrabenstein, Maike (2004), *Kinder und Schrift im Englischunterricht der Grundschule: eine theorie- und empiriegeleitete Studie zur Diskussion um die Integration von Schriftlichkeit – Teil 1*. Berlin: dissertation.de – Verlag im Internet.

Ross, Tony (1989), *I Want a Cat*. London: Random House.

Rymarczyk, Jutta (2008), Früher oder später? Zur Einführung des Schriftbildes in der Grundschule. In: Böttger, Heiner (ed.), *Fortschritte im Frühen Fremdsprachenlernen. Ausgewählte Tagungsbeiträge Nürnberg 2006*. München: Domino Verlag, 170–182.

Smith, Frank (1997), *Reading Without Nonsense*. Third Edition. New York: Teachers College Press.

Vygotsky, Lev S. (1986), *Thought and Language*. Cambridge, MA: The MIT Press.

Jutta Rymarczyk / Annika Musall

Reading skills of first graders who learn to read and write in German and English

Erstklässler, deren Englischunterricht das Schriftbild mit einbezog, wurden am Ende ihres ersten Lernjahres auf ihre Lesefähigkeit getestet. Eine Replikation der Studie von Wimmer et al. (1990) zum Leseverstehen des Deutschen sowie eine analog angelegte Testreihe zum Englischen zeigte, dass die Kinder durchaus in der Lage sind, die gleichzeitige Einführung des deutschen und des englischen Schriftbildes zu bewältigen. Ferner lässt sich kein negativer Transfer von der englischen Schriftsprache auf die deutsche feststellen. Die dritte Forschungsfrage der Studie, wie weit entwickelt die Lesefertigkeiten der Kinder sind, ist differenziert zu betrachten. Zum einen ist hier festzuhalten, dass die Kinder sich sehr stark der deutschen Phonem-Graphem-Korrespondenz bedienen, wenn sie englische Wörter und Pseudowörter vorlesen. Andererseits zeigte sich aber deutlich, dass die Ergebnisse im Leseverstehen, dem leisen Lesen, deutlich besser waren als die im lauten Lesen.

Der Beitrag diskutiert die Resultate der Studie im Kontext der aktuellen Forschung zum Schriftspracherwerb in der Grundschule und plädiert schließlich für die Berücksichtigung der Schriftform von Beginn des Fremdsprachenunterrichts an.

1. First data on second graders' written skills in regular and immersion foreign language classrooms

In summer 2006 in the German federal states Baden-Wurttemberg and Rhineland-Palatinate, the first children had completed years 1 and 2 of primary school with English as a Foreign Language (EFL) classes that had widely excluded the written form. The primary curriculum of Rhineland-Palatinate does not explicitly ask for this exclusion but just mentions year 4, the last year of primary education in this federal state, as the point in time when the learners should show some competence in the written skills: "Sie verfügen über erste Erfahrungen mit dem Schriftbild einer Zielsprache. Sie sind in der Lage, zentrale Wörter und einfache Sätze zu lesen und aufzuschreiben" (They have gained some initial experience of the written form of a target language. They are able to read and write down central words and easy sentences (translation J.R.)), (Ministerium für Bildung,

Frauen und Jugend Rheinland Pfalz 2004: 7f.). Baden-Wurttemberg is more precise in that they clearly allocate the written skills to years 3 and 4 (Ministerium für Kultus, Jugend und Sport Baden-Württemberg 2004: 68).

However, it was hard to believe that learners at the end of their second year of EFL-classes really had no idea about English spelling and no wish to use the written form. Because of this 95 children from four different classes were given 10 minutes to note down English words they were familiar with. The 93 resulting word lists clearly showed that the children had a fairly good idea of English written words (Rymarczyk 2008a). The four classes involved in this first data collection (which later was to become the pilot study of the research project "Two-way literacy acquisition English-German in years 1 + 2") produced lists with an average of 19.3 words. Their English spelling as such, however, did not correspond to conventional English orthography. Instead the children had invented their own spelling by transferring their German phonemic strategy to their English writing. This means they used the English sound forms of the words and matched these sounds with letters as they do in German where this is widely possible due to the transparent letter-sound-correspondence of the language. Thus the children ended up writing words like "weit", "nein" or "veif" (cf. Fig. 1).

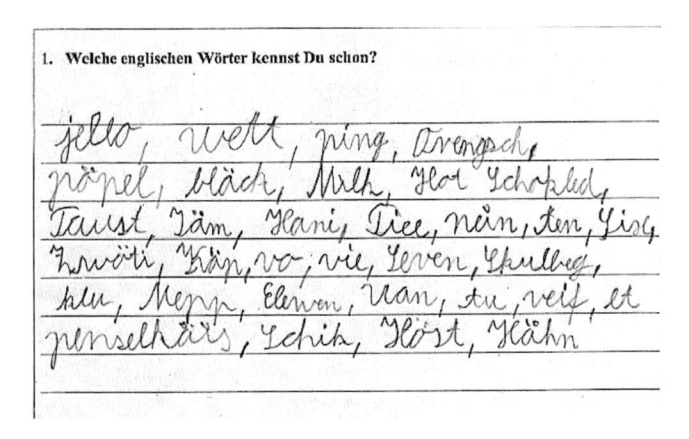

Fig. 1, Rule-based invented spelling

The example in Figure 1 clearly shows that the child proceeded systematically at different levels: At the lexical level the words are listed in semantic fields: first, colours (yellow, white, pink, orange, purple, black) and then breakfast (milk, hot chocolate, toast, jam, honey, tea). At the orthographic level the invented spelling is easily spotted due to its systematic nature: Most obvious are the capital letters for nouns (e. g. "Milk") and the German umlauts (e. g. pöpel, bläck).

The use of invented spelling as such is neither extraordinary nor alarming. Contrary to this, there are many authors – referring to both English and German – who claim that the children's idiosyncratic writing supports their literacy acquisition process (Gentry 2006: xiii; Scheerer-Neumann 1998: 56; Steinig/Huneke 2002: 94). However, it is important to consider that the systematic use of invented forms in a foreign language which is mainly taught orally might have a detrimental effect on the learners' progress. Our data show that many children used their invented spelling systematically, i.e. they had begun to develop their own spelling rules as illustrated in Figure 1: Whenever the diphthong /aɪ/ was needed, the child used the letters <ei> (cf. Fig. 1). Across the four second grades of the pilot study, 28.2 % of the mistakes made were instances of rule-based invented spelling.

Without orthographic input to assist the children, there is the danger of fossilization of incorrect spelling rules. The resulting detrimental effect on the learning process is twofold: first, the learning process is unnecessarily prolonged and second, the children's motivation suffers when they are forced to dismiss their own rules to accept the correct ones (cf. Rymarczyk 2008b).

These results suggested that early instruction in written English might be beneficial. In order to investigate this presupposition, a second data collection[1] was conducted. It was carried out with second graders at northern German early immersion schools in summer 2007. There, English is the medium of instruction from the very beginning and the written form is not withheld from the children but introduced naturally, e. g. to read short texts. We tested 80 immersion students in three classes. They listed an average of 21.3 words. Here only 3.2 % of the mistakes made were instances of rule-based invented spellings. The lower percentage of invented spelling, along with the number of words that the children correctly spelled suggests a more advanced acquisition level of the written form. The children in the immersion classes who had worked with the written form of English showed much better results[2] (cf. Figure 2).

---

1 The second data collection was later seen as the pre-study to the project „Zweitalphabetisierung Englisch in den Grundschulklassen 1+2" (Two-way literacy acquisition English-German in years 1 + 2).
2 In these immersion classes English is the language of instruction for up to 70 % of the lessons. Of course, this high amount of contact time with English supports the children's written foreign language skills by e. g. supporting their phonemic awareness. We do not claim that the use of the written form alone leads to the learners' success but rather that they actually achieve these good results while – or even although! – they are using the written form.

	No written English regular classrooms (pilot study)	Instruction in written English immersion classrooms (pre-study)
average number of words listed	19.34 words	21.28 words
words spelled correctly	30.43 %	60.96 %
words spelled incorrectly	69.57 %	39.04 %
amount of rule-based invented spelling in total number of mistakes[3]	28.16 %	3.19 %

Fig. 2, Comparison of English classes with and without literacy instruction

Due to these findings, the main research project into parallel acquisition of the written forms in German and English was started: „Two-way literacy acquisition English-German in years 1 + 2".

2. First graders' written skills in regular foreign language classrooms

The main investigation examined how first graders in regular, i.e. non-immersion classrooms, deal with the written form after one year of EFL-classes. Luckily we had found teachers who were willing to cooperate and introduce written English although the curriculum in the federal state of Baden-Wurttemberg strongly suggests not to start with the written form before grade 3 (Ministerium für Kultus, Jugend und Sport Baden-Württemberg 2004: 68). They introduced written English rather implicitly by e.g. attaching word cards to objects in the classroom and by providing the written text when picture books were read out to the children or when songs were learnt. They did not follow any explicit phonics programme.

2.1 Research questions and methodology of the main investigation

Our investigation was led by three research questions:

---

[3] Please note that the rule-system the children base their invented spelling on is probably far more developed than indicated by these numbers. Just because a specific instance of invented spelling did not turn up more than once in a word list that was compiled in 10 minutes, this does not mean that the writer did not adhere to an underlying rule when putting down this specific invented form.

1 Are first graders in regular classrooms able to cope with the simultaneous introduction of English and German written forms?
2 Is there any negative transfer in the children's written skills from English to German?
3 How accomplished are their written skills in English?

In order to answer these questions the Austrian investigation by Wimmer et al. (1990) into the universality of the logographic stage in literacy acquisition, as suggested e. g. by Frith, was replicated. According to Frith (1998) the so-called logographic stage is the first stage in the literacy acquisition process. It is characterized by a holistic word recognition based on visual cues (logos) rather than on any matches of sounds and letters. In their study Wimmer et al. (1990) conclude that the logographic stage, though probably important as the first phase in the English literacy acquisition, is not relevant in German. They claim that in German with its transparent phoneme-grapheme-correspondence the children hardly confine themselves to matching visual memories of words to sound forms as it is characteristic of the logographic stage. Instead, the transparency of German phoneme-grapheme-correspondences immediately allowed the children to use alphabetic strategies, i.e. to match letters to sounds. Wimmer et al.'s study reports that children reached the alphabetic level[4] after only eight months of literacy instruction. This result was found with all students, average and even poor learners, the latter being his test group (ibid.).

This study was replicated to see whether there was any negative transfer from English to German. We assumed that if the contact our first graders had had with written English had been detrimental to their achievements in reading and writing German, they would not have been able to use the more advanced strategies of the alphabetic phase. Instead, they would still have been at the logographic level, using its more basic strategies which lend themselves perfectly to reading and writing English at a beginners' level.

Wimmer et al. tested 56 children who had been suggested by teachers of 24 classes as being either poor learners or average learners. The 28 poor learners were assigned to the test group and the 28 average learners were assigned to the control group. Standardized tests[5] were used to examine the children's read-

---

4 In Frith's model of the literacy acquisition process the alphabetic level is the second of three levels: logographic – alphabetic – orthographic level. In a more elaborate version of the model there are six levels but the basic threefold structure remains nevertheless (cf. Frith 1998).
5 Wimmer et al. used the *Diagnostischer Lesetest für die 1. und 2. Klasse* (DLT 1–2) by R. Müller adapted to the Austrian context by Weyermüller, Sebanz & Bodner (1978) and the *Diagnostischer Rechtschreibtest für die 1. und 2. Klasse* by R. Müller adapted to the Austrian context by Weyermüller & Zlabinger (1978).

ing and writing abilities in order to confirm the teachers' judgements. An examination of their letter knowledge served the same purpose. All tests conducted proved the accuracy of the teachers' judgements.

In our study we used the updated versions of the standardized tests (Müller 1984; 2004) employed by Wimmer et al. to select our subjects. Teacher judgements were not taken into consideration because we wanted to select subjects whose results resembled those of the Austrian children as closely as possible. With this aim in mind we tested 280 learners from 14 classes. Eventually we could select 53 subjects whose results matched those of the Austrian group. 28[6] of these children were assigned to the test group and 25 to the control group. Our study examined both the children's reading and writing abilities as the Wimmer et al. study did, but in the following we will only report in detail on the reading.

To test the children's reading abilities a list of 36 words was to be read out (cf. Fig. 3).

Real words (12)	Pseudo words (12) + (12)	
	Visually similar	**Visually non-similar**
Auto	Aufo	Eufo

Fig. 3, Material to test German reading skills

The list consisted of 12 real words, 12 visually similar pseudo words and 12 visually non-similar pseudo words. The real words were taken from the children's German course books and the pseudo words were systematically derived from these real words. The initial letter of the visually similar pseudo words e.g., was always changed for the visually non-similar pseudo words (*A*ufo → *E*ufo).

The words were presented individually; each of them twice: first in a short presentation of only one second and then without any time limit[7]. The children knew that there were non-existent words without meaning.

If the children employed a logographic reading strategy, the real words might be read correctly. In contrast to this, pseudo words cannot be read by means of a logographic strategy since the children do not possess any visual memory of the non-existing words.

---

6   For the English real word/ pseudo word test there are only results from 26 test children because two students did not do the whole test. In accordance with Wimmer et al.'s procedure we stopped the test when a child did not provide four reading attempts in succession.

7   The unlimited time span was set by Wimmer et al. (1990). To make this viable we broke up after a maximum time span of two minutes or when it was absolutely clear that a subject would not make any further attempt to read the item.

2.2 Results of the reading test

Figure 4 provides the results of our replication of Wimmer et al.'s reading test and Wimmer et al.'s results themselves. Our subjects' results are labelled „eE" for „early English", whereas the results of the 1990 study are referred to by „noE" for „no English". The first numbers in each line and slot represent the number of words read correctly during the first presentation of a word which lasted for one second. The numbers in brackets show the number of German words read correctly in the second, long presentation.

Word category	Control group	Test group	Total
real words (max. 12)	noE 10.5 (1.3) eE 8.1 (3.0)	noE 6.9 (2.9) eE 3.5 (6.7)	noE 8.7 (2.1) eE 5.8 (4.9)
pseudo words visually similar (max. 12)	noE 8.2 (2.9) eE 5.7 (5.0)	noE 4.3 (3.5) eE 1.9 (6.5)	noE 6.3 (3.2) eE 3.8 (5.8)
pseudo words visually non-similar (max. 12)	noE 8.0 (3.0) eE 5.0 (5.4)	noE 3.7 (4.0) eE 2.2 (6.4)	noE 5.8 (3.6) eE 3.6 (5.9)

Fig. 4, Comparison of reading results achieved by Wimmer et al.'s subjects and ours

During the short presentation the control group (early English (eE)) correctly read out 8.1 real words, 5.7 visually similar pseudo words and 5.0 visually non-similar pseudo words. The test group (eE), being comprised of poor learners, still correctly read out 3.5 real words, 1.9 visually similar pseudo words and 2.2 visually non-similar pseudo words (cf. Fig. 4). This means that in our replication of the 1990 study the children we tested showed similar though poorer results. However, there was no divergence of more than three words in any of the categories between our subjects who had received early English classes including literacy instruction and Wimmer et al.'s subjects who had no English classes at all.

A repeated measures analysis with word category (3) as within-subjects factor and group (2) as between-subjects factor proved both factors to be highly significant: $F(2,104) = 50.9$, $p < .001$ and $F(1,52) = 19.4$, $p < .001$. The interaction was not significant: $F < 1.0$. The averages show that real words were correctly read more often than any of the two categories of pseudo words. Between the visually similar and visually non-similar pseudo words there were no big differences. These findings also held true for Wimmer et al.

Our results, i. e. the high number of German real words read correctly, seem to suggest a tendency towards logographic readings in both test and control groups.

There are four aspects, however, which do not support this interpretation but instead suggest the use of an alphabetic reading strategy.

First, the number of pseudo words read correctly during the short presentation. Our subjects read about a third of the pseudo words correctly – which is not possible using a logographic strategy.

Second, there is a very high correlation between the number of correctly read pseudo words (visually similar and non-similar) and the number of correctly read real words: $r = .92, p < .001$. Such a correlation is to be expected if real words are read with the only possible strategy for reading pseudo words, namely the alphabetic strategy.

Third, the use of the alphabetic strategy is also supported by the fact that both the number of correctly read real words and pseudo words increased significantly during the long presentations: $t(53) = 12.4, p < .001$. If the logographic strategy with its holistic word recognition had been employed, the lexical items would have mainly been read within a short time span. Reading an item by means of the alphabetic strategy takes longer since the individual graphemes have to be analysed and matched onto phonemes. In accordance with the increase in the total number of items read during the long presentations there is the finding that this increase is greater for pseudo words than for real words: $F(2,104) = 6.8, p < .001$. It is also obvious that the long presentation is more beneficial for poor learners than for average learners: $F(1,52) = 5.7, p < .05$. All these results were also arrived at by Wimmer et al.

In our data, however, a fourth aspect presented itself. Our poor learners read many more pseudo words correctly in the long presentation (12.9) than in the short presentation (4.1). Here, our results differ from Wimmer et al. (long presentation: 7.5; short presentation: 8), thus giving an additional reason to claim that the children make use of the alphabetic instead of the logographic strategy. After all, pseudo words cannot be read by means of the logographic strategy and need more time to be sounded out because there is no corresponding entry in the reader's mental lexicon which can be accessed immediately. To wrap it up: The most important result of both analyses is that even poor learners – and now I am referring to both the 1990 and our current study – were able to read (in the sense of "to articulate") an average of 13 out of 24 German pseudo words during the long presentations (cf. Fig. 4).

This leads to the answers to our research questions 1 and 2. The first question "Are first graders in regular classrooms able to cope with the simultaneous introduction of English and German written forms?" can be answered positively. Since the children in our study who learned English from the very beginning showed results comparable to the results of children without any EFL classes, they seemed to cope quite well. Please remember that this result includes the test groups, i.e. poor learners. When overtaxing by early foreign language learning (FLL) – and especially early FLL which includes first steps into literacy! – is mentioned, it is generally with particular reference to poor learners. But, as our results show, neither early English nor early contact with the English written form has any detrimental effect on poor learners' achievements in German.

This result is backed up by a study from Switzerland which looked into the EFL-competence third-graders had achieved after one year of EFL-classes (Haenni Hoti 2007). Answering a questionnaire, 85% of the teachers involved agreed "generally" or "wholly" (*stimmt eher* or *stimmt genau*) that the children's German language competence did not suffer because of the EFL classes. 44% of these teachers even stated that they "generally" (*eher*) did not think that a second foreign language in grade 5, which still belongs to primary school in Switzerland, overtaxed students, including the poor ones (ibid., p. 26). A comparison of children from cantons with EFL classes starting in grade three and from Luzern where no English is taught in this grade shows no significant differences in their reading comprehension at the end of year three. The finding that two to three lessons of English per week show neither any positive nor any negative influence on the children's reading competence in German (ibid., p. 28) once more underlines our results.

The second question "Is there any negative transfer in the children's written skills from English to German?" can clearly be negated. Just like the "German only" learners in Wimmer et al.'s investigation the students in our study made use of the alphabetic strategy when reading German and were not influenced by their familiarity with English which is supposed to require the logographic strategy during the first step of the literacy acquisition process in a much more distinct way than German. The children do not show any tendency to use the logographic strategy. If they did use the logographic strategy to read in English, it was not transferred to German. Thus, still another fear voiced against the early introduction of the written form can be dispelled.

In order to answer the third research question "How accomplished are their written skills in English?" with respect to the first graders' reading skills we must turn to the tests that were conducted with English word lists. The test and the test material were designed according to the test for German. Since the children's English course books for grade one work with an oral approach, we were careful to choose real words which the teachers had introduced via flashcards or posters (cf. Fig. 5).

Real words (12)	Pseudo words (12) + (12)	
	Visually similar	**Visually non-similar**
car	cas	pas

Fig. 5, Material to test English reading skills

The pseudo words that we built from these real words follow English phonological patterns. The following beginning of one of the English lists that the children read shows that all pseudo words can be pronounced, yet the task is quite demanding for first graders: „Playway, mooth, clote, one, chresenake, tus, yellow, milt, onomwan, mouth".

Because of this it was no surprise that the number of correctly read words was very low (cf. Fig. 6). In the following table, too, the first numbers show the numbers of words read correctly in the short presentation whereas the numbers in brackets refer to the words read correctly in the second, long presentation.

	Control group	**Test group**	**Total**
real words (max. 12)	2.0 (1.4)	0.2 (0.4)	1.1 (0.9)
pseudo words visually similar (max. 12)	0.3 (0.4)	0.0 (0.1)	0.2 (0.3)
pseudo words visually non-similar (max. 12)	0.2 (0.4)	0.0 (0.1)	0.18 (0.2)

Fig. 6, English reading results

Considering these numbers you must keep in mind that these first graders had a maximum of two hours of EFL per week. They were not explicitly instructed in the written form, either. Although the children had had contact with the written form via flashcards, posters, big books etc., they did not have any explicit training in reading. Writing was not dealt with at all. These circumstances should be kept in mind when the allegedly poor results are discussed.

As low as these numbers are, they still serve our purpose. They show that the children used an alphabetic strategy with English. An average of 0.2 pseudo words were correctly read during the short (one second long) presentation. Although this number is very low, the words, being pseudo words, could not have been read with a logographic strategy. Furthermore, as with the German words, the use of the alphabetic strategy is supported by

a) the correlation between the number of correctly read pseudo words and the number of correctly read real words ($r = .64, p < .001$), and

b) the significant increase in the number of correctly read real words and pseudo words during the long presentation ($t\,(51) = 5.7, p < .001$). Only the number of real words read by the control group is actually lower in the long presentation. In all other cases the children read more words correctly in the long presentation. Again, the increase in number is greater for pseudo words than for real words: $F\,(2,100) = 15.8, p < .001$, and poor learners benefited more from the long presentation than average learners: $F\,(1,50) = 13.7, p < .01$.

2.3 A close analysis of the mistakes made in the English reading test

The most obvious piece of evidence that the children applied an alphabetic strategy can be seen when examining the mistakes the children made. When they wrongly read a pseudo word, this usually led to "non-words" that begin with the first letter of the word presented. In order to illustrate this phenomenon, a closer look at one test child's reading mistakes can be helpful (cf. Fig. 7).

1	real word	/mʌŋkɪ/ *monkey* for *monkey*
1	real word	/mʌŋkɪ/ *monkey* for *mokney*
27	non-words (+ 1st letter)	e. g. /snɔkɪ/ for *snoke*
2	non-words (- 1st letter)	e. g. /iːɔn/ for *lion*
5x	no reading attempt	

Fig. 7, Example of individual reading

Instead of *snoke* /snəʊk/, e. g., the boy read /snɔkɪ/, a "non-word" that begins with the first letter of the visually similar pseudo word presented. A mistake like this is to be expected when alphabetic readers decode the letter sequence from left to right but make mistakes for several reasons. The most obvious reason is that they lack some of the necessary letter-sound-correspondences. In contrast to this, logographic readers produce different mistakes. They either produce a real word which shares some graphemic features with the original word (please note that the boy read *monkey* when the original word was *mokney*) or they do not even attempt to read the word.

The distribution of the different types of mistakes the boy made clearly supports the assumption that the boy employed the alphabetic strategy when reading the list of words given to him. Of the 36 words, he read one correctly in the long presentation: *monkey*. Then he read one real word instead of the pseudo word (*monkey* for *mokney*), 27 non-words with the beginning of the original words and two non-words with beginnings different from the original words. Five words he did not attempt to read at all. This means that this child made six mistakes which indicate a logographic strategy (one real word for a pseudo word + five times no reading attempt) vs. 29 mistakes which indicate an alphabetic strategy (cf. Fig. 7). These results make a strong case for the alphabetic strategy.

2.4 Reading English with German phoneme-grapheme-correspondences

As clear cut as this may be, the most obvious piece of evidence for the use of the alphabetic strategy lies in the specific way the children read out the English words. Most incorrectly read words were read "German-style", i.e. by applying the German phoneme-grapheme-correspondence (PGC) to the English words. The test child whose mistakes are presented in Figure 7 read 28 non-words this way. This specific way of reading can be found across all three categories of words that were part of the reading test. The boy read e.g. /kat/ for the real word <cat>, /elepla:nt/ for the visually similar pseudo word <eleplant> and /ba:rtle/ for the visually non-similar pseudo word <bartle>.

This way of reading is not surprising in view of the fact that the children's literacy was explicitly supported only in the German classes. The boy's reading style was no exception (cf. Fig. 8). The first lines show the average numbers of correctly read English words in both short and long presentations (cf. Fig. 6) and the second lines show the average numbers of words which were read according to the German PGC in short and long presentations.

	Control group	Test group	Total
real words (max. 12)	3.4	0.6	2.0
	6.3	6.4	6.4
pseudo words visually similar (max. 12)	0.7	0.1	0.5
	7.3	6.6	7
pseudo words visually non-similar (max. 12)	0.6	0.1	0.3
	8.4	6.9	7.7

Fig. 8, Correctly read English words and reading based on German PGC

Far more words were pronounced on the basis of the German PGC than on the English one. Some children read a few words in a mixed way – partly German, partly English: One child, e. g., read *mouth* as /maʊt/ and the pseudo words *Plagway* and *Slagway* as /plagveɪ/ and /slagveɪ/, respectively.

Although the children are on their way, they do not seem to have made any substantial progress in their acquisition of the English written form. Our results are very positive as far as the use of the alphabetic strategy is concerned but seem to be devastating with regard to the children's EFL achievement. Especially the high number of English words read out with the German PGC might lead to the conclusion that the children sounded out the words without knowing them, i.e. without knowing their meaning.

Obviously, the tendency to employ the PGC of a transparent and regular language when reading an opaque and irregular language is not confined to the pair German - English. Weth (this volume) reports the same phenomenon for young German learners of French and Lázaro Ibarrola (this volume) for young Spanish learners of English. Although the children understand the French or English sound forms, they do not produce them when they read aloud. Both Weth and Lázaro Ibarrola thus conclude that the learners do not recognize the words they read, i. e. cannot extract their meaning.

However, this does not necessarily seem to be the case. Fortunately, several children in our study had commented on the way they had read out the words and provided the German meanings without having been prompted to do so. Again, this held true across all three categories used in the test; the right column in Figure 9 shows what the boy read and the comments he made.

<rabbit>		„/rabɪt/, ich glaub', das heißt auf Deutsch ‚Hase'." (I think this means „Hase" in German.)
<applo>	visually similar	„/aplo/"
<doven>	visually non-similar	"/doven/"
<flower>		"/flovə(r)/, /flovə(r)/!"
<shoudlers>	visually similar	„/ʃoʊdlə(r)s/, das heißt auf Deutsch ‚Schulter'! (This means „Schulter" in German.)

Fig. 9, Words read with German PGC and comments on their meanings

2.5 A word-picture match showing silent reading skills

The children's comments propelled us to design an additional test. By asking the children to match written words and pictures we were able to see how many vocabulary items they actually knew regardless of whether or not they were able to correctly read them out loud. The vocabulary items were identical to the real words of the initial reading test. One test sheet contained 10 reading items and 15 pictures, among them the corresponding pictures (cf. Fig. 10, here the filled in version of the boy whose oral results are presented in figures 7 and 9).

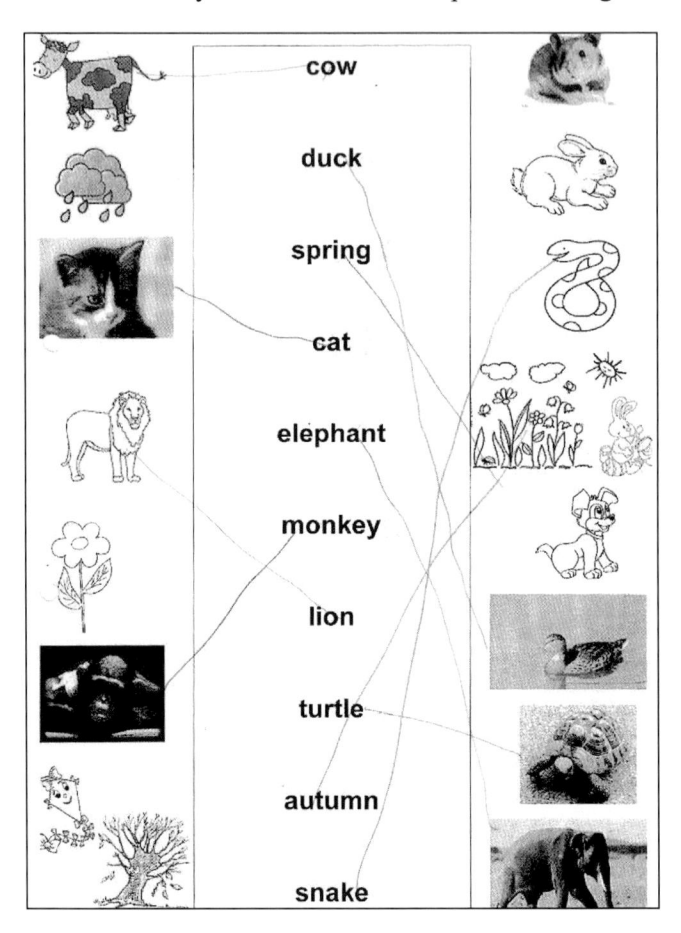

Fig. 10, Word-picture matching test

The test child read 11 of 12 real words with a German PGC. Due to this high number one might conclude that this child did not understand the words he read out. Examining his test sheet, however (Fig. 10), we see that his vocabulary knowledge is actually very good. He correctly matched nine words to the corresponding pictures. His only mistake was *autumn* which he matched with the picture for *spring*, a lexical item from the same word field which consequently lends itself easily for slips of the tongue or slips of the pen. Please note that although the boy had sounded out almost all words incorrectly, he recognized their meaning, i. e. he was able to read the words silently.

This relation of poor oral reading and good silent reading was widespread among the first graders (n = 51) we tested. As far as real words are concerned, the test group (26 students) correctly read out only 5 % yet recognized 58 % of the items in the word-picture test. The control group (25 students) correctly read out 28.3 % and recognized 78 % in the word-picture test. Obviously, it is especially the poor learners whose achievement is not fully recognized if we focus on their oral skills and do not take all facets of their competence into account. This conclusion is also arrived at by Kötter whose case studies of individual children show that learners' poor pronunciation might mask their true foreign language competence in a negative way (Kötter, to appear).

Finally answering our third research question „How accomplished are their written skills in English?" we have to conclude that the first graders' reading skills are much more refined in silent than in oral reading. Again, this is not too surprising because the children were never required to read orally in their EFL classes. Silent reading, however, they were able to practice daily.

We do not want to challenge the didactic principle that literacy teaching has to be sensitive to the learners' knowledge of spoken English as established by most researchers today (among others Cameron 2003: 108). Rather, it should be carefully distinguished between oral and silent reading. Just because children can e. g. read the English names they were given in their English class, we should not jump to the conclusion that there is a close connection between oral production and reading skills (for an example of this conviction cf. Reisener 1975: 185). A statement like Reisener's „Das Lesen, so läßt sich behaupten, ist relational und proportional vom vorher betriebenen und gepflegten Sprechen abhängig" (Reading, so one may state, is relationally and proportionally dependent on the speaking practised and exercised before, J.R.) (ibid.) has to be modified. Support from this view comes from different angles: Today we know that learners do not necessarily have to be able to speak or enunciate clearly if they are to learn reading. Psycholinguists claim that „[r]eading should be based on speech understanding and not on speech production" and „[r]eading can be learned without speaking" (Steinberg & Sciarini 2006: 80). Studies into teaching English as a foreign language report that fourth graders could not read out a story which they had just got to know orally before. They employed the German PGC to such a degree that their reading out loud was hardly understandable. Contrary to this, children who had the opportunity to become familiar with the text by listening to audio tapes and by print were able to read out the text almost flawlessly (Diehr & Rymarczyk 2008: 6).

As incompatible as the differing results of silent and oral reading might seem, they remind us of the assumption which underlies all stage models of literacy acquisition, namely that learning to read and write is a process in which connections between the written form, the sound form and the meaning of a lexical item are gradually formed (Ehri 1999: 82). The exact way in which this connection-forming process takes place might depend on the teaching method. Frisch's data (to appear), e. g., show that the phonics approach does not only support second graders' English oral reading skills but also their reading comprehension, i. e. silent reading. Ehlers reports that young learners (grade 4, n = 1089) in her data showed better results in reading comprehension than in listening comprehension. However, there seems to be a connection between the children's overall performance and their dominant strength in either listening or reading comprehension. The stronger the children actually are, the more clearly their reading comprehension results outdo their listening comprehension scores. Out of the weaker subjects (36,60%) who had achieved an overall score of 67%-80%, more children achieved this score in listening than in reading comprehension: 43,20% compared to 22,30% respectively. The stronger group (24,10%) who achieved a total of 81%-91% showed a different picture: 15% achieved the score in listening compared to 28,80% in reading comprehension. And the top group (6,29% achieving a total score of 92%-100%) showed a very clear dominance in reading over listening comprehension: only 3,8% scored the top points in listening compared to 26,60% in reading (Ehlers, unpublished manuscript). Ehlers assumes that the teachers tend to use more written material than current methodology with its primacy of oracy suggests (oral communication, October 2009). This idea is certainly not far fetched as the results of the Swiss study show. The teachers in Haenni Hoti's investigation (2007: 21) declared that they work a lot with the written form – how much can be seen in the comparison to the oral activities listed in the lower part of Figure 11.

Written activities				
Wie häufig haben Sie das mit der Klasse in diesem Schuljahr (3. Klasse) im Englischunterricht gemacht? (How often did you do this with the class in this term (year 3) in the English lessons?)	häufig (often)	manchmal (sometimes)	selten (rarely)	nie (never)
Die Kinder englische Texte und Geschichten lesen lassen (z. B. im Pupil's Book) (Have the children read English texts and stories (e. g. in the Pupil's Book))	46.4 %	39.3 %	14.3 %	0 %
Die Kinder englische Wörter oder einfache Sätze abschreiben lassen (Have the children copy English words or simple sentences)	57.1 %	42.9 %	0 %	0 %
Die Kinder einfache englische Sätze oder Texte frei aufschreiben lassen (Have the children write English sentences or texts freely)	0 %	53.6 %	39.3 %	7.1 %
Oral activities				
CD mit Musik oder Gesprächen darauf anhören Listen to CDs with music or conversations	67.9 %	25.0 %	7.1 %	0 %
Der Klasse englische Texte und Geschichten vorlesen Read English texts and stories to the class	21.4 %	53.6 %	17.9 %	7.1 %

Fig. 11, Distribution of teachers' answers with regard to oral and written classroom activities (translations by J.R.) (cf. Haenni Hoti 2007: 21)

Although our insights into the early literacy acquisition process are still fragmentary, there seems to be more and more consensus about the early introduction of the written form of the foreign language. Teachers seem to integrate reading and writing into early EFL-classes according to their subjective theories and researchers present positive results as to the beneficial effects of the written form.

3. Conclusion

The conclusion we would like to draw is that the written form of English should be taught right from the start of EFL-classes or at least not be withheld. Our data support teachers' subjective theories and current research studies. The children in our investigation basically seem to skip the logographic stage which was found to be relevant to the acquisition of reading and writing in English. Instead of the logographic strategy they employ the alphabetic strategy which they are familiar with from their German classes. This might give the children a slightly bumpy start reading and writing English, but after a while they might actually benefit from being familiar with the alphabetic strategy. After all, researchers like Ehri (1999), e. g., claim that even English learners in early literacy phases profit from the alphabetic strategy.

Current language policy should be changed. We strongly recommend written English to become part of the curriculum in first grade.

References

Cameron, Lynne (2003), Challenges for ELT from the expansion in teaching children. In: *ELT Journal*, Volume 57/2, April 2003, 105–112.
Diehr, Bärbel & Rymarczyk, Jutta (2008), Zur Basis von Lese- und Schreibversuchen in Klasse 1 und 2. 'Ich weiß es, weil ich es so spreche.' In: *Grundschulmagazin Englisch*. 1/2008, 6–8.
Ehri, Linnea C. (1999), Phases of Development in Learning to Read Words. In: Oakhill, Jane & Beard, Roger (eds.) (1999), *Reading Development and the Teaching of Reading*. Oxford: Blackwell, 79–108.
Frisch, Stefanie (to appear), Zum Umgang mit dem englischen Schriftbild im Englischunterricht der Grundschule. In: Kötter, Markus & Rymarczyk, Jutta (eds.).
Frith, Uta (1998), Psycholinguistische Aspekte orthographischen Wissens. In: Augst, Erhard (ed.). *New Trends in Graphemics and Orthography*. De Gruyter. Berlin, New York. 218 - 233.

Gentry, J. Richard (2006), *Breaking the Code. The New Science of Beginning Reading and Writing.* Portsmouth. NH: Heinemann.

Haenni Hoti, Andrea (2007), NFP56-Projekt: Englisch und Französisch auf der Primarstufe. 1. Zwischenbericht an die teilnehmenden Schulen, an Bildungsbehörden und weitere Interessierte. Ergebnisse zum Englisch in der dritten Klasse. http://www.fe.luzern.phz.ch/fileadmin/media/fe.luzern.phz.ch/nfp56_zwischenbericht.pdf (08.10.2009).

Kötter, Markus (to appear), Lern(er)biographien im Frühbeginn: Fallbeispiele aus der Begleitforschung von Englischunterricht in Klasse 3 und 4. In: Kötter, Markus & Rymarczyk, Jutta (eds.).

Kötter, Markus & Rymarczyk, Jutta (eds.) (to appear), *Fremdsprachenunterricht in der Grundschule: Forschungsergebnisse und Vorschläge zu seiner weiteren Entwicklung.* Frankfurt a. M.: Peter Lang.

Ministerium für Bildung, Frauen und Jugend Rheinland Pfalz (ed.) (2004), Weiterentwicklung der Grundschule. Rahmenlehrplan Grundschule. Teilrahmenplan Fremdsprache. URL: http://grundschule.bildung-rp.de/fileadmin/user_upload/grundschule.bildung-rp.de/Downloads/Rahmenplan/Rapla-FS-Druckfassung.pdf (06.10.2009).

Ministerium für Kultus, Jugend und Sport Baden-Württemberg (ed.) (2004), *Bildungsplan 2004. Bildungsstandards für Englisch. Grundschule – Klassen 2, 4.* http://bildung-staerkt-menschen.de/service/downloads/Bildungsplaene/Grundschule/Grundschule_Bildungsplan_Gesamt.pdf (06.10.2009).

Müller, Rudolf (2004²), *Diagnostischer Rechtschreibtest (DRT 1).* Göttingen: Beltz.

Müller, Rudolf (1984), *Diagnostischer Lesetest zur Frühdiagnose von Lesestörungen (DLF 1–2).* Weinheim: Beltz.

Scheerer-Neumann, Gerheid (2003⁶), Rechtschreibschwäche im Kontext der Entwicklung. In: Naegele, Ingrid & Valtin, Renate (eds.). *LRS – Legasthenie in den Klasen 1 - 10.* Bd. 1 Weinheim, Basel: Beltz. 45 - 65.

Steinberg, Danny D. & Sciarini, Natalia V. (2006²), *An Introduction to Psycholinguistics.* Harlow: Pearson Longman.

Steinig, Wolfgang & Huneke, Hans-Werner (2002), *Sprachdidaktik Deutsch: Eine Einführung.* Berlin: Schmidt.

Reisener, Helmut (1975), Bericht über das Lüneburger Versuchsprojekt: Englischunterricht im Eingangsbereich der Primarstufe. In: Niedersächsisches Kultusministerium (ed.). *Schulversuche und Schulreform. Bd. 8. Englisch im Primarbereich.* Hannover: Schroedel, 163–199.

Rymarczyk, Jutta (2008a), Früher oder später? Zur Einführung des Schriftbildes in der Grundschule. In: Böttger, Heiner (ed.) *Fortschritte im Frühen Fremdsprachenlernen. Ausgewählte Tagungsbeiträge. Nürnberg 2007.* München: Domino. 170–182.

Rymarczyk, Jutta (2008b), Zum Umgang mit Schrift im frühen Fremdsprachenunterricht. In: *Take Off*, 4/ 2008, 49.

Wimmer, Heinz; Hartl, Michael; Moser, Ewald (1990), Passen ‚englische' Modelle des Schriftspracherwerbs auf ‚deutsche' Kinder? Zweifel an der Bedeutsamkeit der logographischen Stufe. In: *Zeitschrift für Entwicklungspsychologie und Pädagogische Psychologie*. Band XXII, Heft 2, 136 - 154.

Amparo Lázaro Ibarrola

English phonics for Spanish children: adapting to new English as a Foreign Language classrooms

Dieser Aufsatz schlägt den Einsatz des Phonics Ansatzes für sehr junge spanische Kinder vor, die Englisch im schulischen Kontext erlernen. Phonics bezieht sich auf ein spezifisches Anfänger-Lese-Programm, das entwickelt wurde, um englischen Kindern Lesen und Schreiben zu vermitteln. Die Methode umfasst die Herausbildung phonologischer Bewusstheit und die kindgerechte Vermittlung von Laut-Buchstaben-Verbindungen. Unterstützte man spanische Kinder darin, die Laut-Buchstaben-Verbindungen des Englischen zu erwerben, könnte (i) graphophonemischer Transfer vermieden werden, (ii) die Aussprache profitieren und (iii) Lesen in der Fremdsprache leichter zu bewältigen sein. Da Lesefähigkeiten generell ausschlaggebend für erfolgreiches Lernen sind, würde der Einsatz von Phonics im Unterricht spanischer Kinder darüber hinaus eine solide Grundlage für das weitere Erlernen der Fremdsprache bilden. Ein weiterer Vorteil ist die einfache Anwendung von Phonics, die eine leichte Integration in den Unterricht ermöglicht. Dieser innovative Vorschlag eröffnet ein neues Forschungsfeld und könnte auf andere europäische Länder mit frühem Englischunterricht ausgeweitet werden.

1. Introduction

This article proposes the use of English phonics with very young Spanish children learning English in school. Phonics refers to a specific beginning reading program to teach English children to read and write. This method involves raising phonological awareness and teaching children how to connect the sounds of the oral language with their graphical representations (letters or groups of letters).

There are good theoretical reasons to believe that adopting this specific reading program with Spanish children could help them not to transfer the graphophonemic rules of Spanish, in other words, not to read English written texts as if they were Spanish. Accordingly, phonics programs could assist Spanish children in the reading process but also in learning English pronunciation. From a broader educational point of view, if phonics makes the reading process in the foreign language easier and more attainable, children will also be more motivated to learn the language and more likely to enjoy reading.

In order to properly highlight the relevance and meaningfulness of the present proposal, it is necessary to examine the situation of English in the Spanish school context (section 2) as well as previous research on reading (section 3). The abundant and varied deal of studies on reading has almost exclusively dealt with reading in the native tongue while the study of how reading is learnt by second language (SL)[1] learners remains scarce (Cheung & Slavin 2005; Stuart 1999). More relevantly for the present work and for the present volume: the study of how reading is learnt by foreign language learners (FL)[2] is virtually non-existent. The absence of research is but the mirror image of English as a Foreign Language (EFL) classroom praxis in the Spanish school context where no systematic approach has yet been taken to tackle reading in English even though children start learning the foreign language in their first school year (when they are 3). This deficiency is somehow the result of the drastic and rapid changes in EFL teaching in the past decade: English has been gradually introduced to younger children but teaching methodologies have not developed at a similar speed.

Thus, the specific methodological proposal we are presenting will contribute bridging the gap between research and class praxis, since it will provide a new tool for teachers and, at the same time, it will open an unexplored and multidisciplinary field of research interweaving research on reading, on second language acquisition, on phonology and on language teaching.

We are also well aware that, even if we are departing from the Spanish context, this proposal could be extended to other EFL school contexts which are also facing the introduction of English with very young learners. In fact, this article is just a theoretical dissertation which we hope lays the foundation of future empirical works which test the validity of phonics (or other beginning reading programs) with children from different language backgrounds, of different ages, in different contexts, etc.

---

1 Second language (SL) learners are those who are learning the target language in a region where that language is broadly spoken. Immigrant children, for instance, learning English in the UK, USA, Canada etc. are English as a Second Language (ESL) learners.
2 Foreign language learners are those who are learning the language in a region where that language is not spoken. Spanish children learning English in Spanish schools, for instance, are English as a Foreign Language (EFL) learners.

2. Learning English in Spanish schools

2.1. Changes in the EFL classroom

Responding to the needs of a new society, open to all kinds of international exchanges, learning languages has progressively gained curriculum space in most teaching institutions all over Europe. To illustrate this, suffice it to mention several initiatives of the European Community, such as the European Year of Languages (2001), the Action Plan on Language Learning and Linguistic Diversity (2004–2006) or the Common European Framework of Reference (CEFR) for languages. On the other hand, within this multilingual mosaic depicting Europe, the growing supremacy of English as a lingua franca has become indisputable. Far from ignoring this, the different educational institutions have devoted great efforts to increase the quantity and quality of English courses.

In Spain, the government has not neglected this concern. Despite having gone through several changes in education laws (LOGSE (1990); LOCE (2002); LOE (2006)), the acquisition of communicative competence in a foreign language has been present in all of them as one of the basic objectives both in primary education (6 school years: age 6–12) and in compulsory secondary education (4 school years: age 14–17). Quoting from the current law (LOE), one objective in primary education is to "acquire, in at least one foreign language, the communicative competence which enables children to express and understand simple messages and to be able to cope with daily situations" (translated from LOE, III, 17(f)). This law also includes the following objective for secondary education: "understand and express yourself in one or more foreign languages in an appropriate manner" (translated from LOE, III, 23(i)).

The main difference is found when we compare the law from 1990 (LOGSE), which does not include the introduction of a foreign language in infant education (3 school years: age 3–6), to the more recent laws from 2002 and 2006 (LOCE and LOE), which do include it in the following words: "The education institutions will promote the incorporation of a foreign language in infant education, especially in the last year" (translated from LOCE, I, 12, 3).

Gradually, the area of EFL has been becoming more important in the Spanish school curriculum, especially in primary school and even more especially in infant education where it had been simply non-existent before. At these levels, despite having differences depending on specific schools or regions, the following general developments have taken place:

Logistical changes:
   The starting age has gone down to the beginning of schooling, when children are 3 years old.
   The number of EFL classes per week has augmented.
   Only English teachers (with a specific degree in English and Language Teaching) are in charge of EFL classrooms. Before these changes, any teacher with a basic level of English could teach this language.
Methodological changes:
   EFL sessions: In EFL classes, teaching English in English has replaced teaching English in Spanish.
   Content and language integrated learning (CLIL) sessions: CLIL instruction, that is, teaching different subjects in English while teaching the language, is being gradually introduced.

In order to illustrate all these modifications with very specific data, we would like to concentrate on the Community of Navarre, which has specific education laws based on the Spanish ones. We show the different changes in the table below.

Education Laws	Onset age	Sessions per week	EFL sessions	CLIL sessions
1992	8	3	3	0
2002	3	5	3	2

The evolution of EFL classes in the Community of Navarre

As can be seen in the table, the 1992 education law (Orden Foral 230/1992: 12/06/1992) established the beginning of EFL classes at the age of 8 and a total number of 3 EFL sessions per week. Ten years later, the next education law for the community (Orden Foral 366: 5/07/2002) establishes English classes in all years, including the early years of infant education. Moreover, the number of sessions is now five per week, three of them for EFL and two of them for teaching different contents through English (CLIL).

As a matter of fact, the law is merely picking up what had become a regular practice in Navarre's schools which, more often than not, had implemented these changes going ahead of the law in answering a social demand. It is also important to point out that these changes are best described as ongoing, since the government is now starting to launch bilingual (English-Spanish) programs in several schools and has planned to spread them gradually all over Navarre, including their introduction in Basque[3] schools.

---

3   Navarre has two official languages, Basque and Spanish. Accordingly it has Basque schools with all subjects in Basque, except for English and Spanish Language.

Obviously, this spectacular increase in the area of English has been followed by an increasing demand for English teachers. The public call for English teachers in Navarre offered 9 posts in 1998; 15 in 2001; 67 in 2003; 157 in 2005; 71 in 2007 and 156 in 2009. The numbers are revealing. However, when it comes to hiring English teachers the schools face the problem that neither teachers nor training programs are properly adapted to the new context. On the one hand, the teaching expertise of those who have been teaching English only three hours per week, starting with 8 year-old students is now insufficient. On the other hand, teacher training programs are still anchored in very traditional syllabuses and need to be drastically modified.

While this happens, teachers do not know how to get the most benefit from the optimal conditions of the English classroom (large number of hours per week and very young learners). It follows that the EFL classes suffer from some serious methodological flaws, such as the one we concentrate on in this article: the lack of method to teach reading in the foreign language.

However, even if this article concentrates on one of these flaws, it would be very unfair to ignore some remarkable achievements. In fact, the growth of English has triggered a great number of research projects providing very valuable contributions for English teachers (Madrid & McLaren (2004); Vez, Guillén & Alario (2002) inter alia). Along the lines of these works, this article also aims at being one more contribution towards the improvement of the academic training of English teachers in primary school and, consequently, of their teaching practices. This contribution concentrates on a very specific methodological intervention, teaching Spanish children to read in English, which, however simple, lays a solid foundation for further learning.

2.2. University programs for EFL teachers

When the Spanish universities devised their language syllabuses for primary school teacher training programs in 1983 (Spanish law for a university reform (*Ley de Reforma Universitaria* (LRU)), most language courses were left in the hands of linguistics and literature scholars, who had never been in a classroom and had never received training in school didactics. Inheritors of their own history, these courses have often remained anchored in epistemological perspectives which, no matter how interesting, were totally unconnected to the teaching profession they were training for.

On the other hand, the celerity of the recent logistical changes described above has not been accompanied by an equally rapid adaptation of these old teacher training programs. Maldonado (2004) in the *Libro Blanco*[4] for the teacher training degree explains that "the deep reformation in the school system, which affected all levels and areas, would have been larger and more effective if it had been accompanied by a deep restructuring of the university teacher training degrees" (translation from Maldonado 2004).

In the case of training programs for English teachers, Spanish universities have always included phonetic courses. However, these courses have usually been devoted to a mere theoretical introduction of English phonology and English transcription. Somehow, it has been commonly and implicitly assumed that pronunciation did not demand specific training and that students would gradually acquire it while learning the language. The same can be said of reading in the foreign language. As a consequence, pronunciation has been traditionally pushed into the background while beginning reading programs in the foreign language have been simply ignored.

It follows that once these university students become school teachers, most of the time they devote little or no time to pronunciation and when they do, it is usually restricted to correcting online and/or to one or two isolated activities typically present in English textbooks. In any case, pronunciation has not been integrated in the daily activities, contrary to grammar, reading, listening or vocabulary. Obviously, teachers devote no time to reading programs because they are not even aware of their existence.

On the other hand, the complexity of the pronunciation of English, as well as the difficulty Spanish students (and teachers!) have when facing the written language and attempting to read it out, provides evidence of the need for more solid training as regards these aspects. This is especially so in infant education and primary school, where students have their first contact with the English language and when they are ready to develop oral and reading skills. However, if English teachers are not taught about the materials, methodologies and possibilities of phonetics and/or reading programs, we cannot expect them to teach pronunciation or reading to their students.

Here comes our proposal. We believe that phonetic courses in EFL teacher training programs should include the didactic possibilities of phonetics, the main one being to teach reading through phonics programs. As stated before, phonics provide teachers with one specific tool to develop phonological awareness among their future students, to improve their pronunciation and to assist them in the reading process by adopting and adapting the methods that English native children use in their own learning-to-read process.

---

4   The so called "Libros Blancos" (literally "white books") collect the main guidelines to design the new courses adapted to the Bologna Process. These books are edited by a national agency of evaluation (ANECA).

At this point, when Spanish degrees are immersed in the Bologna process, a process which hoists the flag of offering education that is closer to real professional practices, it is our hope that the new degrees make room for proposals (like ours) which really aim at connecting university contents and teaching practices.

3. The reading process

3.1. Key issues in the reading process

The process of learning to read, also known as literacy[5], is complex and usually requires a teacher to guide the children. Literacy can be also defined as the sine qua non requirement for further school learning. The importance of this process is evidenced by the fact that it has been extensively and widely researched in all languages, including the two concerning the present work (English and Spanish) (Alegría & Morais 1979; Bryant & Bradley 1985; Cassany 1987, 1993; Clemente & Domínguez 1999; Domínguez 1996a,b; Graves 1991; Pressley 1999; Solé 1992; Teberosky 1991; Tolchinsky 1993; among others).

Leaving aside the details, there are two main approaches to introduce literacy: phonological and whole language methods. Both approaches have been the object of a lively debate and have their corresponding defenders and detractors (Chall 1983). Whole language methods are based on a direct access to meaning via the visual image of words without paying attention to the letters or groups of letters that compose these words and without analysing the sounds corresponding to these letters. On the other hand, phonological methods teach to identify letters with their corresponding sounds and, then, departing from this connection, children construct the sound of the word, recognize it and link it to its meaning.

Without engaging in this long-standing debate, which would be beyond the scope of the present work, we have decided to follow a phonological approach. This approach seems more appropriate for our students who are also acquiring literacy in Spanish and will therefore transfer the connection of letters and sounds from this language. It is thus our belief that a phonological approach will help them to become aware of the different and complex connections between letters and sounds in the new language.

Once we are located in a phonological approach, even if there are different opinions about how the reading process takes place, it is commonly acknowl-

---

5 In the present article the term literacy is used in its narrow sense, which identifies literacy acquisition with learning to read (learning how the writing system works). In a broader sense literacy involves wider and more sophisticated competencies (Perfetti & Marron 1995).

edged that phonology plays an important role in this process[6] (Byrne & Fielding-Barnsley 1991; Carrillo & Sánchez-Meca 1990; Cunningham 1990; Jorm & Share 1983; Read, Zhang, Nie & Ding 1986). The very nature of the alphabetic systems evidences this, since it is a graphic system defined as a phonological representation of the oral language. The term phonological awareness is thus coined. Tunmer (1989) defines it as the ability to reflect on the phonological segments of the oral language. In other words, it refers to the ability to analyse and segment the sound structure of the oral language.

Two key issues about the role of phonological awareness in the reading process are of special relevance to the present work. First of all, the fact that phonological awareness is restricted to the initial stage of the reading process (Clemente 2001; Johnston 1998; Scarborough, Ehri, Olson, & Fowler 1998). Following Clemente (2001), when we learn to read we initially use phonology by transforming every letter into its corresponding sound in the oral language. However, once we are advanced readers we base our reading on the orthographic dimension, that is, we identify the written word immediately when seeing its graphic representation and without the need of phonologically constructing it. Second, abundant research has found tight connections between phonological awareness and high rates of success in reading (Bryant & Bradley 1983; Carrillo & Sánchez Meca 1990; Cunningham 1990; Domínguez 1996a; Liberman, Shankweiler, Fischer & Carter 1974; Morais, Cluytens & Alegría 1984). What is more, the contrary has also been proved: lack of phonological awareness predicts difficulties in reading (Juel, Griffith & Gough 1986).

Jiménez & Ortiz (1995) underline the necessity to determine the exact nature of the connection between phonological awareness and the reading process, more specifically to determine whether phonological awareness is the reason for or the consequence of the reading process. This question raises a controversial issue: is it necessary to use explicit instruction to develop phonological awareness and to teach reading? On the one hand, several authors (Morais, Cary, Alegría & Bertelson 1979; Read et al. 1986) have claimed that phonological awareness cannot be spontaneously acquired and methodological intervention is thus necessary. By contrast, Ehri and Wilce (1980, 1987) found that some children were able to learn to read without the need of phonological reflection. Whatever the case may be, Griffith and Olson (1992) have proved that, regardless of the method used to teach reading, those children with higher levels of phonological awareness exceeded the rest in their reading abilities. It follows that, even if a child might become phonologically aware with no teaching intervention, it seems that helping the child to

---

6   For a different view see Scholes (1998) and the corresponding answer by Johnston (1998).

acquire this awareness with didactical methods will facilitate the reading process and this, beyond all doubt, is desirable from the point of view of education.

Turning to another strand of evidence in favour of instruction for reading, as Adams (1990) and Johnston (1998) claim, even if research struggles to determine exactly why phonological awareness raising methods are successful, their years of success in the classroom (where teachers use them and children learn to read) act as a guarantor for their validity.

Therefore, we conclude that an explicit didactic intervention to develop phonological awareness is beneficial for the reading process. The following points summarize the main findings about phonological awareness which are relevant for our proposal to use phonics with Spanish children:

(i) Phonological awareness plays a crucial role in the initial stage.
(ii) Phonological awareness is related to successful reading.
(iii) Phonological awareness facilitates the reading process (although children might learn to read without developing this awareness).
(iv) Explicit didactic intervention to develop phonological awareness (although not indispensable) is beneficial for the reading process.

3.2. Phonological awareness in Spanish children learning English

In the English-speaking world, reading is often taught through phonics[7] programs. These programs show the connections between letters and sounds, which are known as grapho-phonemic principles. Consequently, these programs help children to acquire the orthographic structure of the oral English they have already acquired.

As stated in the introduction, most works on learning to read have focused on the native language. We are aware that the process of learning to read in a foreign language will, definitely, be a different one. If we concentrate on the present case, Spanish learners of English in school, our students have learnt the alphabet in Spanish together with the Spanish letter-sound relationships and, when facing reading in English, what they need is to learn the new relationships between letters and sounds.

Although no research to date has reported results from FL students, some recent works have enhanced the value of teaching to read in the two languages involved in bilingual programs (Cheung & Slavin 2005: 242). These authors have highlighted the importance of teaching children to read in both languages and

---

7 For the alternative whole language methods see Holdaway (1979).

have found "particularly strong evidence favoring paired bilingual programs, in which students are taught to read both in their native language and in English".

Regarding literacy in SL learners, Stuart (1999) carried out a study with 95 5-year-old inner-city children learning English in London (most children were speakers of Sylheti, a language of Bangladesh). This author used a commercially available method to teach these children to read in English (The Phonics Handbook by Lloyd 1992, reedited in 1995) and the whole program was administered by the regular teachers who received some basic instruction on how to use these methods. The study also included control groups, which just used big books for reading practice. After 12 weeks using the program in the classrooms (one hour per week), Stuart found positive and significant effects in the development of reading and writing in the phonics groups, where children significantly outperformed those of the control groups. This author also found that teachers only need minimal training to learn how to use these materials, which is an important issue, given that the efficacy of any didactic strategy must weigh logistical possibilities against effectiveness on learning. In other words, if phonics were too demanding for teachers they could never be integrated as a regular teaching practice.

All the abovementioned issues lead us to formulate the hypothesis that teaching children how to read in the foreign language they are learning would benefit both the reading process and the language learning process. Based on Stuart's (1999) findings we also believe that the school teachers would be the appropriate agents to administer these programs.

In the next section, we show the specific nature of phonological awareness in our Spanish students of English.

4. Spanish children learning to read in English

The process of learning to read per se is more complex in English than it is in Spanish mainly because written English differs enormously from oral English. While Spanish (standard) uses 29 letters to represent 24 phonemes, English (RP variety) uses 26 letters to represent 44 phonemes. In addition, English presents quite a few pronunciation irregularities while Spanish presents almost none. Not surprisingly, the reading process has deserved far more attention in the English speaking world than in Spanish speaking countries and there are large numbers of works developing pedagogical materials based on phonological awareness to teach English children to read (Bishop 1986; Fitzpatrick 1997; Hohmann 2002; Jager, Goorman & Llundberg 1997; Lloyd 1992, 1995; McCracken & McCracken 1996 inter alia).

Despite this intrinsic difficulty of the reading process in English, which has led to such strenuous efforts to help English children to read, Spanish EFL learners in school have to face the reading process with no specific help. In fact, they are only taught the alphabet (names of the letters) which, as it has been proved, does not help to improve the reading process (Ball & Blachman 1991).

The usual procedure in English classrooms goes as follows: teachers allow children to start reading English by transferring the connections between letters and sounds that they are acquiring in Spanish and they correct them online. In other words, children start reading English words as if they were Spanish and teachers correct their errors as they come across them but with no systematic approach. This means that children have to infer the grapho-phonemic rules of English by themselves. This also means that the reading process is difficult and discouraging for the students. To make matters worse, the process is also very slow because children have only 5 hours per week of English and only a very small amount of this time is devoted to reading aloud and correcting errors.

The subjects of our proposal would be infant and primary school students. At present, pupils usually acquire basic reading skills in Spanish in infant education (age 3–5). When they arrive in the first year of primary school (6 years old) they are able to read and understand isolated words, sentences and in some cases short texts. On the other hand, they have been learning English orally for three years in infant education. This means that they are acquainted with English sounds and they are able to understand school instructions in English as well as to produce some basic words and functional chunks.

In the first years of primary school English teachers start introducing the written text in their lessons, however, as explained before, no specific approach to reading is applied; children are simply left to infer the grapho-phonemic rules of English as they are corrected online. It follows that children have to face a double difficulty: (I) the intrinsic complexity of the English language and (II) the grapho-phonemic transfer from Spanish, as we summarize with some examples[8]:

I. Intrinsic complexity of the English grapho-phonemic relationships:

1. A system of 26 letters and 44 phonemes.
2. A system with a large number of irregular pronunciations.
3. A system with no biunivocal connections between phonemes and graphical representations:
   i) One letter can be equivalent to several phonemes:

---

8   For the sake of simplicity, we concentrate on RP English in the examples and we only provide a very general summary of the key aspects in the comparison of Spanish and English grapho-phonemics. For a detailed description and comparison of these phonological systems see, for example, Alcaraz and Moody (1999), Finch and Ortiz Lira (1982) and Mott (2000).

letter <g> can be pronounced:
  (a) /g/ as in 'gate' /geɪt/
  (b) /dʒ/ as in 'gin' /dʒɪn/
  (c) /ʒ/ as in 'garage' /'gærɑːʒ/
  (d) silent as in 'sign' /saɪn/
 ii) One phoneme can be represented by several letters or combinations of letters:
   Phoneme /ʌ/ can be graphically represented by the following letters:
    (a) <u> as in 'but' /bʌt/
    (b) <oo> as in 'flood' /flʌd/
    (c) <o> as in 'love' /lʌv/
    (d) <ou> as in 'country' /'kʌntri/
    (e) <oe> as in 'does' /dʌz/

II. Transfer from Spanish grapho-phonemic rules:

1. Spanish and English do not share the phonological system. Spanish has 24 phonemes while English has 44. Some phonemes are the same but most of them are either similar but different or simply do not exist in one of the two languages.
2. Spanish and English do not share the grapho-phonemic rules. In Spanish, grapho-phonemic rules tend to be univocal (one letter or one combination of letters is always pronounced similarly) and, as we said before, it is not the case in English, as we exemplify with letter <a>:
  i) English: letter <a> can be pronounced:
    (a) /æ/, as in 'cat' /kæt/
    (b) /eɪ/, as in 'cake' /keɪk/
    (c) /ɑː/, as in 'car' /kɑː/
    (d) /eə/ as in 'care' /keə/
    (e) /ə/ as in 'arrive' /ə'raɪv/
    (f) /ɔ/ as in 'warrior' /'wɔriə/
    (g) /ɔː/ as in 'ball' /bɔːl/
    (h) /ɪ/ as in 'advantage' /əd'vɑːntɪdʒ/
  ii) Spanish: letter <a> is always pronounced:
    /a/ as in 'casa' /'kasa/

Obviously, there are additional difficulties in the case of Spanish children: They still have a very low command of English and they have very limited exposure to the English language if we compare them to bilingual, immersion or second language children (let alone native English children!).

As a consequence, the transference of the grapho-phonemic rules of Spanish will result in children not recognizing familiar words when they see their graphical representation (the written word). In other words, they will not initially be able to connect written and oral English, as we illustrate with one example:

1. A child is orally familiar with the word 'ear' /ɪə/ and is able to associate it with its corresponding meaning and with the Spanish word *oreja*.
2. The child faces the written form 'ear' and does not identify it with its oral form /ɪə/ or its meaning. When asked to read it out he reads /ear/ due to the transference of Spanish grapho-phonemic rules.

As a consequence, the child has to memorize the written form and its meaning instead of accessing the meaning through the phonology of the word, that is, through its pronunciation. As a result, phonology is left aside and pronunciation is 'contaminated' by Spanish grapho-phonemic transfer.

At this point, it is important to clarify that the child will always adapt the pronunciation of the English words to his Spanish phonological system, as this is a general trend in learning a foreign language (Gallardo del Puerto, Lecumberri & Cenoz 2001). However, departing from a native English grapho-phonemic pattern (for example, /teɪk/ for 'take') and then pronouncing it with a Spanish accent (with dental unaspirated /t/ instead of alveolar aspirated /t/) is far more desirable than directly reading English words according to Spanish graphophonemic rules (/take/ for 'take').

In short, the grapho-phonemic transfer from Spanish will directly propitiate an incorrect pronunciation. For this reason, we use phonics to teach Spanish children to read in English in infant and primary education. These children may still pronounce some English words with their Spanish accent, but they will not read English words as if they were Spanish.

5. Conclusions

In conclusion, if we do not assist children in the reading process the consequences below might follow:

1. The pronunciation of English will be damaged by the grapho-phonemic transfer from Spanish.
2. Reading comprehension will be delayed because children do not identify written forms with their corresponding oral forms (that they may have already acquired).
3. The complexity of the process will discourage the child.

All this provides us with a solid theoretical background to hold fast to the belief that methodological intervention through phonics will help Spanish children to establish the correct relationships between letters and phonemes in English. In conclusion, to facilitate the step between oral and written English by the use of phonics programs would be highly beneficial for our students. This will benefit pronunciation, the reading process and, above all, the acquisition of English. It can initially be done by adopting the same methods that English children use, later adapting these methods to the specific needs of Spanish speakers.

We also need to bear in mind that the classroom is the only environment where these children are exposed to English. Thus, it becomes even more necessary to find the best methodology to really make the most of this limited exposure to the language. In addition, it is in Primary school where children will develop their basic reading skills as well as their initiation in the foreign language. This means that it is the best time to build strong foundations for good reading and good pronunciation. As Cheung and Slavin (2005: 243) explain:

"it is in the earliest years of formal education that children define themselves as learners, largely on the basis of reading success. The early elementary years are of particular importance for English language learners, as this is the time when they are most likely to be struggling both to learn a new language and to learn to read".

In other words, teaching literacy in English fits well with the new status of English in Spanish schools. In fact, it lays the cornerstone for success in a school context where children start learning English from the beginning of their school life and where, along with EFL classes, CLIL programs are fast gaining ground.

More generally speaking, this proposal will also contribute to the basic objective in primary school of boosting children's interest in reading and in the foreign language. Logistically speaking, phonics programs are highly suitable for the classroom, since these methods are not expensive or difficult to implement by teachers.

The novelty of this proposal will benefit the field of educational innovation, the field of language acquisition and the field of phonetic research and research on reading. It is our hope that different school contexts which face teaching English at early ages implement the use of beginning reading programs. This would further illuminate (shed light on) this topic, offer guidelines for future research and provide schools with useful tools with which to improve their teaching practices. Finally, the implementation of these methods with children from different first language backgrounds could generate new programs adapted to the peculiarities of every context and language and, if using phonics programs proves to be successful, these programs should be included in university syllabuses as well as in school textbooks.

References

Adams, Marilyn Jager (1990), *Beginning to read.* Cambridge, Mass.: MIT Press.
Alcaraz, Enrique & Moody, Bryn (1999), *Fonética inglesa para españoles* (4th edn.). Alcoy: Marfil.
Alegría, Jesús & Morais, José (1979), Le developpement de l'habilité d'analyse phonétique de la parole et l'apprentisage de la lecture. *Archives de psychologie* 47, 251–270.
Ball, Eileen W., & Blachman, Benita A. (1991), Does phoneme awareness training in kindergarten make a difference in early word recognition and developmental spelling? *Reading Research Quarterly* 26, 49–66.
Bishop, Margaret M. (1986), *The ABC's and All Their Tricks: The Complete Reference Book of Phonics and Spelling.* London: Mott Media.
Bryant, Peter & Bradley, Lynette (1983), Categorizing sounds and learning to read a causal connection. *Nature* 301, 419–421.
Bryant, Peter & Bradley, Lynette (1985), *Children's reading problems: psychology and education.* Oxford: Basil Blackwell.
Byrne, Brian & Fielding-Barnsley, Ruth (1991), Evaluation of a program to teach phonemic awareness to young children. *Journal of Educational Psychology* 83, 451–455.
Carrillo, María Soledad & Sánchez-Meca, Julio (1990), Segmentación fonológica-silábica y adquisición de la lectura: un estudio empírico. *Comunicación, lenguaje y educación* 9, 109–116.
Cassany, Daniel (1987), *Describir el escribir. Cómo se aprende a escribir.* Barcelona: Paidós.
Cassany, Daniel (1993), *Reparar la escritura. Didáctica de la corrección de lo escrito.* Barcelona: Graó.
Chall, Jeanne S. (1983), *Learning to Read: The Great Debate.* New York: McGraw-Hill.
Cheung, Alan & Slavin, Robert E. (2005), Effective Reading Programs for English Language Learners and Other Language-Minority Students. *Bilingual Research Journal* 29.2, 242–267.
Clemente, María (2001), *Enseñar a leer.* Madrid: Pirámide.
Clemente, María & Domínguez, Ana Belén (1999), *La enseñanza de la lectura. Enfoque psicolingüístico y sociocultural.* Madrid: Pirámide.
Cunningham, Anne Elizabeth (1990), Explicit versus Implicit Instruction in Phonemic Awareness. *Journal of Experimental Child Psychology* 50, 429–444.
Domínguez, Ana Belén (1996a), El desarrollo de habilidades de análisis fonológico a través de programas de enseñanza. *Infancia y Aprendizaje* 76, 69–81.

Domínguez, Ana Belén (1996b), Evaluación de los efectos a largo plazo de la enseñanza de habilidades de análisis fonológico sobre el aprendizaje de la lectura y de la escritura. *Infancia y Aprendizaje* 76, 83–96.

Ehri, Linnea C. & Wilce, Lee S. (1980), The influence of orthography on readers' conceptualization of the phonemic structure of words. *Applied Psycholinguistics* 1, 371–385.

Ehri, Linnea C. & Wilce, Lee S. (1987), Does learning to spell help beginners learn to read words? *Reading Research Quarterly* 18, 47–65.

Finch, Diana F. & Ortiz Lira, Héctor (1982), *A course in English phonetics for Spanish speakers*. London: Heineman.

Fitzpatrick, Jo (1997), *Phonemic Awareness: Playing With Sounds to Strengthen Beginning Reading Skills*. Cyprus: Creative Teaching Press.

Gallardo del Puerto, Francisco; García Lecumberri, María L. & Cenoz, Jasone (2001), L3 English vowel and consonant discrimination in learners with different ages of first exposure. In: Iglesias, Luis & Doval Suárez, Susana (eds.) *Studies in Contrastive Linguistics. Proceedings of the 2nd International Contrastive Linguistics Conference*. Santiago de Compostela: Universidad de Santiago de Compostela, 419–426.

Graves, Donald H. (1991), *Didáctica de la escritura*. Madrid: Morata-MEC.

Griffith, Priscilla & Olson, Mary W. (1992), Phonemic Awareness Helps Beginning Readers Break the Code. *Reading Teacher* 45, 7: 516–523.

Hohmann, Mary (2002), *Fee, Fie, Phonemic Awareness: 130 Pre-reading Activities for Preschoolers*. Detroit: High/Scope Press.

Holdaway, Don (1979), *The foundations of literacy*. Sydney, NSW: Ashton Scholastic.

Jager, Marilyn; Goorman, Barbara R. & Llundberg, Ingvar (1997), *Phonemic Awareness in Young Children: A Classroom Currículum*. Baltimore, M. D.: Brookes Publishing Company.

Jiménez, Juan E. & Ortiz, María del Rosario (1995), *Conciencia fonológica y aprendizaje de la lectura. Teoría, evaluación e intervención*. Madrid: Síntesis.

Johnston, Rhona S. (1998), The case for orthographic knowledge: Response to Scholes (1998) The case against phonemic awareness. *Journal of Research in Reading* 21, 195–200.

Jorm, Anthony F. & Share, David L. (1983), Phonological Recording and Reading Acquisition. *Applied Psycholinguistics* 4, 103–147.

Juel, Connie; Griffith, Priscilla L. & Gough, Philip B. (1986), Acquisition of literacy: A longitudinal study of children in first and second grade. *Journal of Educational Psychology* 78, 243–255.

Liberman, Isabelle; Shankweiler, Donald; Fischer, F. William & Carter, Bonnie (1974), Explicit syllable and phoneme segmentation in the young child. *Journal of Experimental Child Psychology* 18, 201–212.

Lloyd, Susan (1992, 1995), *The Phonics Handbook: A Handbook for Teaching Reading, Writing and Spelling*. Essex, England: Jolly Learning.

Madrid, Daniel & McLaren, Neil (2004), *TEFL in Primary Education*. Granada: Universidad de Granada.

McCracken, Marlene J. & McCracken, Robert A. (1996), *Spelling Through Phonics*. Winnipeg, Canada: Peguis Publishers.

Mott, Brian (2000), *English Phonetics and Phonology for Spanish Speakers*. Barcelona: EUB.

Morais, José; Cary, Luz; Alegría, Jesús & Bertelson, Paul (1979), Does awareness of speech as a sequence of phones arise spontaneously? *Cognition*, 7, 323–331.

Morais, José; Cluytens, Mireille & Alegría, Jesús (1984), Segmentation abilities of dyslexics and normal readers. *Perceptual and Motor Skills* 58, 221–222.

Perfetti, Charles A. & Marron, Maureen A. (1995), *Learning to read: Literacy Acquisition by Children and Adults (Technical Report 95–07)*. Philadelphia, PA: National Center on Adult Literacy.

Pressley, Michael (1999), *Cómo enseñar a leer*. Barcelona: Paidós.

Read, Charles; Zhang, Young-Fei; Nie, Hong-Yin & Ding, Bao-Qing (1986), The ability to manipulate speech sounds depends on knowing alphabetic reading. *Cognition* 24, 31–44.

Scarborough, Hollis S.; Ehri, Linnea C.; Olson, Richard K. & Fowler, Anne E. (1998), The fate of phonemic awareness beyond the elementary school years. *Scientific Studies of Reading* 2, 115–142.

Scholes, Robert (1998), The case against phonemic awareness. *Journal of Research in Reading* 21, 177–188.

Solé, Isabel (1992), *Estrategias de lectura*. Barcelona, ICE Universidad de Barcelona: Graó.

Stuart, Morag (1999), Getting ready for reading: Early phoneme awareness and phonics teaching improves reading and spelling in inner-city second language learners. *British Journal of Educational Psychology* 69, 587–605.

Teberosky, Ana (1991), *Aprendiendo a escribir*. Barcelona: ICE/Horsori.

Tolchinsky, Liliana (1993), *Aprendizaje del lenguaje escrito*. Anthropos: Barcelona.

Tunmer, William E. (1989), The role of language-related factors in reading disability. In: Shankweiler, Donald & Liberman, Isabelle (eds.) (1989), *Phonology and reading disability: Solving the reading puzzle*. Ann Arbor: University of Michigan Press, 91–131.

Vez, José Manuel; Guillén, Carmen & Alario, Carmen (2002), *Didáctica de la lengua extranjera en educación infantil y primaria*. Madrid: Síntesis.

Other documents:

Agencia Nacional de Evaluación de la Calidad y Acreditación (2004). *Libro blanco del Título de Grado de Magisterio*. Volúmenes I y II. [Online:
Council of Europe. (2001). Common European Framework of Reference for Languages: Learning, Teaching, Assessment. Strasbourg: [Online: http://www.coe.int/t/dg4/linguistic/Source/Framework_EN.pdf. 10.08.2009].
Ley Orgánica de Reforma Universitaria (11/1983, de 25 de agosto). [Online: http://www.boe.es/boe/dias/1983/09/01/pdfs/A24034-24042.pdf. 10.08.2009].
LOCE: Ley Orgánica de Calidad de la Educación (10/2002 de 23 de diciembre). Publicada en el Boletín Oficial del Estado nº 307 de 24 de diciembre de 2002. [Online: http://www.boe.es/boe/dias/2002/12/24/pdfs/A45188-45220.pdf. 10.08.2009].
LOE: Ley Orgánica de Educación (2/2006, de 3 de mayo). Publicada en el Boletín Oficial del Estado número 106, de 4 de mayo de 2006. [Online: http://www.boe.es/boe/dias/2006/05/04/pdfs/A17158-17207.pdf. 10.08.2009].
LOGSE: Ley Orgánica de Ordenación General del Sistema Educativo (1/1990, de 3 de Octubre). Publicada en el Boletín Oficial del Estado nº 238 de 4 de octubre de 1.990. [Online: http://www.boe.es/boe/dias/1990/10/04/pdfs/A28927-28942.pdf. 10.08.2009].
Orden Foral 230/1992 de 12 de junio. Publicada en el Boletín Oficial de Navarra nº 88. [Online (in a summarized form): http://www9.euskadi.net/euskara_araubidea/Legedia/legeak/gaztelan/nafarroa/92c230.pdf. 10.08.2009].
Orden Foral 366/2002 de 5 de julio. Publicada en el Boletín Oficial de Navarra nº 105. [Online: http://www.navarra.es/home_es/Actualidad/BON/Boletines/2002/105/Anuncio-5/. 10.08.2009].
Volumen I: http://www.aneca.es/media/150404/libroblanco_jun05_magisterio1.pdf. 10.08.09
Volumen II: http://www.aneca.es/media/150408/libroblanco_jun05_magisterio2.pdf. 10.08.09]

Stefanie Frisch

Bewusstmachende Verfahren beim Umgang mit dem Schriftbild im Englischunterricht der Primarstufe – erste Ergebnisse der LiPs Studie

Up to the present, empirical studies investigating reading-related issues in the primary English as a Foreign Language (EFL) class have been rare (Diehr & Rymarczyk 2008, Duscha 2007, Reichart-Wallrabenstein 2004, Rymarczyk 2008, Wunsch 2006). This paper outlines the findings of a questionnaire study conducted in 2008, which surprisingly revealed that written English is most commonly introduced according to the whole word method. However, in both English and German first language (L1) contexts most children learn to read and write according to a different approach – namely phonics in English speaking countries and Lautiermethode (German for 'sounding out graphemes') in Germany. In the light of this discontinuity the present paper explores whether and how phonics can be modified and adjusted for the German EFL context. Additionally, a brief account is given of a qualitative study (N = 11) in which firstgraders learn English grapheme-phoneme correspondences with the help of consciousness-raising activities in order to support them in reading aloud a short English text. On the basis of observations and analyses of learner texts, conclusions are drawn as a basis for further study.

1. Einleitung: Der Bedarf an Forschungsergebnissen zum Lesen im Englischunterricht der Grundschule

In der Didaktik des frühbeginnenden Englischunterrichts besteht im Bereich des Lesens großer Forschungsbedarf. Zum einen liegen nur wenige empirische Erkenntnisse zur Bedeutung des Schriftbildes für das Fremdsprachenlernen vor (Diehr & Rymarczyk 2008; Duscha 2007; Reichart-Wallrabenstein 2004; Rymarczyk 2008; Wunsch 2006). Zum anderen fehlt es an Wissen darüber, welche schriftsprachigen Angebote Lernende erhalten und wie sie diese Angebote lernförderlich nutzen können. Auf Grund der Besonderheiten der geschriebenen englischen Sprache wird ein spezifisches Unterrichtsangebot für den Englischunterricht benötigt. Das englische Schriftsystem, welches über eine schwach ausgeprägte Buchstaben-Laut-Entsprechung (*deep orthography*) verfügt (vgl. Stubbs 1996: 1442), stellt gerade Fremdsprachenlerner einer Muttersprache mit einer stark ausgeprägten Buchstaben-Laut-Entsprechung (*shallow orthography*) (wie z. B. dem Deutschen) (a.a.O.) vor eine große Herausforderung und birgt ein erhöhtes Fehlerrisiko in sich (vgl. Wimmer, Klampfer & Frith 1993: 325). In diesem Beitrag werden sowohl die Lehrenden als auch die Lernenden in den Blick genommen. Zunächst werden erste Erkenntnisse aus einer Fragebogenstudie zu den von Praktikern bevorzugten Leselehransätzen zusammengetragen (N = 43). Da sich im englischsprachigen Raum erst seit wenigen Jahren der *Phonics* Ansatz als Standardverfahren etabliert hat, soll außerdem der Frage nachgegangen werden, ob und wenn ja, auf welche Weise dieses Verfahren lernförderlich auf den deutschen Kontext übertragen werden kann. Im Rahmen der LiPs Studie (Lesen im Englischunterricht der Primarstufe; vgl. Diehr in diesem Band) wurden in einem ersten Schuljahr englische Graphem-Phonem-Relationen bewusst gemacht, um die Lernenden dabei zu unterstützen, einen kurzen englischen Text laut vorzulesen. Aus den Beobachtungen und Ergebnissen werden Konsequenzen für eine weitere Untersuchung gezogen, die in Nordrhein-Westfalen durchgeführt wird.

2. Das Schriftbild im Englischunterricht der Grundschule

Der Umgang mit dem Schriftbild im Englischunterricht der Grundschule wurde in Deutschland kaum untersucht, da in den bisherigen Konzeptionen des frühen Fremdsprachenlernens der Beginn in Klasse 3 vorgesehen war und der Schwerpunkt auf die Entwicklung der mündlichen Kompetenzen gelegt wurde. Es wird außerdem befürchtet, dass es zu Interferenzen zwischen der Muttersprache und den englischen Schriftbildern kommt (vgl. Schmid-Schönbein 2006: 3). In jüngster Zeit mehren sich jedoch die Stimmen, die von einer positiven Auswirkung des Schriftbildes auf das Fremdsprachenlernen ausgehen. Es lassen sich vor allem zwei Argumentationsstränge finden, die einen lernförderlichen Einfluss des Schriftbildes auf die Sprachentwicklung der Grundschulkinder hervorheben. Zum einen wird angenommen, dass der Einsatz des Schriftbildes eine Lernerleichterung darstellt, weil die Lernenden eine visuelle Unterstützung zur Segmentierung des Lautstroms in einzelne Wörter und Buchstaben erhalten, wodurch die Bedeutungsbildung (vgl. Mindt & Wagner 2009: 120; Schmid-Schönbein 2006: 3) und die Aussprache von schwierigen Lauten (vgl. Bassetti 2009: 193) erleichtert werden kann. Zum anderen wird auf die Rolle des Schriftbildes bei der Entwicklung von Sprachbewusstheit (*language awareness*) verwiesen. Erst durch die grafische Repräsentation von Wörtern werden Wortverwandtschaften und Ähnlichkeiten mit der Muttersprache sowie morphologische Regelmäßigkeiten deutlich (vgl. Koda 2008: 76; Mindt & Wagner 2009: 120; Wunsch 2006: 16).

2.1 Curriculare Vorgaben zum Einsatz des Schriftbildes

In den Bundesländern Baden-Württemberg, Brandenburg, Nordrhein-Westfalen und Rheinland-Pfalz wird eine Fremdsprache ab der 1. Klasse unterrichtet (vgl. Gompf 2009: 2). Die Empfehlungen der verschiedenen Curricula zum Einsatz des Schriftbildes unterscheiden sich sowohl in der Frage nach dem geeigneten Zeitpunkt als auch in der Frage nach dem Umfang des schriftlich einzuführenden Wortmaterials. In Brandenburg und Nordrhein-Westfalen sollen die Lernenden von Anfang an dem Schriftbild von Einzelwörtern begegnen (vgl. MBJS BB 2008: 21; MSW NW 2008: 8). Am Ende der Grundschulzeit sollen sie kurze Texte lesen und verstehen können. Weil in Baden-Württemberg eine zeitversetzte Einführung in Klasse 3 vorgesehen ist, wird das englische Schriftbild in den Klassen 1 und 2 völlig ausgeklammert (vgl. MKJS BW 2004: 68). Die Leistungserwartungen ähneln den Vorgaben der Bundesländer Nordrhein-Westfalen und Brandenburg. Die Lernenden sollen am Ende von Klasse 4 in der Lage sein, kurze klar strukturierte Texte zu verstehen (vgl. MKJS BW 2004: 78). Im Teilrahmenplan für Fremdsprachen in Rheinland-Pfalz werden keine genauen Angaben zum Zeitpunkt der Einführung des Schriftbildes gemacht. Am Ende der vierten Klasse sollen die Lernenden in der Lage sein, zentrale Wörter und einfache Sätze zu lesen und zu schreiben (vgl. MBFJ RP 2004: 8). In keinem der Lehrpläne lassen sich nähere Hinweise zum Umgang mit dem englischen Schriftbild finden. Es wird zwar darauf verwiesen, dass die Lernenden allmählich ein Verständnis für die Beziehung zwischen gesprochener und geschriebener Sprache entwickeln sollen (vgl. MSW NW 2008: 6). Es bleibt jedoch unklar, ob sich die Lernenden die englischen Wörter als Ganzes einprägen sollen, oder ob sie die englischen Graphem-Phonem-Verbindungen kennenlernen sollen.

2.2 Empirisch begründete Erkenntnisse zur Bedeutung des Schriftbildes für das Fremdsprachenlernen

Empirische Befunde zu der Annahme, dass das Schriftbild einen lernförderlichen Einfluss auf die Entwicklung der fremdsprachlichen Kompetenzen hat, liefern Duscha (2007) und Reichart-Wallrabenstein (2004). Duscha untersucht in einer quantitativen Studie, welchen Einfluss der Einsatz des Schriftbildes auf die Behaltensfähigkeit, die Aussprache, das Hörverstehen und das freie Sprechen von Drittklässlern hat. Dazu vergleicht er den Lernerfolg von fünf Klassen, die mit Schrift unterrichtet wurden, mit dem von fünf anderen Klassen, die ohne Schrift unterrichtet wurden. Die Ergebnisse zeigen, dass sich die Verwendung des Schriftbildes signifikant positiv auf die Fähigkeit ein Gedicht auswendig vorzutragen und auf die Fähigkeit ein Bild frei zu beschreiben auswirkt. Weiterhin stellt Duscha fest, dass die Aussprache und das Hörverstehen der Schülerinnen und Schüler, die mit Schriftbild unterrichtet wurden, besser ausgebildet sind, als die der Schülerinnen und Schüler, die dem Schriftbild nicht begegnet sind. Bei der Behaltensfähigkeit von Vokabeln zeigen sich wiederum keine Unterschiede in den Ergebnissen der beiden Lerngruppen (vgl. 2007: 300). In einer qualitativen Studie beobachtet Reichart-Wallrabenstein, wie Drittklässler mit dem englischen Schriftbild umgehen. Sie erkennt, dass die Lernenden beim eigenständigen Lesen von Bilderbüchern verschiedene Strategien anwenden, um die Texte, die zum Teil unbekannten Wortschatz enthalten, zu verstehen: Sie beginnen Wörter, die sie nicht verstehen, laut zu lesen, sie übersetzen den Text Wort für Wort, sie vergleichen englische Wörter mit deutschen und sie stellen einen Bezug zu den Illustrationen und dem Kontext der Geschichten her (vgl. Reichart-Wallrabenstein 2001: 30). Reichart-Wallrabenstein kommt zu dem Schluss, dass Drittklässler in der Lage sind, über das englische Schriftbild nachzudenken und Hypothesen über mögliche Regelmäßigkeiten zu bilden (Reichart-Wallrabenstein 2004). Diese Ergebnisse unterstützen die Vermutung, dass junge Lernende vom Einsatz des Schriftbildes z. B. für die Entwicklung der Sprachbewusstheit profitieren können. In dem Forschungsprojekt ‚Zweitalphabetisierung Englisch', das seit 2006 in Baden-Württemberg durchgeführt wird (in Baden-Württemberg wird seit 2004 Englisch ab Klasse 1 unterrichtet), untersucht Rymarczyk u. a. den Kenntnisstand im Schreiben von Zweitklässlern, die dem Schriftbild in den ersten beiden Lernjahren nicht begegnet sind (Rymarczyk 2008; Rymarczyk in diesem Band). In der Erhebung schreiben die Lernenden am Ende des zweiten Schuljahres die ihnen bekannten englischen Wörter auf. Rymarczyk kann zeigen, dass Zweitklässler ihr Vorwissen aus dem Erstschriftspracherwerb auf den Zweitschriftspracherwerb transferieren. Ohne eine explizite Einführung in das englische Schriftsystem schreiben die Lernenden auf der Grundlage der deutschen Graphem-Phonem-Relation (z. B. *kau* für *cow*, Rymarczyk 2008: 178). Aufgrund dieser Beobachtungen kommt Rymarczyk zu dem Schluss, dass das Ausklammern des englischen Schriftbildes einen negativen Effekt auf das Sprachenlernen hat. Es führt dazu, dass die Lernenden ihre eigenen Konzepte über die Schreibung entwickeln und in Form des sogenannten *invented spelling* umsetzen (ebd.; Diehr & Rymarczyk 2008).

2.3 Umgang mit dem Schriftbild aus der Perspektive der Lehrkräfte

Anhand einer Fragebogenstudie, an der sich 43 Lehrkräfte aus 15 verschiedenen Schulen in Baden-Württemberg beteiligt haben, wird ermittelt, welchen Stellenwert die Lehrkräfte dem Lernbereich Lesen im Englischunterricht zuweisen, welche Probleme beim Umgang mit dem Schriftbild gesehen werden und nach welchen Leselehrverfahren das englische Schriftbild in den Grundschulklassen derzeitig eingeführt wird. Es ist nicht überraschend, dass 70% der befragten Lehrerinnen angeben, dass das Schriftbild einen sekundären Stellenwert in ihrem Unterricht hat, da der baden-württembergische Lehrplan die Entwicklung der mündlichen Fähigkeiten als Hauptaufgabe des Englischunterrichts in der Grundschule versteht (MKJS BW 2004: 68). Immerhin sehen 28% der Befragten die Entwicklung der Lesefertigkeiten dennoch als eine zentrale Aufgabe des Englischunterrichts. Das Schriftbild wird als Merkhilfe angeboten (46%), zur Entwicklung der Sprachbewusstheit eingesetzt (33%) und als Lernerleichterung für das Fremdsprachenlernen verstanden (19%). Etwas weniger als die Hälfte der Lehrkräfte (44%) sieht keine Probleme beim Umgang mit dem englischen Schriftbild bzw. macht bei dieser Frage keine Angaben. 56% der befragten Lehrpersonen befürchten, dass durch die Integration des Schriftbildes Aussprachefehler entstehen können und vor allem Schülerinnen und Schüler mit einer Lese-Rechtschreibschwäche benachteiligt werden. Wie also versuchen diese Lehrkräfte die genannten Probleme zu vermeiden? 34 der befragten Lehrerinnen, also 74%, führen das Schriftbild nach der Ganzwortmethode ein (Abb. 1)[1]. Den Lernenden wird das Schriftbild auf Wortkarten präsentiert, nachdem die Bedeutung und die Aussprache gesichert sind. Die Besonderheit des Vorgehens besteht darin, dass die Lernenden das Schriftbild unanalysiert als Ganzes – quasi als Bild – in ihrem mentalen Lexikon abspeichern müssen. Dies ist ein unerwarteter Befund, da die Lernenden im Deutschunterricht in der Regel im Sinne der Methodenintegration, d.h. nach einem analytisch-synthetischen Ansatz Lesen und Schreiben lernen (vgl. Marx 2007: 107). Die Lernenden erhalten bei diesem Verfahren von Anfang an sowohl Hilfestellungen, um Wörter aus dem Kontext zu erschließen, als auch Anleitung zum Dekodieren der Wörter auf der Grundlage der Graphem-Phonem-Korrespondenz (Schründer-Lenzen 2004: 107). Nach dem integrierten Verfahren gehen fünf Lehrerinnen vor.

---

[1] Eine Lehrerin kreuzt alle Antwortmöglichkeiten an.

Nach welchem Verfahren führen Sie das Schriftbild im Englischunterricht der Grundschule ein?

Verfahren	Anzahl
Ganzwortmethode	~35
Buchstabiermethode/Lautiermethode	~1
Integrierte Methode	~6
Lesen durch Schreiben	~4
?	~2

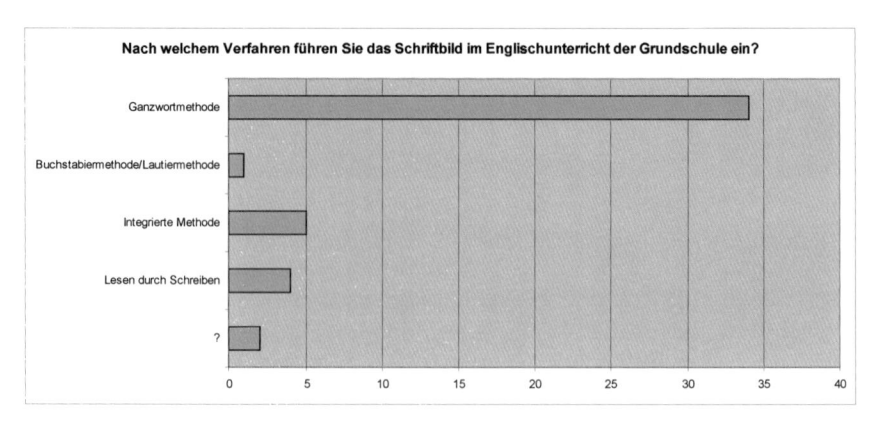

Abb. 1: Verfahren zur Einführung des Schriftbildes

Die Buchstabier- bzw. Lautiermethode kommt bei einer der befragten Lehrerinnen im Englischunterricht zum Einsatz. Vergleichbar mit dem englischen *Phonics* Ansatz lernen die Schülerinnen und Schüler systematisch die Buchstaben-Laut-Beziehungen kennen. In der Regel wird im Rahmen eines Fibellehrgangs das Lesen von dekodierbaren Wörtern trainiert (Marx 2007; Schründer-Lenzen 2004). Vier Lehrerinnen unterrichten in Anlehnung an den von Reichen entwickelten Leselernansatz ‚Lesen durch Schreiben' (1988). Im Deutschen erhalten die Kinder eine Anlauttabelle, mit der sie eigene Texte schreiben können. Das Lesen wird nicht explizit trainiert. Reichen geht davon aus, dass sich durch das Produzieren von Texten die Lesefertigkeiten automatisch mitentwickeln.

Die Ganzwortmethode bietet den Lernenden dagegen keine expliziten Hilfen für das Verstehen der Besonderheiten der englischen Graphem-Phonem-Relationen. Sie vertraut darauf, dass Lernende diese Relationen selbstständig entdecken. Erkenntnisse aus der Forschung zum Lesen des Englischen als Erstsprache zeigen, dass kompetente Leser Wörter nicht als Ganzes lesen, sondern dass sie Verbindungen zwischen den Graphemen des Schriftbildes und Phonemen des Lautbildes herstellen (vgl. Adams 1990: 412; Ehri 1998; Rayner & Pollatsek 1989; Tunmer & Hoover 1992: 183; Urquhart & Weir 1998: 51). Zum Lesen des Englischen als Fremdsprache liegen bisher aber noch keine Forschungsergebnisse vor. Die Lehrkräfte sind daher noch darauf angewiesen, nach subjektiven Theorien und nach Versuchs- und Irrtumsverhalten vorzugehen.

3. Alphabetisierung in der Erst- und Fremdsprache

In den Bundesländern, in denen Englisch bereits in der ersten Klasse eingeführt wird, sind die Schülerinnen und Schüler nicht viel älter als Muttersprachler, wenn diese das Lesen und Schreiben lernen. Auch englische Leseanfänger stehen vor der Aufgabe, ein opakes Schriftsystem zu entschlüsseln. Es stellt sich die Frage, ob und auf welche Weise sich Leselehrverfahren, die im englischsprachigen Raum eingesetzt werden, auch für den deutschen Kontext eignen.

3.1 Erstalphabetisierung Englisch

Zahlreiche Untersuchungen wurden in englischsprachigen Ländern (Australien, UK, USA) im Auftrag der Regierungen durchgeführt, um Kenntnisse über den Einfluss von zwei Leselehransätzen auf die Entwicklung der Lesefertigkeiten zu gewinnen (Chall 1967; Johnston & Watson 2005; National Reading Panel 2000; Rose 2006). Der Spracherfahrungsansatz (*whole language approach*) stellt die Bedeutung des Vorwissens des Lesers und seine Fähigkeiten, Informationen aus dem Kontext zu erschließen (*top down skills*) in den Vordergrund. Die Schülerinnen und Schüler lernen, Wörter anhand von Schlüsselmerkmalen zu lesen (z. B. anhand der Anfangsbuchstaben); zudem werden sie angeleitet, Voraussagen über den Inhalt des zu lesenden Textes zu treffen, um die Bedeutung der Wörter aus dem Kontext zu erschließen (vgl. Goodman 1970: 29; Liberman & Liberman 1992: 356f.). Dabei werden die Leseanfänger darin bestärkt, während des Lesens immer wieder zu prüfen, ob das Gelesene Sinn ergibt, wodurch Verständnisfehler vermieden werden sollen (vgl. Goodman 1970: 32). Im *Phonics* Ansatz hingegen werden die Dekodierungsfähigkeiten des Leseanfängers geschult (*bottom up skills*), da diese als Voraussetzung für einen erfolgreichen Aufbau der Lesefertigkeit verstanden werden. Es hat sich gezeigt, dass Lernende, die nach den sogenannten *Phonics* Programmen unterrichtet werden, über eine bessere Leseleistung verfügen als Schülerinnen und Schüler, die nach dem Spracherfahrungsansatz bzw. nach dem Ganzwortansatz das Lesen lernen (Camilli, Vargas & Yurecko 2003; Chall 1967; Evans & Carr 1985; Johnston & Watson 2005, 2007; National Reading Panel 2000; Rose 2006). Die Ergebnisse haben dazu geführt, dass im englischsprachigen Raum heute überwiegend anhand des *Phonics* Verfahrens unterrichtet wird (AG DEST 2005; DFES 2006; National Reading Panel 2000; Rose 2006).

In den *Phonics* Programmen lernen die Schülerinnen und Schüler explizit, wie die Buchstaben der geschriebenen Sprache und die Laute der gesprochenen Sprache in Beziehung stehen (vgl. DFES 2007; Stahl 2001: 336; Johnston & Watson 2007).

Da die phonologische Bewusstheit – also die Fähigkeit die Laute einer Sprache zu hören und von anderen zu unterscheiden – eine wichtige Voraussetzung darstellt, um Lesen zu lernen, üben die Lernenden zunächst Laute in Wörtern zu identifizieren und Wörter in ihre Einzellaute zu segmentieren (Phase 1). In Phase 2 lernen die Schülerinnen und Schüler die Buchstaben-Laut-Beziehung von Konsonanten und Kurzvokalen, da diese relativ regelmäßig sind (z. B. <a> - /æ/, <e> - /e/, <i> - /ɪ/ und <o> - /ɒ/), und sie dekodieren einsilbige Wörter nach dem Muster Vokal-Konsonant (VK Wörter, z. B. *at*) bzw. nach dem Muster Konsonant-Vokal-Konsonant (KVK Wörter, z. B. *hat*). Wörter, die häufig in Erstlesetexten auftauchen und in dieser Phase noch nicht anhand der eingeführten Graphem-Phonem-Relationen dekodiert werden können (z. B *the, to, I*), werden als Ganzwörter eingeführt. In Phase 3 lernen die Kinder die Buchstaben-Laut-Beziehung von Doppelkonsonanten, Langvokalen und weiteren hochfrequenten Wörtern. Die Lerner werden angeleitet KVK Wörter, zweisilbige Wörter und Überschriften zu dekodieren. In Phase 4 kommen Wörter mit dem Muster KKVK (z. B. *stop*) und KVKK (z. B. *tent*) hinzu. In Phase 5 werden schließlich Alternativartikulationen von Graphemen eingeführt. Insbesondere im zweiten Lernjahr, also in Phase 6, wird die Aufmerksamkeit auf das morphematische Prinzip des englischen Schriftsystems gerichtet (z. B. auf das Plural -s oder das Suffix -ing, das die Verlaufsform anzeigt). Der Schwerpunkt liegt auf der schnellen Erfassung von Buchstabenclustern, um die Lesegeschwindigkeit zu erhöhen. Durch die automatisierte Buchstabencluster- bzw. Worterkennung kann sich der Leser stärker auf die Sinnerschließung konzentrieren. Der Leselehrgang im englischsprachigen Raum ist sehr zeitintensiv und erstreckt sich vor allem über die ersten beiden Schuljahre (vgl. Tab. 1).

Merkmal des *Phonics* **Ansatzes**[2]	Systematische Bewusstmachung von Graphem-Phonem-Korrespondenzen
Phasen	1) Training der phonologischen Bewusstheit: allgemeine Lautdiskriminierung, Rhythmus und Reim, Alliteration, mündliche Lautsegmentierung und -verschmelzung
	2) Einführung von 19 Konsonanten und Kurzvokalen. Erlesen dekodierbarer VK Wörter und KVK Wörter und Einführung hoch frequenter, nicht dekodierbarer Wörter.
	3) Einführung von 25 Buchstaben (Doppelkonsonanten, Langvokale). Erlesen dekodierbarer KVK Wörter, zweisilbiger Wörter und von Überschriften. Einführung weiterer

---

2 Der *Phonics* Ansatz umfasst das Lesen- und Schreibenlernen. In der Übersicht werden nur die auf das Lesenlernen bezogenen Inhalte dargestellt.

	hoch frequenter, nicht dekodierbarer Wörter. Einführung der Buchstabennamen. 4) Erlesen dekodierbarer KKVK und KVKK Wörter, mehrsilbiger Wörter (z. B. *desktop*) und Sätze. Einführung weiterer hoch frequenter, nicht dekodierbarer Wörter. 5) Alternativartikulation von Graphemen. Training der schnellen Erfassung von Buchstabenclustern (z. B. <igh> – /aɪ/). Erlesen von Sätzen. Einführung weiterer hoch frequenter, nicht dekodierbarer Wörter. 6) Eigenständiges lautes und leises Lesen unbekannter Texte. Übung der lautrichtigen Betonung von mehrsilbigen Wörtern. Training des Leseverstehens.
Dauer	1–2 Jahre

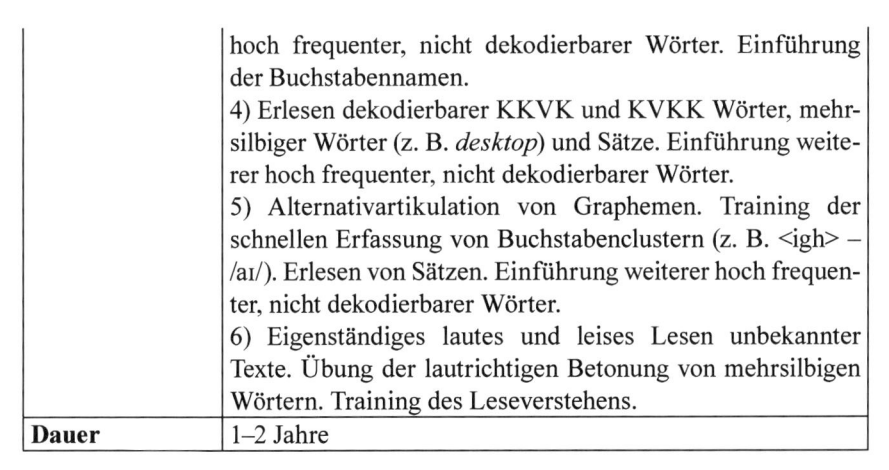

Tab. 1 *Vorgehen des Phonics Ansatzes (DFES 2007; Johnston & Watson 2007)*

3.2 Bewusstmachende Verfahren im Fremdsprachunterricht

Im Englischunterricht der Grundschule stehen in der Regel 90 Minuten Unterrichtszeit pro Woche zur Verfügung. Es ist in dieser kurzen Zeit nicht möglich, junge Fremdsprachenlernende in der gleichen Weise und im gleichen Umfang wie Muttersprachler an das Schriftbild heranzuführen, da der *Phonics* Ansatz sehr zeitaufwendig ist. Aufgrund des Erfolgs des *Phonics* Ansatzes im englischsprachigen Raum erscheint es jedoch sinnvoll, zu untersuchen, welche Buchstaben-Laut-Beziehungen sich für die explizite Einführung im Kontext des frühen Fremdsprachenlernens eignen. Mindt und Wagner gehen davon aus, dass ein regelgeleitetes bzw. bewusstmachendes Vorgehen bei eindeutigen Graphem-Phonem-Relationen die Entwicklung des Leseverstehens unterstützten kann (vgl. 2009: 124f., 197). Die Bedeutung von bewusstmachenden Verfahren für das Fremdsprachenlernen wurde bisher vor allem im Kontext des Grammatikunterrichts diskutiert (Eckerth 2008; Ellis 1992; Kuhn 2006; Mindt 2006). Ellis skizziert vier Merkmale, die seiner Meinung nach die Besonderheit eines bewusstmachenden Verfahrens ausmachen (vgl. 1992: 234):

a) Die Aufmerksamkeit der Lernenden wird auf ein spezifisches sprachliches Phänomen gerichtet.
b) Die Lernenden erhalten Beispielmaterial, anhand dessen das besondere Merkmal veranschaulicht wird.
c) Die Lernenden erbringen eine kognitive Abstraktionsleistung, um das sprachliche Phänomen zu verstehen.

d) Die Lernenden werden angeregt, ihre Erkenntnisse in Form einer Regel zusammenzufassen. Dies ist jedoch nicht zwingend notwendig.

Bei bewusstmachenden Verfahren handelt es sich demnach um eine explizite Auseinandersetzung mit einem sprachlichen Phänomen. Anders als im deduktiven Grammatikunterricht wird die Regel aber nicht durch die Lehrkraft präsentiert, sondern die Lehrkraft schafft Bedingungen, unter denen die Lernenden auf induktive Weise die sprachliche Besonderheit und ggf. auch die Regel selbst entdecken. Diesem Vorgehen liegt die folgende Annahme zugrunde: „It is perfectly possible to develop an explicit understanding of how a grammatical structure works without learning much in the way of grammatical terminology" (Ellis 1992: 234).

Nicht jedes sprachliches Phänomen eignet sich jedoch für eine explizite Erarbeitung im frühen Fremdsprachenunterricht. DeKeyser zufolge sind sehr einfache und sehr schwierige Regeln nicht für das explizite Lernen geeignet (vgl. 2003: 332). Für die Beurteilung des Schwierigkeitsgrades der zu lernenden Regel müssen vor allem zwei Bereiche in den Blick genommen werden. Erstens spielt die subjektive Schwierigkeit eine Rolle, die als das Verhältnis der inhärenten sprachlichen Komplexität zu der Fähigkeit des Lernenden mit dieser Regel umzugehen verstanden werden kann. Die Regel „When two vowels go walking, the first does the talking" (Adams 1990: 269) ist an sich sehr einfach. Sie setzt jedoch voraus, dass die Lernenden zum einen mit den englischen Buchstabennamen vertraut sind (<a> = /eɪ/, <e> = /i/, <i> = /aɪ/, <o> /əʊ/, <u> = /juː/) und dass sie zum anderen verstehen, was ein Vokal ist und ihnen alle englische Vokale bekannt sind. Um die Regel zu begreifen, muss der Lernende außerdem erfassen, dass mit "does the talking" die Artikulation des Buchstabens gemeint ist und nicht des Lautes, durch den er in der Regel realisiert wird. Erst wenn diese Bedingungen erfüllt sind, kann die Regel für das Erlesen der Wörter *rain, bean, tie, coat* und *cue* hilfreich sein. Zweitens spielt die objektive Schwierigkeit eine Rolle. Dazu muss die Komplexität, die Häufigkeit der Verwendung der Regel, ihre Auffälligkeit und Abstraktheit berücksichtigt werden. Als *rule of thumb* stellt DeKeyser fest: "The harder it is to learn something through simple association, because it is too abstract, too distant, too rare, too unreliable, or too hard to notice, the more important explicit learning processes become" (2003: 334).

Es bleibt also zu klären, welche subjektiven und objektiven Schwierigkeiten die englische Graphem-Phonem-Relation für junge Fremdsprachenlernende in sich birgt. Die meisten Schülerinnen und Schüler verfügen bereits zu einem gewissen Grad über Vorkenntnisse im Umgang mit einer Alphabetschrift, wenn sie dem englischen Schriftbild begegnen (Abschnitt 2.2). Die Kinder haben eine phonologische Bewusstheit für die Laute der deutschen Sprache entwickelt. Sie kennen am Ende des ersten Halbjahres die meisten Graphem-Phonem-Korrespondenzen des deutschen Schriftsystems und sie können Einzelwörter und zum Teil schon kurze Texte lesen. Es kann davon ausgegangen werden, dass auf diese Vorkenntnisse beim Dekodieren englischer Wörter oder Lesen eines englischen Textes zurückgegriffen werden kann (vgl. Grabe & Stoller 2002: 52; Koda 2008: 71f.). Die objektive Schwierigkeit liegt in der Komplexität des englischen Schriftsystems. Es ist nicht anzunehmen, dass die Lernenden in der Lage sind, sich die englischen Graphem-Phonem-Relationen selbstständig zu erschließen. Diese Erkenntnisse haben wichtige Impulse für die Untersuchung des Zweitschriftspracherwerbs in einem ersten Schuljahr gegeben.

4. Anlage und Durchführung der LiPs-Vorstudie

Die oben skizzierten Erkenntnisse aus der englischen Leseforschung und zum Fremdsprachenlernen wurden zum Ausgangspunkt einer Studie genommen, in der die Auswirkungen von explizitem Wissen über englische Graphem-Phonem-Korrespondenzen auf die Fähigkeiten einen kurzen Text zu lesen und zu verstehen, untersucht wurden.

4.1 Gruppe der beteiligten Lernenden

Die Untersuchungsgruppe setzt sich in dieser qualitativen Studie aus 11 Schülerinnen und Schülern eines ersten Schuljahres in Baden-Württemberg zusammen (Tab. 2). Die Lernenden hatten bis zum Zeitpunkt der Untersuchung zehn Monate Englischunterricht erhalten, in dem die Klassenlehrerin den Schwerpunkt auf die Entwicklung des Hörverstehens und des Sprechens gelegt hatte. Die Lernenden waren dem englischen Schriftbild bis zu Beginn der Untersuchung nicht begegnet.

Bundesland	Baden-Württemberg
Jahrgangsstufe	1. Schuljahr
Grundgesamtheit	N = 11 Schülerinnen und Schüler (3 Mädchen, 8 Jungen)
Herkunftssprache	Deutsch
Standort der Grundschule	Ländlich
Vorkenntnisse im Umgang mit dem englischen Schriftbild	Keine
Methodisch-didaktischer Ansatz	Immersiv-reflexiv (MKJS BW 2004)

Tab. 2: Untersuchte Schülerpopulation

4.2 Analyse des Textes

Im englischsprachigen Raum lernen die Kinder das Lesen häufig anhand der sogenannten *Phonics Reader*. Die Texte der *Floppy's Phonics* Reihe von Oxford University Press sind beispielsweise in sechs Schwierigkeitsniveaus gestuft (von *stage 1+* bis *stage 6*). Sie enthalten Wörter, die von den Lernenden auf der Grundlage ihres Wissens über englische Graphem-Phonem-Relationen dekodiert werden können. Für diese Studie wurde der *stage 1+* Text *Cat in a Bag* (Hunt & Brychta 2007a) ausgewählt. Die Geschichte folgt einem sehr einfachen Handlungsstrang und umfasst 64 Wörter. Wilf bekommt Besuch von seinen Freunden Biff, Kipper und Chip. Er führt ihnen einen Zaubertrick vor, bei dem er eine kleine Stofftierkatze geschickt in einem Beutel verschwinden lässt und schließlich aus einem Zylinder wieder hervor zaubert. Auf der Textebene wird nicht verraten, auf welche Weise Wilf dieser Trick gelingt. Mit Hilfe der Bilder wird es allerdings möglich, das Geheimnis hinter dem Zaubertrick zu lüften.

Sprachlich wird der Fokus in diesem Erstlesetext auf die Übung der Laute /b/, /d/, /ɪ/ und /n/ gerichtet. Die Laute /æ/, /g/, /h/, /k/, /ɒ/, /m/, /p/, /s/, /t/ werden als bekannt vorausgesetzt. Für die Gruppe der untersuchten Lernenden wurde der Schwerpunkt auf die Graphem-Phonem-Korrespondenz (GPK) <a> - /æ/, <u> - /ʌ/, <o> - /ɒ/ gelegt, da sich diese von der deutschen Graphem-Phonem-Verbindung unterscheiden. Die Buchstaben-Laut-Relationen <e>, <a> - /ə/ (in *the* und *a*) und <e> - /iː/ (in *he*) kommen auch in der Geschichte vor, konnten aber aufgrund der begrenzten Zeit nicht explizit eingeführt werden. Darüber hinaus enthält der Text Laute, die für deutsche Fremdsprachenlerner besondere artikulatorische Schwierigkeiten in sich bergen. Die Laute /ɬ/, /ð/ und /w/ gibt es im Deutschen nicht, und die Laute /b/, /d/, /g/ und /z/ werden im Auslaut von deutschen Muttersprachlern häufig stimmlos artikuliert (Tab. 3).

Sprachliche Analyse des Leselerntexts *Cat in a Bag* (Hunt & Brychta 2007a)	
a) Phonologische Analyse	
Von der deutschen GPK abweichende Vokallaute	/æ/, /ʌ/, /ɒ/, /iː/, /ə/
Von der deutschen GPK abweichender Halbvokallaut	/w/
Von der deutschen GPK abweichende Konsonantenlaute	/ɬ/, /ð/
Stimmhafte Konsonanten im Auslaut	/b/, /d/, /g/, /z/

b) Lexikalische Analyse	
Inhaltswortschatz	*bag, cat, hat, tin, tub*
Namen	*Wilf*
Funktionswortschatz	unbestimmter Artikel *a* bestimmter Artikel *the* Personalpronomen *he, his* Präpositionen *in, on*
onomatopoetischer Wortschatz	*tap*
c) Grammatische Analyse	
Zeitform	Verben in der Vergangenheit *had, put*
Satzbau	Positive Aussagen SPO SPO + adverbiale Bestimmung des Ortes

Tab. 3: Sprachliche Analyse **Cat in a Bag**

Der Inhaltswortschatz umfasst die Objekte, die Wilf zum Zaubern benötigt: *bag, cat, hat, tin, tub*. Der Text beinhaltet darüber hinaus sowohl den unbestimmten als auch den bestimmten Artikel, die Präpositionen *in* und *on*, die Personalpronomen *he* und *his* und das onomatopoetische Wort *tap*, welches das Geräusch des Zauberstabs versprachlicht. Die Geschichte wird in der Vergangenheit erzählt und setzt sich aus Subjekt-Prädikat-Objekt Sätzen (z. B. *Wilf had a cat.*) und Subjekt-Prädikat-Objekt Sätzen ergänzt durch eine adverbiale Bestimmung des Ortes (z. B. *He put the cat in the bag.*) zusammen.

4.3 Didaktische Ziele

In sieben Unterrichtsstunden wurden die Erstklässler darauf vorbereitet, den kurzen Erstlesetext *Cat in a Bag* (Hunt & Brychta 2007a) laut vorzulesen.

Zeitpunkt der Untersuchung	Dauer der Untersuchung	Lehrverfahren	Getestete Fähigkeiten	Messinstrument
Juni 2008	4 Wochen (7 Unterrichtsstunden)	Bewusstmachung von Graphem-Phonem-Korrespondenzen mit Schriftbild: <a> - /æ/ <u> - /ʌ/ <o> - /ɒ/	Phonologische Rekodierung Leseverstehen	Lautes Lesen + Videoaufnahme (Dokumentation der Lesefehler) Leseverstehenstest
		Training der phonologischen Bewusstheit ohne Schriftbild: <th> - /ð/ <w> - /w/ <l> - /ɫ/ <e>, <a> - /ə/		

Tab. 4: Design der LiPs-Vorstudie

Um ein Auswendiglernen der Geschichte zu vermeiden, wurde der Inhaltswortschatz (Tab. 3) im Zusammenhang einer anderen Geschichte eingeführt, in der Kippers Familie Einkaufen geht (Hunt & Brychta 2007b). Die Geschichte wurde mit Hilfe der Bilder und den Prinzipien des *storytelling* folgend (Wright 2005) eingeführt und von den Schülerinnen und Schülern in einem kleinen Rollenspiel nachgespielt (Abb.2).

Einführung des Schriftbildes anhand eines bewusstmachenden Verfahrens in Anlehnung an den Phonics Ansatz

Nachdem die Aussprache der neu eingeführten Wörter und Phrasen gesichert war, wurde das Schriftbild auf Wortkarten eingeführt. Die Schülerinnen und Schüler ordneten zunächst den Gegenständen die Wortkarten zu, die den Kurzvokal /æ/ enthielten (Tab. 5, Merkmal b). In einem nächsten Schritt wurden die Lernenden gebeten, zu beschreiben, was ihnen bei der Aussprache der Wörter auffiel. Ihre Aufmerksamkeit wurde durch die Lehrperson gezielt auf ein sprachliches Phänomen gerichtet (Tab. 5, Merkmal a). Die Kinder stellten fest, dass der Buchstabe <a> anders als im Deutschen ausgesprochen wird, nämlich ähnlich wie das deutsche <ä> (Tab. 5, Merkmal c). Auf einem Lernplakat wurden alle Wörter gesammelt, in denen die Lernenden ein /æ/ hörten (Tab. 5, Merkmal d).

Merkmale bewusstmachender Verfahren	Beispiel
a) Die Aufmerksamkeit der Lernenden wird auf ein spezifisches sprachliches Phänomen gerichtet.	Die Aufmerksamkeit der Lernenden wird auf die Graphem-Phonem-Relation <a> - /æ/ gerichtet.
b) Die Lernenden erhalten Beispielmaterial, anhand dessen das besondere Merkmal veranschaulicht wird.	Präsentation von Wörtern mit der ausgewählten Graphem-Phonem-Relation auf Wortkarten.
c) Die Lernenden erbringen eine kognitive Abstraktionsleistung, um das sprachliche Phänomen zu verstehen.	Die Lernenden verbalisieren die Abweichung der englischen Graphem-Phonem-Relation von der deutschen.
d) Die Lernenden werden angeregt, ihre Erkenntnisse in Form einer Regel zusammenzufassen. Dies ist jedoch nicht zwingend notwendig.	Auf einem Lernplakat werden als Merkhilfe Wörter gesammelt, in denen das Graphem <a> als /æ/ artikuliert wird.

Tab. 5 Merkmale bewusstmachender Verfahren mit Beispiel

In den darauffolgenden Stunden wurde mit der Bewusstmachung der Graphem-Phonem-Relationen für die Kurzvokale /ʌ/ in *mum* und *tub*, und /ɒ/ in *Floppy, got, mop, on, pot, top* in gleicher Weise vorgegangen. Mit dem Spiel *My English Sounds* (Lehrerin zeigt auf eines der Lernplakate, Lernende versuchen so schnell wie möglich, den richtigen Laut zu nennen) wurde die Aussprache der typisch englischen Vokale gezielt geübt.

Training der phonologischen Bewusstheit

In Anlehnung an den *Phonics* Ansatz (Tab. 1) wurde als weitere Übung für die Entwicklung der phonologischen Bewusstheit und der Lesefertigkeit das Segmentieren von Wörtern in ihre Einzellaute (z. B. *cat* à /k/ - /æ/ - /t/) geübt. Die für deutsche Muttersprachler schwierig zu artikulierenden Laute /ɬ/, /ð/ und /w/, die Artikulation des bestimmten und unbestimmten Artikels und die stimmhaften Konsonanten /b/, /d/, /g/ und /z/ im Auslaut (Tab. 3) wurden im Zusammenhang des angeleiteten Rollenspiels implizit geübt (Abb. 2).

S1 (Kipper): I **want a** cat.	S1 (Chip): I **want a** bag.
S2 (Mum): Do you like **th**is cat?	S2 (Mum): Do you like **th**is bag?
S1 (Kipper): Yes, I call her **Wi**lbur.	S1 (Chip): Yes, it's nice.

Abb. 2: Beispieldialoge

4.4 Datenerhebung

In der letzten Stunde der Sequenz erhielt die Lerngruppe die unbekannte Geschichte *Cat in a Bag* mit dem Hinweis, dass sie nun eine weitere Geschichte von Kipper und seinen Freunden lesen können. Nachdem die Lernenden die Geschichte selbstständig leise gelesen hatten, wurden sie aufgenommen, während sie die Geschichte laut lasen. Der Text enthielt keine unbekannten Wörter. Durch die Wahl einer neuen Geschichte konnte sichergestellt werden, dass die Kinder den Text tatsächlich dekodierten und nicht aus dem Gedächtnis auswendig wiedergaben. Im Anschluss an die Aufnahmen bearbeiteten die Kinder einen Leseverstehenstest, indem sie acht Bildern aus der Geschichte die passenden Sätze zuordneten. In Anlehnung an den Leseverstehenstest der EVENING Studie (Groot-Wilken, Engel & Thürmann 2007) wurde ein Aufgabenformat gewählt, das die zu erschließende Aussage auf die Satzebene beschränkt. Die Lernenden mussten die acht Satzaussagen sehr genau lesen, da die Sätze zum Teil den gleichen Wortschatz enthielten: z. B. *Wilf had a bag. He put the cat in the bag.* und *Wilf had the cat in his hat.* Damit wurde vermieden, dass die Lernenden nur das Wort *cat* lasen und dem Bild richtig zuordneten, auf dem eine Katze abgebildet war, ohne den Satz verstanden zu haben.

4.5 Ergebnisse

Die Lernenden lesen den Erstlesetext in einer ihrem Entwicklungsstand angemessenen Lesegeschwindigkeit, die vergleichbar ist mit der eines englischen Leseanfängers. Die Werte liegen zwischen 38 und 64 Wörtern pro Minute (WpM) (Durchschnitt aller Schülerinnen und Schüler: 54 WpM). Auch im Deutschen lesen Schülerinnen und Schüler am Ende des ersten Schuljahres Texte mit bekannten Wörtern mit einer Geschwindigkeit von ca. 49 bis ca. 62 WpM (vgl. Klicpera & Gasteiger-Klicpera 1993: 50), da der Alphabetisierungsprozess noch nicht abgeschlossen ist. Englische Muttersprachler lesen am Ende des ersten Lernjahres zwischen ca. 22,5 und 56 WpM (vgl. z. B. Speece & Ritchey 2005:

396). Die Lesegenauigkeit[3] der Lernenden, der hier untersuchten Gruppe liegt bei 76% (69%-89%). Dies entspricht etwa den Werten eines deutschen Leseanfängers, der eine Liste mit neuen Wörtern auf Deutsch liest (ca. 72%, vgl. Klicpera & Gasteiger-Klicpera 1993: 14). Wimmer, Klampfer und Frith stellen fest, dass die Lesegenauigkeit englischer Erstklässler im Vergleich niedriger ist (vgl. 1993: 326). Die Autoren geben jedoch keine Prozentzahlen an.

Beim Lesen des englischen Textes treten bei der Untersuchungsgruppe zum Teil Transferfehler auf. Sieben Lernende lesen den Namen *Wilf*, fünf das Inhaltswort *tub*, zwei das Personalpronomen *he*, sechs den bestimmten Artikel *the* und sieben Lernende das onomatopoetische Wort *tap* mit deutscher Phonation. Die für deutsche Muttersprachler typische Auslautverhärtung tritt nur bei dem Verb *had* (4 Lernende) und bei dem Personalpronomen *his* (6 Lernende) auf. Die Inhaltswörter *bag* (8 Lernende) und *tub* (10 Lernende) werden überwiegend korrekt mit stimmhaftem Auslaut gelesen (Tab. 6). Es kann angenommen werden, dass die Lernenden die Aussprache implizit durch die Verwendung im Unterricht gelernt haben. Bei den ebenfalls nur implizit geübten Lauten /ə/, /ɫ/, /ð/ und /w/ treten sehr viele Aussprachefehler auf. Sie werden nur von vier Schülerinnen und Schülern ein bzw. zwei Mal lautrichtig artikuliert (Tab. 7). Dies hängt vermutlich damit zusammen, dass die Lernenden den Inhaltswörtern *bag* und *tub* häufiger begegnet sind, als den Wörtern *Wilf, had, his, the* und *a*. Es ist interessant zu sehen, dass vielen der Lernenden aufgefallen ist, dass die Grapheme <th> in *the* nicht als /t/ artikuliert werden. In 64% der Fälle lesen die Lernenden im Anlaut /d/, drei Mal /w/ und ein Mal /h/.

Lesefehler differenziert nach Phonemen												
Besonderheit	Von der deutschen GPK abweichende Vokallaute					Von der deutschen GPK abweichender Halbvokallaut	Von der deutschen GPK abweichende Konsonantenlaute		Stimmhafte Konsonanten im Auslaut			
Phonem	æ	ɒ	ʌ	ə	iː	w	ɫ	ð	b	d	g	z
Fehler	19%	18%	61%	59%	23%	58%	51%	92%	3%	33%	5%	56%
Anzahl der Lernenden	4	3	8	10	3	7	7	11	1	4	3	6

Tab. 6 Dokumentation der Lesefehler nach Phonemen

---

3   Die Lesegenauigkeit errechnet sich aus dem Anteil der fehlerhaft artikulierten Phoneme zur Gesamtheit der Phoneme des Textes.

Bei den explizit eingeführten Laut-Buchstaben-Verbindungen treten deutlich weniger Fehler auf. Es fällt auf, dass alle Lernenden in den Wörtern *had* und *hat*, alle bis auf zwei Lernende in den Wörtern *cat* und *on* und alle bis auf einen Schüler in *bag* die Kurzvokale /æ/ und /ɒ/ lautrichtig artikulieren. Diese Wörter zählen zu den Lexemen, bei denen die wenigsten Lesefehler auftreten (Tab. 6). Es kann angenommen werden, dass die Lernenden die explizit eingeführten englischen Graphem-Phonem-Verbindungen herstellen und für das Lesen dieser Wörter nutzen können. Drei weitere Ergebnisse unterstreichen diese Annahme. Zum einen machen die Lernenden Übergeneralisierungsfehler beim Lesen des unbestimmten Artikels *a*. Anstelle des Schwa Lautes /ə/ lesen sie /æ/ (10 Lernende). In englischen Schulen wird der unbestimmte Artikel als sogenanntes *tricky word* eingeführt (vgl. Johnston & Watson 2007: 36), und die Schülerinnen und Schüler erfahren, dass sie sich einige Wörter als Ganzes einprägen müssen. Auch das Personalpronomen *he* gehört zu den *tricky words*. Für die weitere Forschung wäre es interessant zu untersuchen, ob die Einführung von *tricky words* auch die Entwicklung der Lesefertigkeit in der Fremdsprache unterstützt.

Lesefehler differenziert nach Lexemen						
Lexeme	Inhaltswörter	Namen	Funktionswörter			Onomatopoetischer Wortschatz
			Artikel	Personalpronomen	Präpositionen	
Fehler	11,6%	55%	71%	29%	3%	36%

Tab. 7 *Dokumentation der Lesefehler nach Lexemen*

Des Weiteren lässt sich aus den zahlreichen Fragen der Kinder, die während der Vorbereitung auf das Lesen der kurzen Geschichte gestellt wurden, die Annahme ableiten, dass die explizit eingeführten Graphem-Phonem-Relationen beim Lesen genutzt wurden. Nachdem den Lernenden bewusst gemacht worden war, dass der Buchstabe <a> im Englischen sehr häufig als /æ/ artikuliert wird, wollte ein Junge wissen, welchen Buchstaben die Engländer denn dann für den Laut /ʌ/ zur Verfügung hätten. Ein Mädchen wollte im Anschluss an die vierte Stunde, in der die Buchstaben-Laut-Beziehung <u> - /ʌ/ bewusst gemacht wurde, wissen, ob *ketchup* ein englisches Wort sei, weil das <u> darin /ʌ/ gesprochen wird. Diese Rückfragen legen den Schluss nahe, dass bereits Sechsjährige über eine metasprachliche Kompetenz verfügen, die ihnen erlaubt, über Sprache bewusst nachzudenken und Muster zu erkennen.

Ein nicht ganz eindeutiger Hinweis für die Annahme, dass die englischen Graphem-Phonem-Relationen verstanden wurden und für das Lesen englischer

Wörter genutzt werden konnten, lässt sich aus den Selbstkorrekturen der Lernenden ableiten. Eine Schülerin liest zum Beispiel „He put **the** /te/ **tub** /ʊ/ tub in **the** /de/ tin". Während des Lesens scheint sie festzustellen, dass sie für das Wort /tʊb/ keinen lexikalischen Eintrag in ihrem mentalen Lexikon findet. Schließlich fällt ihr offenbar die englische Graphem-Phonem-Relation für den Kurzvokal <u> wieder ein und somit ist sie doch noch in der Lage, das Wort *tub* lautrichtig zu artikulieren. Da die Geschichte Bilder enthält, wäre jedoch auch die Deutung möglich, dass sie das Bild zu Hilfe nimmt, darauf eine Tupperdose erkennt, für die sie den entsprechenden Eintrag in ihrem mentalen Lexikon findet und so zu der richtigen Aussprache geleitet wird.

Das Wort *tub* wird nur von zwei Schülerinnen und Schülern durchgehend und von vier Kindern ein Mal lautrichtig artikuliert. Die bewusstgemachte Graphem-Phonem-Relation konnte für das laute Lesen des Wortes nicht genutzt werden. Es bleibt zu untersuchen, ob die Lernenden lediglich mehr Übung benötigt hätten oder ob sie zu diesem Zeitpunkt von der Menge der eingeführten Graphem-Phonem-Korrespondenzen überfordert waren. Ellis zufolge ist „[c]onsciousness-raising […] unlikely to result in immediate acquisition. More likely, it will have a *delayed* effect" (1992: 239). Es stellt sich außerdem die Frage, welche Auswirkung ein länger angelegter *Phonics*-informierter Unterricht auf die Lesefertigkeiten von jungen Lernenden hat.

Im Leseverstehenstest schneiden die meisten Schülerinnen und Schüler sehr gut ab. Sieben der elf Kinder ordnen alle Sätze den Bildern richtig zu. Zwei Schülerinnen und Schüler verstehen 88% der Sätze richtig (sieben richtige Zuordnungen) und zwei Schüler kreuzen 63% der Sätze richtig an (fünf richtige Zuordnungen). Diese Ergebnisse unterstreichen die Annahme, dass den Lernenden der Wortschatz in dem neuen Text bekannt ist und inhaltlich verstanden wird.

Zusammenfassend lässt sich feststellen, dass die LiPs-Vorstudie zu folgenden Ergebnissen geführt hat:

a) Die Erstklässler können einen kurzen englischen Text in einer Lesegeschwindigkeit lesen, die sowohl der Erwartung an Leseanfänger beim Lesen deutscher Texte am Ende von Klasse 1 als auch der Lesegeschwindigkeit von englischen Muttersprachlern entspricht.
b) Der Fehlerumfang entspricht dem Durchschnitt eines Leseanfängers in Klasse 1 beim Lesen unbekannter Wörter.
c) Die Bewusstmachung der Graphem-Phonem-Relationen <a> - /æ/ und <o> - /ɒ/ wirkt sich positiv auf die Artikulation von Wörtern mit diesen Kurzvokalen aus. Die Bewusstmachung der Graphem-Phonem-Relation <u> - /ʌ/ hat diese Wirkung nicht.

d) Durch die Bewusstmachung der Graphem-Phonem-Relationen, beginnen die Erstklässler über die Besonderheiten des englischen Schriftsystems nachzudenken und Fragen zu stellen.
e) Die Annahme, dass deutsche Fremdsprachenlernende die Phoneme /b/ und /g/ im Auslaut stimmlos artikulieren, hat sich bei den Lexemen *tub* und *bag* nicht bestätigt.
f) Beim lauten Lesen des Textes *Cat in a Bag* treten die wenigsten Aussprachefehler beim Lesen von Inhaltswörtern auf.
g) Die Erstklässler können den Inhalt eines unbekannten Textes mit bekanntem Wortschatz verstehen.

5. Ausblick

Aus den Übergeneralisierungsfehlern, den gestellten Fragen zur englischen Graphem-Phonem-Korrespondenz und den vorgenommenen Selbstkorrekturen lässt sich schließen, dass bewusstmachende Verfahren, speziell die explizit eingeführten Regelmäßigkeiten, ein lernförderliches Unterrichtsangebot darstellen. Die geringe Lesegenauigkeit wirft jedoch die Frage auf, ob das explizite Beschäftigen mit einzelnen Graphem-Phonem-Relationen des englischen Schriftsystems die Kinder zu diesem Zeitpunkt überfordert hat. In der ersten Klasse haben die Kinder die Regeln der Graphem-Phonem-Beziehung des deutschen Schriftsystems noch nicht automatisiert. Es ist anzunehmen, dass sie zunächst eine gewisse Lesesicherheit im Umgang mit der Erstschriftsprache erlangen müssen, bevor sie systematisch an das englische Schriftsystem herangeführt werden können. Die Vorbereitung auf die Aufgabe, einen englischen Text zu lesen, hätte vielleicht mit einem Ganzwortverfahren zu ähnlichen oder besseren Ergebnissen geführt. In einer Langzeitstudie soll auf der Grundlage der hier diskutierten Ergebnisse der Einfluss eines Ganzwortansatzes mit dem eines *Phonics* basierten Ansatzes auf die Entwicklung der Lesefertigkeit verglichen werden (vgl. Frisch 2009: 158). Dazu wird eine komparative Studie in zwei parallelen zweiten Klassen durchgeführt. In der Experimentalgruppe wird den Lernenden die englische Graphem-Phonem-Relation bewusst gemacht. Die Kontrollgruppe begegnet dem Schriftbild ausschließlich auf Wortkarten. Abgesehen von diesem Unterschied arbeiten die Schülerinnen und Schülern in beiden Klassen mit der gleichen Anzahl und der gleichen Auswahl an Schriftbildern. Anhand von Videoaufnahmen und Leseverstehenstests werden die Fähigkeit zur phonologischen Rekodierung und das Leseverstehen von unbekannten Texten mit bekanntem Wortmaterial untersucht. Die Ergebnisse dieser Studie können dann einen Beitrag zur empirischen Fundierung der Diskussion um die Frage nach dem geeigneten Umgang mit dem Schriftbild im Englischunterricht der Grundschule leisten.

Literaturverzeichnis

Adams, Marilyn Jager (1990), *Beginning to read: Thinking and learning about print*. Cambridge, Massachusetts: MIT Press.

[AG DEST] Australian Government. Department of Education, Science and Training (Hrsg.) (2005). Teaching Reading. Report and Recommendations. National Inquiry into the Teaching of Literacy. [Online: http://www.dest.gov.au/nitl/report.htm. 22.08.2009].

Bassetti, Benedetta (2009), Orthographic input and second language phonology. In: Piske, Thorsten (Hrsg.), *Input matters in SLA*. Bristol et al.: Multilingual matters, 191–206.

Camilli, Gregory, Vargas, Sadako & Yurecko, Michele (2003), Teaching Children to Read: The fragile link between science and federal education policy. *Education Policy Analysis Archives* 11.15. [Online: http://epaa.asu.edu/epaa/v11n15/. 22.08.2009].

Chall, Jeanne (1967), *Learning to Read. The Great Debate*. New York: McGraw-Hill.

DeKeyser, Robert (2003), Implicit and explicit learning. In: Doughty, Catherine L. & Long, Michael H. (Hrsg.), *The Handbook of Second Language Acquisition*. Oxford et al.: Blackwell, 313–348.

[DFES] Department for education and skills (Hrsg.) (2006), Primary National Strategy. The Primary Framework for literacy and mathematics: core position papers underpinning the renewal of guidance for teaching literacy and mathematics. [Online: http://nationalstrategies.standards.dcsf.gov.uk/node/85021. 16.02.2010].

[DFES] Department for education and skills (Hrsg.) (2007), Letters and Sounds: Principles and Practice of High Quality Phonics. [Online: http://nationalstrategies.standards.dcsf.gov.uk/node/84969. 15.02.2010].

Diehr, Bärbel & Rymarczyk, Jutta (2008), Zur Basis von Lese- und Schreibversuchen. 'Ich weiß es, weil ich es so spreche.' *Grundschulmagazin Englisch – The Primary English Magazine* 1, 6–8.

Duscha, Michael (2007), *Der Einfluss der Schrift auf das Fremdsprachenlernen in der Grundschule. Dargestellt am Beispiel des Englischunterrichts in Niedersachsen*. [Online: http://bib1lp1.rz.tu-bs.de/docportal/servlets/MCRFileNodeServlet/DocPortal_derivate_00004267/Dissertation.pdf?hosts=local. 16.02.2010].

Eckerth, Johannes (2008), Investigating consciousness-raising tasks: pedagogically targeted and non-targeted learning gains. *International Journal of Applied Linguistics* 18: 2, 119–145.

Ehri, Linnea C. (1998), Grapheme-Phoneme Knowledge is Essential for Learning to Read Words in English. In: Metsala, Jamie L. & Ehri, Linnea C. (Hrsg.), *Word Recognition in Beginning Literacy.* Mahwah New Jersey/London: Lawrence Erlbaum Ass., 3–40.

Ellis, Rod (1992), *Second Language Acquisition and Language Pedagogy.* Bristol: Multilingual Matters.

Evans, M.A. & Carr, T.H. (1985), Cognitive abilities, conditions of learning, and early development of reading skill. *Reading Research Quarterly* 20, 327–350.

Frisch, Stefanie (2009), Phonics in the German Primary EFL Class. *VIEWS* 18: 3. (Special Edition: Conference Proceedings: Bridging the Gap between Theory and Practice), 157–159.

Goodman, Kenneth S. (1979), Behind the Eye: What Happens in Reading. In: Goodman, Kenneth S. & Niles, Olive S. (Hrsg.), *Reading. Process and Program.* Urbana, Ill.: National Council of Teachers of English, 2–38.

Gompf, Gundi (2009), *Fremdsprachenlernen ab Klasse 1. Synopse 2008/2009.* [Online: http://www.kles.org/pdf-dateien/Kommentierte_Synopse_2008–2009.pdf. 16.02.2010].

Grabe, William & Stoller, Fredricka L. (2002), *Teaching and Researching Reading.* London: Pearson Education.

Groot-Wilken, Bernd, Engel, Gaby & Thürmann, Eike (2007), Listening and Reading Comprehension. Erste Ergebnisse einer Studie zu Englisch ab Klasse 3 an nordrhein-westfälischen Grundschulen. *Forum Schule* 18: 1. [Online: http://www.grundschulverband.de/fileadmin/grundschulverband/Download/aktuell/Gaby_Engel_STS_Soest.pdf. 16.02.2010].

Hunt, Roderick & Brychta, Alex (2007a), *Cat in a Bag. (Oxford Reading Tree).* Oxford: Oxford University Press.

Hunt, Roderick & Brychta, Alex (2007b), *The Dog Tag. (Oxford Reading Tree).* Oxford: Oxford University Press.

Johnston, Rhona & Watson, Joyce (2005), A Seven Year Study of the Effects of Synthetic Phonics Teaching on Reading and Spelling Attainment. In: *Insight.* [Online: http://www.scotland.gov.uk/Publications/2005/02/20682/52383. 16.02.2010]

Johnston, Rhona & Watson, Joyce (2007), *Teaching Synthetic Phonics.* Exeter: Learning Matters Ltd.

Klicpera, Christian & Gasteiger-Klicpera, Barbara (1993), *Lesen und Schreiben. Entwicklung und Schwierigkeiten.* Bern: Huber.

Koda, Keiko (2008), Impacts of prior literacy experience on second-language learning to read. In: Koda, Keiko & Zehler, Annette M. (Hrsg.), *Learning to Read Across Languages. Cross-Linguistic Relationships in First- and Second-Language Literacy Development.* New York et al.: Routledge, 68–69.

Kuhn, Tatjana (2006), *Grammatik im Englischunterricht der Primarstufe. Theoretische Grundlagen und praktische Unterrichtsvorschläge.* Heidelberg: Winter.
Marx, Peter (2007), *Lese- und Rechtschreiberwerb.* Paderborn: Schöningh.
[MBFJ RP] Ministerium für Bildung, Frauen und Jugend Rheinland-Pfalz (Hrsg.) (2004), *Rahmenplan Grundschule. Teilrahmenplan Fremdsprache.* Mainz: Sommer Druck und Verlag.
[MBJS BB] Ministerium für Bildung, Jugend und Sport Brandenburg (Hrsg.) (2008), *Rahmenlehrplan für moderne Fremdsprachen. Erste Fremdsprache. Begegnung mit fremden Sprachen.* Hans Gieselmann Druck- und Medienhaus GmbH & Co KG.
Mindt, Dieter (2006), Von der Imitation zur bewussten Verwendung von Sprachmitteln: Ein neues Unterrichtsmodell. In: Schlüter, Norbert (Hrsg.), *Fortschritte im frühen Fremdsprachenlernen.* Berlin: Cornelsen, 68–74.
Mindt, Dieter & Wagner, Gudrun (2009), *Innovativer Englischunterricht für die Klassen 1 und 2.* Braunschweig: Westermann.
[MKJS BW] Ministerium für Kultus, Jugend und Sport des Landes Baden-Württemberg (2004), *Bildungsplan 2004. Grundschule.* Villingen-Schwenningen: Neckar-Verlag.
[MSW NW] Ministerium für Schule und Weiterbildung Nordrhein-Westfalen (2008), *Lehrplan Englisch für die Grundschulen des Landes Nordrhein-Westfalen. 16.6.2008.* [Online: http://www.standardsicherung.schulministerium.nrw.de/lehrplaene/upload/klp_gs/GS_LP_E.pdf. 16.02.2010].
National Reading Panel (2000), *National Reading Panel Reports Combination of Teaching Phonics, Word Sounds, Giving Feedback on Oral Reading Most Effective Way to Teach Reading.* [Online: http://www.nationalreadingpanel.org/Press/press_rel_4_13_00_1.htm. 16.02.2010].
Rayner, Keith & Pollatsek, Alexander (1989), *The Psychology of Reading.* London: Prentice Hall.
Reichart-Wallrabenstein, Maike (2001), Das leere Blatt, Dinosaurier und die Lesekonferenz. Schrift im Englischunterricht der Grundschule einmal anders. *Grundschulunterricht* 4. Sonderheft Fremdsprachen, 27–30.
Reichart-Wallrabenstein, Maike (2004), *Kinder und Schrift im Englischunterricht der Grundschule. Eine theorie- und empiriegeleitete Studie zur Diskussion um die Integration von Schriftlichkeit. Band 1: Text.* Berlin: dissertation.de.
Reichen, Jürgen (1988), *Lesen durch Schreiben. Wie Kinder selbstgesteuert Lesen lernen* (3. Auflage). Sundern: SABE Verlag.
Rose, Jim (2006), *Independent review of the teaching of early reading. Final report.* [Online: http://www.standards.dfes.gov.uk/phonics/report.pdf. 16.02.2010].

Rymarczyk, Jutta (2008), Früher oder später? Zur Einführung des Schriftbildes in der Grundschule. In: Böttger, Heiner (Hrsg.), *Fortschritte im Frühen Fremdsprachenlernen. Ausgewählte Tagungsbeiträge Nürnberg 2006.* München: Domino Verlag, 170–182.

Schmid-Schönbein, Gisela (2006), Vom Lesen zum Schreiben. Der Weg zum kommunikativen Gebrauch des Englischen. *Primary English* 4, 3–5.

Schründer-Lenzen, Agi (2004), *Schriftspracherwerb und Unterricht. Bausteine professionellen Handlungswissens.* Opladen: Leske + Budrich.

Speece, Deborah L. & Ritchey, Kristen D. (2005), A Longitudinal Study of the Development of Oral Reading Fluency in Young Children At Risk for Reading Failure. *Journal of Learning Disabilities* 38: 5, 387–399.

Stahl, Steven A. (2001), Teaching Phonics and Phonological Awareness. In: Neuman, Susan B. & Dickinson, David K. (Hrsg.), *Handbook of Early Literacy Research. Volume 1.* New York/London: The Guilford Press.

Stubbs, Michael (1996), The English writing system. In: Hartmut, Günther (Hrsg.), *Schrift und Schriftlichkeit – ein interdisziplinäres Handbuch internationaler Forschung. Writing and its use. 2. Halbband.* Berlin: De Gruyter, 1441–1445.

Tunmer, William E. & Hoover, Wesley A. (1992), Cognitive and Linguistic Factors in Learning to Read. In: Gough, Philip E., Ehri, Linnea C. & Treiman, Rebecca (Hrsg.), *Reading Acquisition.* Hillsdale, NJ: Lawrence Erlbaum Ass., 175–214.

Urquhart, Sandy & Weir, Cyril (1998), *Reading in a Second Language. Process, Product and Practice.* London: Longman.

Wimmer, Heinz, Klampfer, Barbara & Frith, Uta (1993), Lesenlernen bei englischen und
deutschen Kindern. In: Heiko Balhorn & Hans Brügelmann (Hrsg.), *Bedeutungen erfinden – im Kopf, mit Schrift und miteinander.* Konstanz: Libelle, 324–329.

Wright, Andrew (2005), *Storytelling with Children.* Oxford: Oxford University Press.

Wunsch, Christian (2006), Schriftbilder. Sprachbewusstsein und Lernhilfe geben. *Primary English* 2, 15–17.

Petra Burmeister

Did you now that 15 difrent Fish arts in the Kiel Canal live? On foreign language writing in partial immersion primary school classrooms

Im Laufe der Grundschulzeit wird die Arbeit mit schriftlichen Texten zunehmend wichtiger. Besonders im Sachfachunterricht werden Inhalte vermehrt mit Hilfe von schriftlichen Texten erarbeitet, dokumentiert und gelernt. Entsprechendes gilt auch für Grundschulen, in denen Sachfächer in einer Fremdsprache unterrichtet werden. Sollten die Schülerinnen und Schüler in solchen immersiven Klassen von Anfang an systematischen Lese- und Schreibunterricht in der Fremdsprache erhalten, um sie zu befähigen, im Sachfachunterricht mit fremdsprachlichen Texten umzugehen, oder reicht die Literarisierung im Deutschen aus?

In diesem Beitrag wird an einigen Beispielen gezeigt, dass Schülerinnen und Schüler einer norddeutschen Grundschule mit partieller Immersion adressatengerechte und sachfachlich anspruchsvolle Texte in der Fremdsprache Englisch schreiben können, obwohl sie keinen systematischen Lese- und Schreibunterricht in der Fremdsprache erhalten haben. Ein 'schriftreicher' Unterricht, der den Kindern von Beginn an vermittelt, wie wichtig und hilfreich die fremdsprachliche Schrift ist, scheint auszureichen, um textuelle Kompetenz im Englischen zu fördern. Jedoch sollte diskutiert werden, ob und wenn ja, wie und ab wann die Rechtschreibkompetenz im Englischen gefördert werden sollte.

1. Introduction

In early total French immersion programs in Canada as well as in similar programs world wide, students are taught reading and writing in the respective second or foreign language (L2) before they are taught literacy skills in their first language. In some immersion programs, first language (L1) literacy instruction might even be delayed for three or more years. However, research in the context of Canadian French immersion has shown that, after the introduction of L1 language arts, the immersion student's L1 literacy skills are as good as the L1 literacy skills achieved by students in non-immersion comparison groups (e. g. Genesee 1987, 2004; Swain & Lapkin 1982; Turnbull, Lapkin & Hart 2001). Research has also revealed that the immersion students, in comparison to their non-immersion peers, develop high levels of L2 reading skills although the students had very little knowledge of the L2 upon starting literacy training in school (e. g. Genesee 1987, 2004; Swain & Lapkin 1982). Furthermore, the immersion student's L2 writing skills are much more advanced than the writing skills achieved by their non-immersion peers in French-as-a-second-language programs although the immersion student's written texts are often unidiomatic and show grammatical weaknesses (e. g. Harley 1984, 1989; Swain & Lapkin 1986). Research in programs in which immersion instruction is delayed until grade three or five has revealed the same positive results as summarized above. In these middle immersion programs, the students learn to read and write in their L1 English and the L2 is taught in daily Core French lessons.

This article focuses on an early partial immersion program at a primary school in Northern Germany in which all subjects are taught in the L2 English except German and in which the students learn to read and write in their L1 German. Research has shown that after four years of primary school, the students' L1 reading skills are at the same level and even surpass the L1 reading skills of non-immersion peers even though for the immersion students 70% of the school day is in the L2 English (Zaunbauer, Bonerad & Möller 2005; Zaunbauer & Möller 2006; Zaunbauer 2007; Zaunbauer & Möller 2007; see also Piske this volume). In this partial immersion program, no textbook-based EFL lessons are offered and the students are not systematically taught English spelling. From the first day of school onwards, parallel to the formal literacy training in the L1, the students experience a 'soft' immersion into English print just by being exposed to plenty of it and they seem to transfer the literacy skills developed in the L1 to the L2. First analyses of students' written texts have shown that although the students make spelling and grammar mistakes, their texts are of high quality especially with regard to subject-matter orientation and textual competence. The students' texts show that L1 and L2 literacy skills can be introduced at the same time and that there is no need to delay the introduction of L2 print until the students have mastered the L1 writing system (for a discussion, see Diehr, Piske and Rymarczyk this volume).

2. Partial immersion at the Claus-Rixen-Primary School in Northern Germany

In Germany, German Language Arts is a compulsory subject in all state schools and students are taught to read and write in German before they are taught literacy skills in any foreign language. This is why there are no state primary schools in Germany with Canadian-like total immersion programs in which instruction in the first language is postponed for a certain amount of time and where students learn to read and write in the L2 (e. g. Genesee 1987). Due to these compulsory German lessons, the amount of immersion instruction at German primary schools cannot exceed 70 %.

The data analysed for this article was collected in the Claus-Rixen-Primary School (CRS), a German state primary school in which all subjects apart from German are taught in the foreign language English during the four years of primary schooling. The CRS is located near Kiel (Schleswig-Holstein, Northern Germany) and caters for middle-class students. The partial immersion program at CRS started in 1999 with one class. Half of the children in this first cohort had attended a neighbouring German-English bilingual kindergarten.

2.1 Literacy instruction in the L1 and the L2

Like their peers in the non-immersion classes, the students in the partial immersion program at CRS learn to read and write in daily 45-minutes German lessons. The L1 literacy training approach used in both, the immersion and non-immersion classes is called *Lesen durch Schreiben* ('reading via writing'; Reichen 2001). The students start writing (and reading) by sounding out words with the help of the so called *'Anlauttabelle'*, a chart which helps to identify the initial sound (*Anlaut*) of a word. The chart depicts pictures of objects and animals together with the letters for the initial sound in the respective word, e. g. the letter <b> is shown next to the picture of a banana (German: *Banane*), or a picture of a pair of scissors is shown next to the letters *Sch / sch* (for /ʃ/ in *Schere*). For letters representing different sounds, two pictures are given, e. g. a picture of a duck and a donkey (German: *Ente* and *Esel*) is placed next to the corresponding initial letters <E/e> (for /eː/ in *Esel* and /ə/ in *Ente*). When the students wish to write a word they segment the word into sounds and search for objects or animals in the chart which 'begin' with the respective sounds. Then they write down the corresponding letters and blend them together into words. With the help of this strategy, the students can start writing all kinds of words 'from scratch'.

The *Lesen durch Schreiben*-approach is based on the assumption that students can find out by themselves, and at their own pace, how the orthographic system of German works and that literacy skills are promoted by letting the students express themselves in writing from the very start. The aims are to develop the students' ability to sound out letters and words and to enable them to write words which are 'phonetically correct'. The instructional focus, at least during the initial phase of literacy training, is explicitly *not* on accuracy and it goes without saying that the students make mistakes because the grapheme-phoneme correspondences in German are not always consistent[1]. Experience at CRS has shown that at the end of grade one, when the students are approximately seven years old, all students have understood the 'alphabetic principle', i. e. that "the speech stream can be divided into sounds, and these sounds are represented by letters or groups of letters." (Peregoy & Boyle [4]2005: 171).

Whereas there is a strong emphasis on literacy training in German, the students in the partial immersion program at CRS are not systematically taught to read and write in the L2 English during their time in primary school. However, from the first day onwards, students are immersed in a "literacy-rich environment" (Peregoy & Boyle [4]2005: 183) with English print on posters, on handouts, or in books. In addition, daily routines such as writing down the tasks for the day on the blackboard or adding new words to the word banks reflect the importance of English writing (Grabe & Kaplan 1996: 266ff.; Lepschy 2007: 44; Peregoy & Boyle [4]2005: 183ff).

During first grade, the students in the partial immersion classes at CRS are allowed to discover the English writing system at their own pace. Some students try to sound out English words and to copy them into their files as soon as they start reading and writing in German. Other students seem to ignore English writing completely as if they want to protect themselves from being overtaxed (Burmeister & Piske 2008: 187). However, at the beginning of grade two, print becomes more and more important and the students are encouraged to read and write in English. Mistakes in students' texts are corrected 'en passant' since the focus is on meaning rather than on form.

2.2 The functions of L2 writing in the partial immersion classroom

The functions of reading and writing in the immersion subjects are the same as in subjects taught in the students' L1. In Science lessons, for example, students need to learn how to obtain information from various written sources, including annotated tables or diagrams and they need to know how to read experimental instructions. They need to be able to record hypotheses, observations and findings, to describe processes, to complete tables, or label diagrams (Gesellschaft für Didaktik des Sachunterrichts 2002: 13).

Just like in Science, reading and writing becomes more and more important in other subjects. The students read song lyrics in Music lessons, write down their

---

1 Results of a longitudinal study comparing the effectiveness of the *Lesen durch Schreiben*-approach and other early literacy approaches in German primary schools are discussed in Hinney, Huneke, Müller & Weinhold 2008 and in Weinhold 2006).

thoughts in Religious Education or read tasks in Mathematics. In addition, they get to know the different types of texts typically used in the respective subject matter.

The L2 input (oral and written) provided by the immersion teachers at CRS is, of course, age-appropriate and structurally rich (e. g. Burmeister & Pasternak 2004: 27, Burmeister 2006: 205; Burmeister & Piske 2008: 187). The written materials such as content-related picture books or science readers published in English-speaking countries are selected on the basis of content relevance and the needs and interests of the students and the language in these books is not altered or simplified. Long-term anecdotal evidence in CRS has shown that the students enjoy reading age-appropriate texts and that they seem to benefit from the authentic, structurally and lexically rich input.

2.3 L2 writing in the partial immersion classes at Claus-Rixen-School

During first grade, writing and reading tasks are usually relatively undemanding for the students. They connect words and pictures by drawing lines and copy words or small phrases. However, in grade four, the demands on the students' writing skills are much higher because they have to be able to describe processes or to record findings after science experiments.

Experience at CRS has shown that the partial immersion students in grades three and four are able to write complex texts for different purposes. Since they have not been not explicitly taught to write English texts, they apparently transfer the textual skills learned in their German lessons, e. g. how to structure texts, how to use cohesive ties in order to achieve a coherent text, or how to tailor texts to a specific audience. The teachers at CRS are convinced that regular (creative) work with a wide variety of texts in the *German* lessons reinforces textual competence in the L2 English. Experience at CRS has also shown that the individual variation between students regarding the quality of their texts is as high in English as it is in German and that the students' marks for written texts correlate in English and German. This anecdotal evidence is supported by the results of international research in the field of L2 writing (e. g. Grabe & Kaplan 1996: 140ff.; Peregoy & Boyle [4]2005: 156f).

3. The analysis of texts written by students in partial immersion classes

School-based investigations have shown that after four years of primary schooling in partial immersion classes at CRS, the students can write functionally adequate texts in the L2 English although L2 writing skills have never been explicitly and systematically taught. How do L2 English writing skills develop? What kinds of text do the students produce? How are their texts structured? How accurate are the texts? Which types of errors do the students make? The last two questions were of particular concern to the teachers in the partial immersion classes because the EFL teachers at the secondary school complained about the high number of spelling mistakes made by the students in partial immersion classes.

In order to evaluate the quality of the students' written texts, a pilot study focusing on the above questions was set up. The preliminary steps were to find out what kinds of texts students produced in class and which kinds of texts could serve as a valid basis for further analyses.

For this purpose, texts written by the partial immersion students of the 2003 cohort at CRS were collected. These texts stem from regular lessons and were not elicited in a controlled, experimental setting. The data comprise of four sets of texts (n = 83) written by the students in grades three and four between June 2006 and June 2007. Two text sets stem from Science lessons, one about "My Neighbourhood" taught at the end of grade three and the other one about "The Kiel Canal" at the end of grade four. The free compositions ("My Christmas holiday", "My Easter holidays") were written during the second half of grade four.

In the following section, some findings of the preliminary analyses will be presented. It is important to note that these findings are purely descriptive because detailed statistical analyses have not been carried out yet.

3.1 Typical features in the partial immersion students' L2 English written texts

The data selected for this section show features which are typical in the sense that they can be found across grades three and four and in the majority of the written texts. The aim is to illustrate – in a descriptive manner – how the third and fourth graders in this partial immersion school write in their L2 and what kind of errors they make.

Since language teachers should focus on what learners *can* do rather than look for what they *cannot* do (European Commission 2001), we should begin with examples showing how well the partial immersion students write in the L2 – although they have not been explicitly taught writing skills nor grammar. For this purpose, the various spelling and grammar mistakes in the excerpts displayed in figures 1 to 5 are not taken into consideration.

The first set of texts was obtained in June 2006, at the end of grade three, in the context of a Science unit about the students' hometown. Their task was to paint a picture of their neighbourhood and to write a text about it. On average, the students wrote 60 words, the shortest text had 45 and the longest 84 words.

The excerpt in figure 1 below shows that the student's text is functionally adequate in the sense that she focuses on the task and uses technical terms appropriate in this 'geographical' context, such as "in the east", "in the south", "in the west". The references like "My *neighours –their, they", "my Grandma – her" make her text coherent.

> Write about the people in your neighbourhood.
> My neighbours in the east are verry kind. Their names are Edid and Hainz. They have goldfishes and wenn I am on holidays they take my rabbits. My Grandma in the south is the best neighbour. I kann take my Rabbit to her. Her name is ██████. The neighbours in the west have a dog caled Artos.

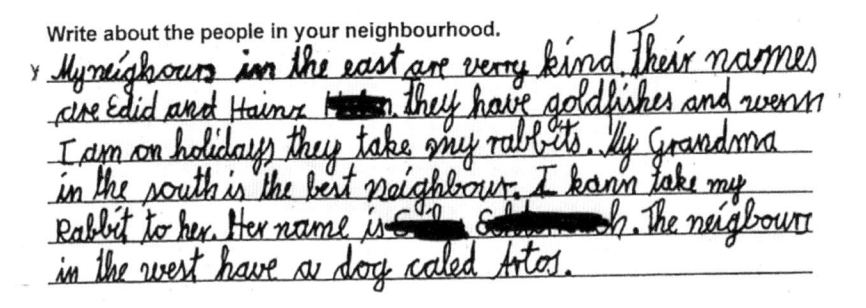

Figure 1: A third grader's Science text about "My neighbourhood".

The ability of the students to write subject-matter oriented texts is especially apparent in the following data obtained at the end of grade four. These texts stem from a regular Science classroom test designed by the teacher in order to evaluate what students had learned in the previous unit about the Kiel Canal. The students had the following tasks: They were first asked to draw the Kiel Canal onto a map of the state of Schleswig-Holstein. They then had to label the two cities located at either end of the Kiel Canal. Finally, they had to put together important facts, e. g. about the locks in the Kiel Canal for an American family visiting Schleswig-Holstein and the Kiel Canal. The average number of words for the three tasks together is 209 (minimum 112, maximum 319).

The title of this article stems from one of the grade four science texts about the Kiel Canal (see figure 2 below). It illustrates the ability of most students to follow the task instructions and tailor their texts to the respective audience.

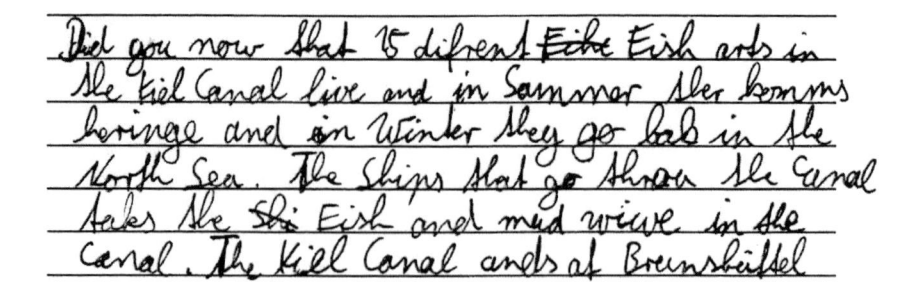

> *Did you now that 15 difrent ~~Eihe~~ Eish arts in the Kiel Canal live and in Sammer ther komms horinge and in Winter they go bab in the North Sea. The Ships that go throu the Canal taks the Sh: Eish and mud wieve in the Canal. The Kiel Canal ends at Brunsbüttel*

Figure 2: A fourth grader's science text about the Kiel Canal.

As required in the task, the student directly addresses the imaginary American family by asking the question "Did you *now ..." and includes information he considers as being important and interesting to know about the Kiel Canal.

In the excerpts below (figures 3 to 5), students write about the locks of the Kiel Canal.

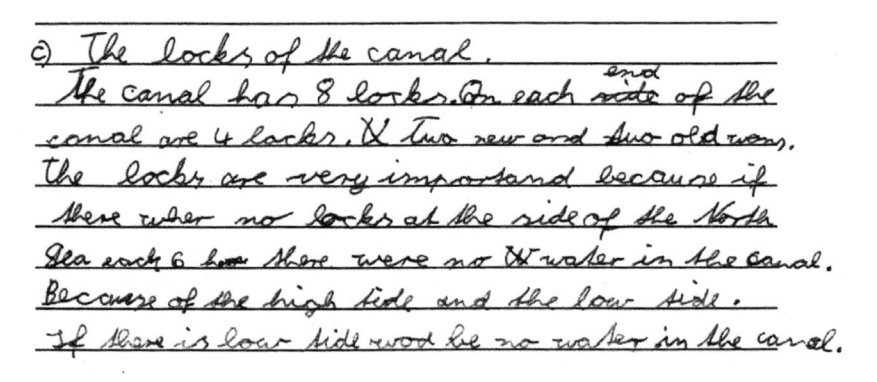

> *c) The locks of the canal.*
> *The canal has 8 locks. On each end of the canal are 4 locks. & Two new and two old wans. The locks are very importand because if there wher no locks at the side of the North Sea each 6 how there were no & water in the canal. Because of the high tide and the low tide. If there is low tide wood be no water in the canal.*

Figure 3: A fourth grader's science text about the locks of the Kiel Canal.

In her text in figure 3 above, the student describes the importance of the locks in the Kiel Canal. She expresses her thoughts with the help of rather complex sentence constructions, e. g. conditional sentences, without having been explicitly taught grammar.

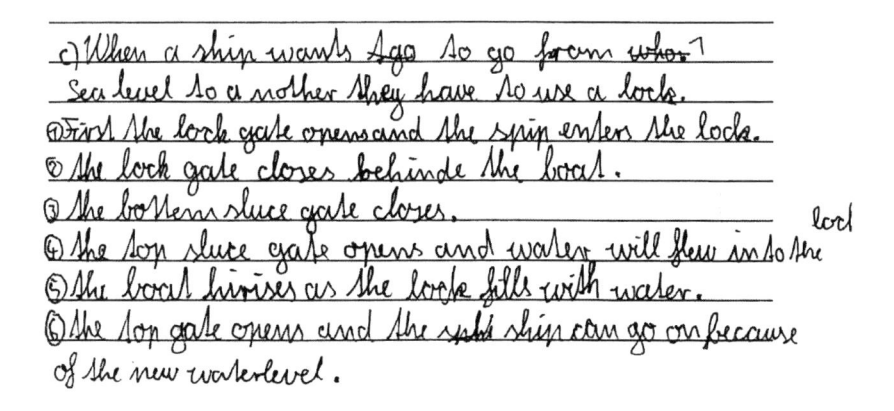

On foreign language writing in partial immersion primary school

> c) When a ship wants to go to go from who?
> Sea level to another they have to use a lock.
> ① First the lock gate opens and the ship enters the lock.
> ② The lock gate closes behinde the boat.
> ③ The bottem sluce gate closes.   lock
> ④ The top sluce gate opens and water will flow into the
> ⑤ The boat hivises as the lock fills with water.
> ⑥ The top gate opens and the ship ship can go on because
> of the new waterlevel.

Figure 4: A fourth grader's science text about the locks of the Kiel Canal

The student in figure 4 describes step by step how a ship lock operates, whereas the student in figure 5 provides the reader with a comprehensive overview about the locks in the Kiel Canal including facts, the process of ship locking and the function of the locks.

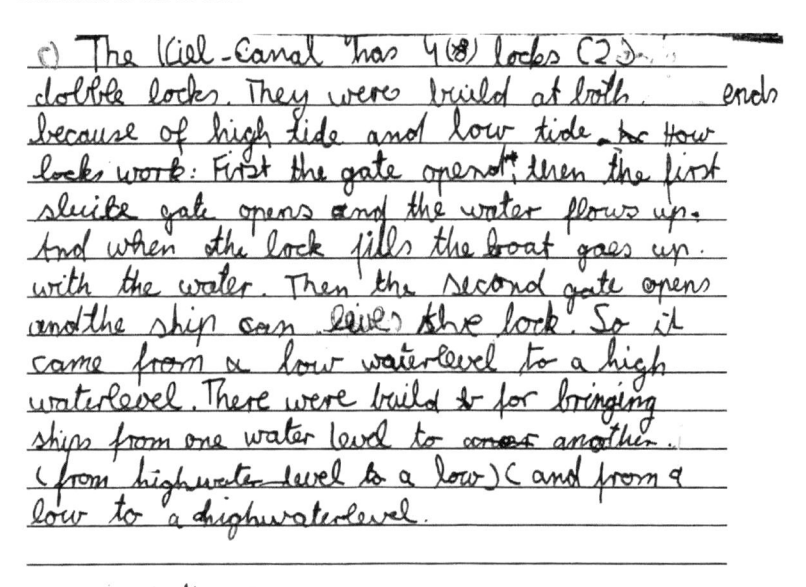

> c) The Kiel-Canal has 4(8) locks (2).
> double locks. They were build at both   ends
> because of high tide and low tide. * How
> locks work: First the gate opens*, then the first
> sluice gate opens and the water flows up.
> And when the lock fills the boat goes up.
> with the water. Then the second gate opens
> and the ship can leve the lock. So it
> came from a low waterlevel to a high
> waterlevel. There were build it for bringing
> ships from one water level to anot another.
> (from highwater level to a low)(and from a
> low to a highwaterlevel.
>
> ✶ and the ship enters the lock

Figure 5: A fourth grader's science text about the locks of the Kiel Canal

The excerpts in figures 3, 4, and 5 above are typical examples of texts with adequate descriptions of complex subject matter. They show that the students are able to describe their recently acquired knowledge in a task-oriented way and to tailor it to the intended audience. Although they have not been taught grammar, the students can formulate sentences in the L2 which are relatively complex.

While the analysis of the science texts yields interesting results with respect to the students' ability to express their content knowledge in the L2, the level of students' L2 overall writing competence is best reflected in the compositions about how they spent their Christmas and Easter vacations (see also Burmeister & Piske 2008: 189 ff.). These texts are the longest in the data, presumably because the students could express themselves freely and apparently enjoyed writing the stories. The average number of words in the 'Christmas compositions' is 143, with a minimum of 56 and a maximum of 232 words. For the 'Easter compositions', the average number of words is 140, with a minimum of 66 and a maximum of 217 words.

In the text below a student describes her New Year's Eve 'adventure':

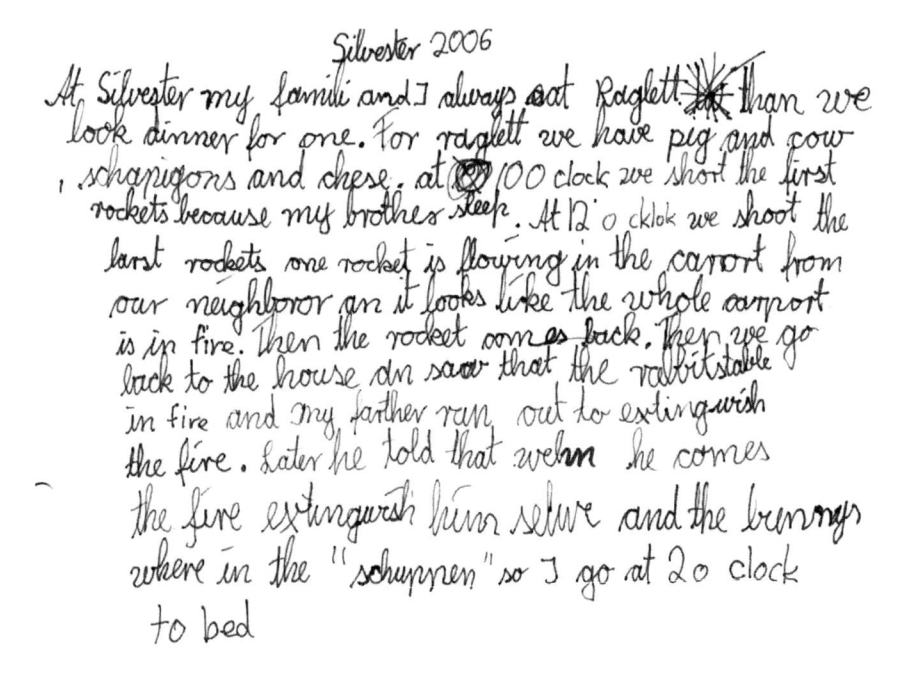

> Silvester 2006
> At Silvester my famili and I always eat Raglett. Than we took dinner for one. For raglett we have pig and cow, schanigons and chese. at 8 00 clock we shoot the first rockets because my brother sleep. At 12 o cklok we shoot the larst rockets one rocket is flowing in the carport from our neighboror an it looks like the whole carport is in fire. Then the rocket comes back. Then we go back to the house an saw that the rabbitstable in fire and my farther ran out to extingwish the fire. Later he told that wehn he comes the fire extingwish him selwe and the bunnys where in the "schuppen" so I go at 2 o clock to bed

Figure 6: A fourth grader's composition about "My Christmas holidays".

Like the texts in figures 1 to 5, the one above is also relatively complex with respect to its syntax, discourse structure and lexical aspects but there are some non target-like forms which – in the opinion of many secondary school teachers – downgrade the quality of the students' texts. Especially spelling errors in words which are frequently used are intolerable for many teachers. In the above text, these are: *famili* for *family*, *larst* for *last*, *wehn* for *when*, *an* for *and*, *farther* for *father*, *himselve* for *himself*, *where* for *were*. Another negative aspect for many teachers is the variable use of tenses within one text. In the composition above, the student correctly begins with the present tense ("*I always eat*") and continues with present tense as well as past tense forms.

The first analyses of the Christmas and Easter texts have shown that some spelling mistakes seem to be very robust in the sense that they can be found throughout grades three and four. One type of error is the omission of letters which represent 'silent' sounds, such as *leand* instead of *leaned*, *ant* instead of *aunt*, *to* instead of *too*, *gos* statt *goes*, *ar* instead of *are*, *evry* instead of *every*, *our* instead of *hour*. In some words, the students insert a letter, such as in the text above in *farther* for *father*, or *larst* instead of *last* (maybe in attempt to express the length of the vowel). In addition, words with initial *wh* are often spelled incorrectly, e. g. *wehn*, *wen*, *wenn* for *when*, *wy* for *why*, *wether* for *whether*.

All in all, the texts analysed so far have shown that, at the end of grade 3, most of the students have left behind what Peregoy & Boyle have classified as the stage of the 'transitional speller' (Peregoy & Boyle [4]2005: 195ff.) and first error counts have shown that only 8% of the mistakes are spelling errors. Phonetic spellings such as *grunup* for *grown-up*, *birstey* for *birthday*, *awy* for *every*, *parinds* for *parents* or *rait* for *right* are relatively rare.[2] Some mistakes show that the students, in their attempt to write English words, base their decisions on analogies when they write *flue* for *flew* (as in *glue*), or *by* for *buy* (as in *cry* and *why*).

The question to be asked is: Do the students in the partial immersion classes at CRS have spelling problems? Can teachers expect a higher level of accuracy after four years and approximately 2500 hours taught in English? Should L2 writing skills be taught explicitly and systematically? If yes, are there appropriate tasks or strategies which foster spelling skills? In other words: What needs to be discussed in Germany in the context of partial immersion education at primary schools is the 'accuracy-problem' which has long been discussed in the context of Canadian Immersion (e.g. Harley 1989; Lyster 1987; Lyster & Ranta 1997; Swain & Lapkin 1986).

---

2   Phonetic spelling is frequently found in texts written by students in regular EFL programs with only two lessons per week (see Diehr & Rymarczyk 2008 and Rymarczyk 2008, a,b).

4. Conclusions

Many foreign language teachers still judge their students' L2 writing skills by mainly focusing on aspects of orthographic and linguistic accuracy. In the case of the question included in the title of this paper (see also figure 2), i. e. **Did you now that 15 difrent Fish arts in the Kiel Canal live?*, these teachers will most probably pay particular attention to the spelling mistakes (**now* for *know*, **difrent* for *different*, **Fish* for *fish*), the lexical error (**arts* based on German *Arten* for *types*) and the syntactic error (German word order pattern in the that-clause) produced by this student. In other words, many teachers still focus on what the students *cannot* do instead of acknowledging what they *can* already do, which is what teachers should concentrate on according to the 'philosophy' guiding the Common European Framework of Reference for Languages (European Commission 2001).

Seen in this light, the positive features in the partial immersion students' texts, such as the use of cohesive ties, the correct use of tenses, lexical variation and syntactic complexity outweigh the impact of orthographic or linguistic errors – especially if we consider that the partial immersion program at Claus-Rixen-School in Kiel aims at fostering oral (and not written) communicative competence and that grammar and spelling are not explicitly taught during the four grades of primary schooling.

However, further analyses have to be carried out in order to learn more about L2 writing in the partial immersion programs. One interesting question, among others, would be to find out to what extent L2 spelling development parallels the development of written skills for L1 German and to what extent different L1 literacy training methods (like the *Lesen durch Schreiben*-approach mentioned in section 2.1) have an impact on the development of L2 writing.

In addition, researchers and teachers need to discuss whether L2 writing skills in primary school immersion programs should be developed in a more systematic way, and if yes, how. There have already been first attempts to foster accuracy in a grade four partial immersion class at Claus-Rixen-School. The teacher made students write sentences connected to the contents of their Science lessons and implemented a 'words-of-the-week' training on the basis of *Dolch-sight word lists*[3]. Unfortunately, only short-term improvements could be observed. It might be worth finding out what kind of *consciousness raising tasks* (Ellis 2003: 162ff.) would be suitable to make the students focus on form in a meaningful way.

The question of whether and how L2 literacy skills should be fostered in primary school is presently the focus of lively discussion in the context of regular

---

3   e.g. http://www.janbrett.com/games/jan_brett_dolch_word_list_main.htm (16.11.2009)

foreign language teaching in Germany. In most German states, foreign language instruction is introduced in grade three with two 45-minute lessons per week. Although the students at the beginning of grade three have already had two years of L1 literacy training, the development of L2 reading and writing skills is often postponed because L2 oral skills should be developed first. In the state of Baden-Württemberg, where foreign language instruction already starts in grade one, the development of L2 literacy skills is delayed until grade three. Many teachers even ban foreign language print from their classroom in order not to overtax and confuse the students with two new writing systems. However, recent research has shown that this delay can lead to problems because the students form hypotheses about the spelling of English words which they cannot verify if print is banned from the classroom. After the instruction of print in grade three, the students then have to relearn the spelling of many L2 words (Diehr & Rymarczyk 2008; Rymarczyk 2008, a, b; Diehr and Rymarczyk this volume).

5. References

Burmeister, Petra (2006). Immersion und Sprachunterricht im Vergleich. In: Pienemann, Manfred; Keßler, Jörg-U. & Roos, Eckhard (eds.) (2006). *Englischerwerb in der Grundschule. Ein Studien- und Arbeitsbuch.* Paderborn: Schöningh/UTB, 197–216.

Burmeister, Petra & Pasternak, Ruth (2004). Früh und intensiv: Englische Immersion in der Grundschule am Beispiel der Claus-Rixen-Grundschule in Altenholz. In: *Fachverband Moderne Fremdsprachen fmf,* Landesverband Schleswig-Holstein (ed.) (2004), *Mitteilungsblatt August 2004,* 24–30.

Burmeister, Petra & Piske, Thorsten (2008). Schriftlichkeit im fremdsprachlichen Sachfachunterricht an der Grundschule. In: Böttger, Heiner (ed.) (2008), *Fortschritte im Frühen Fremdsprachenlernen. Ausgewählte Tagungsbeiträge Nürnberg 2007.* München: Domino, 183–193.

Diehr, Bärbel & Rymarczyk, Jutta (2008). „Ich weiß es, weil ich so spreche". Zur Basis von Lese- und Schreibversuchen in Klasse 1 und 2. *Grundschulmagazin Englisch/The Primary English Magazine,* 1, Februar/März 2008, 6–8.

Ellis, Rod (2003). *Task-based Language Learning and Teaching.* Oxford: Oxford University Press.

European Commission (ed.) (2001). *Common European Framework of Reference for Languages: Learning, Teaching, Assessment.* Cambridge: Cambridge University Press.

Genesee, Fred (1987), *Learning Through Two Languages: Studies of Immersion and Bilingual Education.* Cambridge, Mass.: Newbury House.

Genesee, Fred (2004). What do we Know about Bilingual Education for Majority-Language Students. In: Bhatia, Tej .K. & Ritchie, William (eds.) (2004). *The Handbook of Bilingualism*. Malden, MA: Blackwell, 547–576.

Grabe, William & Kaplan, Robert B. (1996). *Theory and Practice of Writing: An Applied Linguistics Perspecitive*. Harlow: Longman.

Gesellschaft für Didaktik des Sachunterrichts (ed.) (2002). *Perspektivrahmen Sachunterricht*. Kempten: Klinkhardt.

Harley, Birgit (1987). How good is their French? Fourth printing of the Special Issue "The Immersion Phenomenon", *Language and Society*, 12/1984. 55–60.

Harley, Birgit (1989). Transfer in the written compositions of French immersion students. In: Dechert, Hans W. & Raupach, Manfred (eds). *Transfer in language production*, 3–19. NY: Ablex.

Hinney, Gabriele; Huneke, Hans-Werner; Müller, Astrid & Weinhold, Swantje (2008). Definition und Messung von Rechtschreibkompetenz. *Didaktik Deutsch* 14, Sonderheft Nr. 2, 107–126.

Lepschy, Almut (2007). Yellow cows and blue horses: Kunstunterricht in der zweiten Klasse – Englisch immersiv. In: *Grundschule* 4/April 2007, 41–44.

Lyster, Roy (1987). Speaking immersion. *Canadian Modern Language Review*, 43(4), 701–17.

Lyster, Roy & Ranta, Leila (1997). Corrective feedback and learner uptake: Negotiation of form in communicative classrooms. *Studies in Second Language Acquisition, 19,* 37–66.

Peregoy, Suzanne F. & Boyle, Owen F. (^{4}2005). *Reading , Writing, and Learning in ESL. A Resource Book for K-12 Teachers*. Boston: Pearson Education.

Reichen, Jürgen (2001). *„Hannah hat Kino im Kopf": Die Reichen Methode Lesen durch Schreiben und ihre Hintergründe für Lehrerinnen und Lehrer, Studierende und Eltern*. Hamburg: Heinevetter-Verlag.

Rymarczyk, Jutta (2008). Früher oder später? Zur Einführung des Schriftbildes in der Grundschule. In: Böttger, Heiner (ed.) (2008). *Fortschritte im Frühen Fremdsprachenlernen. Ausgewählte Tagungsbeiträge Nürnberg 2007*. München: Domino, 170–182.

Rymarczyk, Jutta (2008a). „Paralleler Schriftspracherwerb in Erst- und Fremdsprache ist unmöglich!" *Take off! Zeitschrift für frühes Englischlernen* 4/2008, 48.

Rymarczyk, Jutta (2008b). Zum Umgang mit Schrift im frühen Fremdsprachenunterricht. *Take off! Zeitschrift für frühes Englischlernen* 4/2008, 49.

Swain, Merrill, & Lapkin, Sharon (1982). *Evaluating Bilingual Education: A Canadian Case Study*. Clevedon, Eng.: Multilingual Matters.

Swain, Merrill & Lapkin, Sharon (1986). Immersion French in secondary schools: "The goods" and "the bads." *Contact, 5* (3), 2–9.

Turnbull, Miles; Lapkin, Sharon & Hart, Doug (2001). Grade 3 Immersion students' performance in literacy and mathematics: province-wide results from Ontario (1998–99). *The Canadian Modern Language Review* 58, 9–26.

Weinhold, Swantje (2006). Entwicklungsverläufe im Lesen- und Schreibenlernen in Abhängigkeit verschiedener didaktischer Konzepte: Eine Longitudinalstudie 1–4. In: Weinhold, Swantje (ed.) (2006). *Schriftspracherwerb empirisch. Konzepte, Diagnostik, Entwicklung.* Baltmannsweiler: Schneider Verlag Hohengehren, 120–151.

Zaunbauer, Anna C.M.; Bonerad, Eva-Marie & Möller, Jens (2005). Muttersprachliches Leseverständnis immersiv unterrichteter Kinder. *Zeitschrift für Pädagogische Psychologie* 19, 233–235.

Zaunbauer, Anna C. M. & Möller; Jens (2006). Ein Vergleich monolingual und teilimmersiv unterrichteter Kinder der zweiten und dritten Klassenstufe. *Zeitschrift für Fremdsprachenforschung* 17, 181–200.

Zaunbauer, Anna C. M. (2007). Lesen und Schreiben in der Fremdsprache – von Anfang an. *Take off! Zeitschrift für frühes Englischlernen* 1/2007, 46.

Zaunbauer, Anna C. M. & Möller, Jens (2007). Schulleistungen monolingual und immersiv unterrichteter Kinder am Ende des ersten Schuljahres. *Zeitschrift für Entwicklungspsychologie und Pädagogische Psychologie* 39, 141–153.

Constanze Weth

„Wörter, Wendungen und Sätze so aus dem Gedächtnis schreiben, dass sie eindeutig erkennbar sind"[1]: Überlegungen zum Umgang mit Schrift im frühen Fremdsprachenunterricht

French (as well as English) orthography is regarded as difficult. French writing is hence not taught systematically in language classes at primary schools in Germany. Nevertheless, young pupils in most of the German federal states do read and write in the foreign language and may gain some insights into the relationship between spoken and written French. The curriculum in Baden-Wuerttemberg claims that after primary school and four years of French lessons, pupils 'may write short, known and often-repeated words and sentences in a recognisable way'. But how must words and sentences be written so that they can be understood by the reader? The article proposes an approach to a definition of 'recognisable' writings. It analyses first the structures of spoken and written French. It then scrutinises the writings of German and French children who are learning to write their first language, before it examines the writing of German pupils learning French as a foreign language.

1. Der Umgang mit Schrift im frühen Fremdsprachenunterricht

Das Lesen und Schreiben des Französischen stellt für Schüler und Lehrende eine Hürde dar, da im Französischen (und Englischen) offenkundig keine eindeutige Relation zwischen der Lautung und dem Schriftbild eines Wortes besteht. Lehrende beklagen, dass die Schüler im Französischen nicht, wie im Deutschen, nach Gehör schreiben könnten. Dabei wird übersehen, dass auch im Deutschen keine Eins-zu-eins-Relation zwischen Laut und Buchstaben besteht. Wie jede Orthographie repräsentieren die Buchstaben vielmehr phonologische Strukturen.[2]

---

1   Das Zitat ist dem Bildungsplan vom Ministerium für Kultus, Jugend und Sport Baden-Württemberg (MKJS 2004: 78, 92) entnommen. Die erste Seitenzahl in der Literaturangabe des Bildungsplans bezieht sich hier und im folgenden Text auf den Rahmenplan Englisch, die zweite auf die identisch lautenden Richtlinien für Französisch. Die Literaturangabe für den Bildungsplan Baden-Württemberg des Ministeriums für Kultus, Jugend und Sport 2004 werden im Folgenden immer mit (MKJS 2004) abgekürzt.
2   Im Deutschen verweist die Orthographie neben Phonemen vor allem auf die Silbenstruktur mit festem und losem Anschluss. Die Repräsentation der betonten und unbetonten Silbe im Deutschen ist vor allem durch die Schreibung von <e> in der Redukti-

Eine Besonderheit des Französischen liegt darin, dass in der Lautung nicht ausgedrückte Morpheme in der Graphie explizit sind.[3] Ohne Kenntnis dieser Funktion von einzelnen Buchstaben und Buchstabengruppen am rechten Wortrand ist das korrekte Schreiben französischer Wörter nicht möglich. Auch ein sinnvolles Erlesen eines Textes kann dann nicht gelingen, da ohne Strukturwissen die französische Orthographie undurchsichtig bleibt.

Bei regelmäßigen Hospitationen im Französischunterricht in 3. und 4. Klassen konnte ich feststellen, dass die Schüler beim Lesen von Wörtern und Sätzen deren Lautgestalt in der geschriebenen Form häufig nicht wiedererkennen. Sie entziffern die Wörter nach dem deutschen Muster und erkennen das – in der Lautung bekannte – Wort in der graphischen Form nicht oder nur durch die Wortlänge und den Anfangsbuchstaben wieder. Der linke Wortrand kann in der Tat relativ eindeutig einer Lautung zugeordnet werden, wenn man die Unterschiede zwischen der deutschen und französischen Symbolisierung beachtet (bspw. wird /u/ im Deutschen als <u>, im Französischen mit <ou> repräsentiert). Der rechte Rand ist dagegen auf der phonologischen Ebene nicht transparent. Hier werden Formen wie *il nage* und *ils nagent* homophon als /il naʒ/ artikuliert. Die Endung <-ent>, die im letzten Beispiel mit keiner Lautung korrespondiert, kann in anderen Fällen aber auch einen Nasalvokal symbolisieren (*aimablement* /ɛmabləmɑ̃/). Zudem wird ein finales <-e> meist gar nicht, wenn es mit Akut versehen ist, aber als /e/ artikuliert.

Beobachtet man das laute Lesen von Schülern im Französischunterricht, zeigen sich diese Schwierigkeiten sehr deutlich. Beim Lesen haben Dritt- und Viertklässler Schwierigkeiten, die bekannten Wörter zu rekodieren, also mit ihrem Wissen über deren Lautung abzugleichen. Die oben genannten Wörter *nage* und *nagent* werden, meiner Beobachtung nach, in verschiedenen Klassen recht willkürlich als *[na.ʒe], *[na.ʒɑ̃], *[na.gɑ̃] oder nach deutscher Akzentstruktur als *[na.gə] oder *[na.gənt] wiedergegeben. Diese Lesarten zeigen Unsicherheiten beim Rekodieren französischer Wörter auf. Sie lassen die Schüler aber auch entdecken, dass die deutsche und französische Schriftsprache unterschiedlich funktionieren.

Richtig lesen und vor allem schreiben kann auf Französisch nur derjenige, der die – in der Phonie nur wenig expliziten – grammatischen Strukturen der Äußerung analysiert und deren entsprechende graphische Form kennt (vgl. Weth im Druck). Auch für Muttersprachler ist die französische Orthographie durch den starken Bezug zur Morphologie äußerst schwierig zu lernen (David 2006; Jaffré & Brissaud 2006).

---

onssilbe abgebildet (leben [le.bən] bzw. [le.bm]; essen [ʔɛs.n]. Das zweite <e> wird nie als [e] oder [ɛ] rekodiert). Vgl. dazu Maas (1992, 2006), Eisenberg (1995).

3 Wie bspw. das finale <-s>, das nominale und adjektivale Pluralformen anzeigt (*chaise – chaises* ‚Stuhl – Stühle').

Im Fremdsprachenunterricht muss die orthographische Struktur des Französischen aber nicht hinderlich, sondern kann sogar hilfreich sein. Sie verdeutlicht den Lernern die – ihnen noch unbekannten – Sprachstrukturen. Eine solche Vorgehensweise geht davon aus, dass auch Grundschulkinder eine Fremdsprache anders erwerben als ihre Erstsprache. Sie geht zudem davon aus, dass alle Kinder in der Grundschule Schreiben und Lesen lernen und dadurch beginnen, Sprachstrukturen zu reflektieren (McBride-Chang 2004; Siebert-Ott 2008; Sprenger-Charolles 2004; Tannen 1982).

Obwohl es mittlerweile umfangreiche Literatur zum Fremdsprachenlernen in der Grundschule gibt (Grau & Legutke 2008; Kierepka, Klein & Krüger 2007) und obwohl Schrifterwerb in der Zweitsprache ein wichtiges Thema in der Schrifterwerbsforschung darstellt (Apeltauer 2007; Ehlers 2006; Maas & Mehlem 2003), gibt es bisher noch keine umfassende Untersuchung zum Lesen und Schreiben in der Fremdsprache der Primarstufe.[4]

Dieser Artikel setzt bei einer im Bildungsplan Baden-Württemberg 2004 formulierten Kompetenzbeschreibung der Fertigkeit Schreiben in der vierten Klasse an. Er versucht zu analysieren, was es bedeutet, wenn Kinder „kurze, bekannte und sehr häufig wiederkehrende [französische] Wörter, Wendungen und Sätze so aus dem Gedächtnis schreiben, dass sie eindeutig erkennbar sind" (MKJS 2004: 78, 92). Wie müssen die Schreibungen beschaffen sein, damit jemand anders – oder der Schreiber selbst etwas zeitversetzt – diese dekodieren und verstehen kann?

Der Beitrag ist folgendermaßen aufgebaut: Er beleuchtet zunächst die curricularen Vorgaben für den frühen Fremdsprachenunterricht in Baden-Württemberg (2). Um sich einem Verständnis anzunähern, was „erkennbare" Schülerschreibungen ausmacht, werden danach die Strukturen der gesprochenen und geschriebenen Sprache Französisch betrachtet (3), anschließend die geschriebenen Lernervarietäten von Schülern mit Französisch und Deutsch als Erstsprache (4) und von Schülern mit Französisch als Fremdsprache (5). Anhand von Schriftbeispielen von Viertklässlern wird eine Analysemöglichkeit vorgestellt, die sich einer Definition von „erkennbaren" Schülerschreibungen annähert (6). Abschließend werden die dargelegten Punkte diskutiert (7).

2. Curriculare Vorgaben für den Fremdsprachenunterricht am Beispiel des Bildungsplans in Baden-Württemberg (MKJS 2004)

Seit die Fremdsprachen in den 1990er Jahren flächendeckend in den Grundschulen Europas Eingang gefunden haben, stellen die Bildungspläne der Länder in

---

[4] Einzelne Artikel sind veröffentlicht von Mertens (2002a, b) und Rymarczyk (2008).

Deutschland, in Einklang mit dem Gemeinsamen Europäischen Referenzrahmen, die mündliche Kommunikation und ganzheitliches Lernen in den Vordergrund. In den Bildungsplänen der Länder Nordrhein-Westfalen, Rheinland-Pfalz und Baden-Württemberg ist das Lesen und Schreiben in der Fremdsprache zwar in den Kompetenzbeschreibungen ausgewiesen, ein didaktischer Zugang zur Auseinandersetzung damit ist aber nur rudimentär gegeben oder fehlt völlig (vgl. Rymarczyk 2008: 171). Für das Land Baden-Württemberg beispielsweise lauten die Richtlinien für den Fremdsprachenunterricht im seit 2003/2004 gültigen Bildungsplan folgendermaßen: Im Fremdsprachenunterricht sollen Interaktion und Kommunikation in der Fremdsprache zu einer „genuin positiven Haltung gegenüber der Sprache" führen. In den ersten beiden Klassen steht das „reflektierte Erleben" von Sprache im Vordergrund. Dieses hat zum Ziel, den Kindern „einen Willen [zu vermitteln], sich in der Muttersprache und in der Zielsprache angemessen verständigen zu können" (MKJS 2004: 68, 82). Die Kompetenzerwartung am Ende der zweiten Klasse ist auf das Verstehen mündlich dargebotener einzelner Wörter und Wendungen unter Bezug auf Situation und Kontext ausgerichtet. In Klasse drei und vier sollen die Schüler die Kompetenz erlangen, „Sprachstrukturen aus der Situation herauszulösen und situationsunabhängiges Sprachwissen aufzubauen" (MKJS 2004: 68, 82). Zeitgleich beginnen sie, in der Fremdsprache zu lesen und zu schreiben. Mit Unterstützung kontextueller Hilfen sollen die Kinder schließlich „kürzere beschreibende und erzählende Texte sowie Korrespondenztexte aus ihrer Erfahrungswelt und bekannten Themenfeldern [lesen], die hauptsächlich aus einfachen sprachlichen Mitteln bestehen." Zudem beginnen sie, „[...] nach schriftsprachlichen Regelhaftigkeiten in der Zielsprache zu suchen, diese auszuprobieren und zu modifizieren" (MKJS 2004: 70, 84). Am Ende von Klasse 4 sind die Kinder laut Bildungsplan schließlich befähigt, in einem kurzen Text Wörter, Wendungen und kurze Texte wiederzuerkennen und auch mündlich wiederzugeben, also den groben Textverlauf und die Hauptaussagen zu verstehen (MKJS 2004: 78, 92). Im Kompetenzbereich Schreiben sind sie in der Lage, „kurze, bekannte und sehr häufig wiederkehrende Wörter, Wendungen und Sätze so aus dem Gedächtnis [zu] schreiben, dass sie eindeutig erkennbar sind". Mit ihren schriftsprachlichen Mitteln können sie „Postkarten, kürzere Briefe oder E-Mails zur Kontaktaufnahme schreiben" (MKJS 2004: 78, 92).

Der Bildungsplan formuliert also eine Schreibkompetenz, die über die Schreibung einzelner Wörter und einfacher Sätze hinausgeht und das Produzieren von Texten zum Ziel hat. Der Bildungsplan weist ebenfalls explizit darauf hin, dass die orthographische Systematik der Fremdsprachen erst in der Sekundarstufe eingeführt wird (MKJS 2004: 71, 85). Er postuliert, dass Verständlichkeit der orthographischen und grammatischen Korrektheit vorausgeht (MKJS 2004: 71, 85) und markiert damit diese beiden Bereiche als nachrangig. Zwar geht der Bildungsplan von einem grundsätzlichen Interesse von Kindern an Schrift aus. Danach beginnen sie ab Klasse 3 „nach schriftsprachlichen Regelhaftigkeiten der Zielsprache zu suchen, diese auszuprobieren und zu modifizieren" (MKJS 2004: 71, 84). Er führt aber nicht aus, auf welcher Basis Kinder zunächst eigene Regeln für die Schreibung der Fremdsprache konstruieren und die Regelhaftigkeiten der französischen Orthographie entdecken (vgl. Rymarczyk 2008: 172).

Die wenigsten Grundschüler erreichen am Ende der vierten Klasse die im Bildungsplan beschriebenen Kompetenzen. Grund dafür ist meines Erachtens nicht in erster Linie eine grundlegende Überforderung der Kinder, sondern eine fehlende didaktische Methodik für den Zugang zur französischen (bzw. englischen) Schriftsprache.

Denn wenn man die im Bildungsplan Baden-Württemberg aufgeführten Kompetenzerwartungen für das Lesen und Schreiben in der vierten Klasse genauer betrachtet, zeigt sich, dass sich diese letztlich nur auf das Erkennen und Reproduzieren von Schriftbildern beschränken. Anstatt Strukturwissen aufzubauen, sollen die Schüler in der Fremdsprachen „bekannte Wendungen, Wörter und Wortanteile *wiedererkennend* zum Kontext in Beziehung setzen [und ...] in schriftlichen Texten einfache Textsortenmerkmale und Gliederungsmerkmale *erkennen*, deuten und zum Textverstehen nutzen" (MKJS 2004: 77, 91. Hervorhebung CW). Um didaktische Methodiken zu erstellen, die aufzeigen, wie Lehrende das „Erkennen" von strukturellen Unterschieden des Deutschen und der neu erlernten Sprache im Unterricht produktiv aufgreifen oder initiieren können, ist das theoretische Wissen über die jeweilige Orthographie grundlegend. Ohne dessen Kenntnis sind die Regularitäten der jeweiligen Schriftsysteme nicht transparent.

3. Strukturen der gesprochenen und geschriebenen Sprache im Französischen und Deutschen sowie ihre Verschriftung

Rymarczyk (2008) hat für das Englische gezeigt, dass Kinder am Ende des zweiten Lernjahres (2. Klasse) in der Lage sind, einzelne Lexeme oder kurze Ausdrücke auf Englisch zu schreiben. Aufgefordert durch die Frage, welche englischen Wörter die Kinder kennen und ob sie sie schon schreiben können, haben die Kinder in den vier Untersuchungsklassen durchschnittlich zwischen 16,7 und 22 Wörter verschriftet. Die meisten dieser Schreibungen waren nach normativen Kriterien nicht korrekt geschrieben, einige Kinder schrieben aber bis zur Hälfte der Items korrekt entsprechend dem Standard (Rymarczyk 2008: 175). Darüber hinaus entdeckte Rymarczyk in den normativ nicht korrekten Schreibungen Regelhaftigkeiten, die sie als „Eigenregel" bezeichnet. Als systematisch wertete sie diese, wenn ein Kind diese Regel mindestens zwei Mal angewendet hatte. Diese Regularitäten entlehnten die Kinder häufig den Regeln der deutschen Rechtschreibung. So repräsentierten sie ein Phonem des Englischen und Deutschen mit deutschem Graphem (/f/ à <v>). Die Texte enthielten Großschreibungen von Nomen, für das Deutsche typische Buchstaben wie Umlaute <ü> und eine Reihe von Schreibungen zur Repräsentation von Auslautverhärtung, Dehnung und Schärfung. Weiterhin näherten sich die Schüler englischen Phonemen, die keine Entsprechung im Deutschen haben (bspw. /θ/), mit Hilfe deutscher Grapheme an (Rymarczyk 2008: 177–178). Diese Strategien sind typisch für Kinder, die in zwei Sprachen alphabetisiert werden.[5] Mehrsprachige Kinder beziehen sich auf die ihnen bekannte Schriftsprache noch stärker, wenn es ihr einziges schriftliches Referenzsystem ist. Das zeigt sich, wenn sie ihre (nicht verschriftete oder im Umfeld der Kinder nicht geschriebene) Familiensprache spontan schreiben (Maas & Mehlem 2003; Weth 2008). In den Schreibungen mehrsprachiger Kinder zeigt sich – neben den Sprachkenntnissen der verschrifteten Familien- oder Fremdsprache – welchen Zugang sie zu den orthographischen Strukturen der Schulsprache haben (Weth 2008: 282). Denn nur wenn ihnen die orthographischen Strukturen dieser Sprache vertraut sind, können sie auf deren Systematik zurückgreifen, um die Familien- oder Fremdsprache zu verschriften.

Um zu verstehen, wie Schüler mit der französischen Schrift beim Lesen und Schreiben umgehen, soll nun nachvollzogen werden, wie das gesprochene und geschriebene Französisch im Kontrast zum Deutschen strukturiert ist.

Die gesprochene und geschriebene Sprache sind, einzelsprachenübergreifend, durch zwei verschiedene Medien abgebildet und dadurch unterschiedlich strukturiert. Das akustische Medium der gesprochenen Sprache besteht aus einem über Schallwellen transportierten Lautkontinuum, ist durch Rhythmus, Akzent und Intonation strukturiert und durch vielfältige Variation in den individuellen und regionalen Sprechweisen charakterisiert. Diese Aspekte der gesprochenen Sprache werden im visuellen Medium der Schrift nicht repräsentiert. Alphabetische Schriften sind also keine Abbildung der gesprochenen Sprache, sondern sind in den regelhaften einzelsprachlichen Strukturen derselben „fundiert"[6]. Durch die Aneinanderreihung von Buchstaben, die Wortausgliederung und die Kon-

---

5 Zum Türkischen vgl. Reich (2002), zum doppelten Schrifterwerb von Französisch und Okzitanisch vgl. Weth (2008: 255–262). In den okzitanischen und französischen Schülerschreibungen ließen sich Strategien der Konvergenz und Divergenz zwischen den beiden in der Schule gelernten Sprachen ausmachen. Die zweisprachig alphabetisierten Kinder haben in ihren Texten orthographische Mittel eingesetzt, um ihre Texte graphisch als ‚Okzitanisch' oder ‚Französisch' zu markieren (Weth 2008: 204).
6 Zu dem Begriff „fundieren" vgl. Maas (1992). Er spricht von der *Fundierung* orthographischer Formen in den phonologischen Verhältnissen der gesprochenen Sprache.

stantschreibungen stellt geschriebene Sprache phonologische, morphologische und syntaktische Strukturen dar. Deutlich wird dies, wenn Expertenleser nicht existierende Nonsens-Wörter lesen. Die im Deutschen möglichen, aber nicht existierenden Wörter *knopke, schrommel* und *quope* werden Expertenleser aller Voraussicht nach als /ˈknɔp.kə/, /ˈʃʀɔm̩əl/ und /ˈkvo.pə/ erlesen. Wäre das Nonsens-Wort *quope* ein französisches Wort, hätten frankophone Leser es wohl ohne zu zögern als /ˈkɔp/ artikuliert. Die unterschiedlichen Lesarten referieren auf die verschiedenen Fundierungen der französischen und deutschen Orthographie im jeweiligen Sprachsystem. Im Deutschen wird durch das finale <-e> bzw. <-el>, <-en>, <-er> die prosodische Struktur mehrsilbiger Wörter angezeigt. Das prosodische Grundmuster des Deutschen ist der Trochäus, bestehend aus zwei Silben mit akzentuierter und Reduktionssilbe (bspw. *Flügel, Reisen, Kater*). Die erste Silbe des Wortes *quope* ist dabei „lose" an die Reduktionssilbe angeschlossen, während die Vokale der ersten Silbe der Wörter *knopke* und *schrommel* „fest" an den folgenden Vokal angeschlossen sind (Maas 1992; Röber 2009). Im Französischen als silbenzählender Sprache spielt der Akzent bei der orthographischen Repräsentation von Wörtern keine Rolle. Das finale <-e> verweist bei der französischen Lesart von *quope* darauf, dass der finale Konsonant artikuliert wird. Hieße das Wort *quopes*, handelte es sich sehr wahrscheinlich um die Pluralform eines Nomen oder Adjektiv. Läse man *quopent*, würde man davon ausgehen, die dritte Person Plural des Verbs *quoper* vor sich zu haben. Die lautliche Realisierung aller flektierten Formen wäre allerdings dieselbe: /ˈkɔp/.

Die regelhaften Strukturen der französischen Orthographie beziehen sich vor allem auf die phonologische, morphologische und lexikalische Struktur (vgl. Catach 1992; Meisenburg 1996). Sie symbolisieren die gesprochene Sprache sehr regelhaft, geben also viele Hinweise, wie das geschriebene Medium in den gesprochenen Code „rekodiert" (Neef 2005) werden muss. Catach (1992) hat dies anhand ihrer Analyse der französischen Orthographie als plurales System dargestellt. Darin symbolisieren bestimmte Grapheme („Phonogramme") einzelne Phoneme, z. B. repräsentiert <r> /ʀ/ oder <on> /ɔ̃/. Kaum mit der Lautung korrespondieren die „Morphogramme". Sie symbolisieren als Stammschreibungen konstant lexikalische Morpheme und Derivationsmorpheme. Die Darstellung von Flexionsendungen bleibt fast ausschließlich auf den graphischen Code beschränkt und hat kaum eine Entsprechung in der Lautung. Hierauf bezieht sich der Begriff *orthographe grammaticale* (Argod-Dutard 1996). „Logogramme" dienen schließlich vor allem der Homonymendifferenzierung und verleihen dem Wort in seiner graphischen Gestalt eine spezifische Physiognomie. Die Eindeutigkeit in der Schreibung hat zur Folge, dass die französische Orthographie die Sprachstruktur sehr deutlich und differenziert abbildet und den Leser somit unterstützt, den Text schnell erfassen zu können. Eine Ableitung von der Lautung zur graphischen Form ist umgekehrt dagegen häufig nicht möglich. Denn lautliche Korrespondenzen sind oft durch den graphischen Kontext mitbestimmt. Da zudem viele Buchstaben für nicht-lautliche Informationen genutzt werden, ist das Kodieren, das Schreiben des Französischen, mit einem hohen grammatischen Strukturwissen verbunden.

Die Nutzung von Schrift im Fremdsprachenunterricht – zumal an den Grundschulen – ist nicht mit einer normativen Sicht auf orthographische Schreibungen zu verwechseln. Letztere betrachtet Orthographie als die normativ gesetzte Recht-Schreibung von Wörtern. Diese werden im traditionellen Unterricht durch häufige Wiederholung geübt, abgefragt und ihre Schreibung als richtig oder falsch bewertet (David 2006). Setzt man sich im Unterricht dagegen mit Schriftstrukturen auseinander, um regelhafte Sprachstrukturen zu verdeutlichen, kann man von der verhältnismäßig geringen Anzahl an Schreibungen, die im Kontext des gegenwärtigen Französisch nicht nachvollziehbar sind, absehen. Überlegt werden muss stattdessen, wie Grundschüler erstens methodisch an die orthographischen Formen des Französischen herangeführt werden, um sie erlesen zu können. Weiterhin bedarf es einer Reflexion darüber, wie mit aus normativer Sicht nicht korrekten Schülerschreibungen umgegangen wird.[7]

4. Geschriebene Lernervarietäten des Französischen und Deutschen als Erstsprache

Die Nonsens-Wörter des vorigen Kapitels haben gezeigt, dass die Beschreibung von Orthographie als eine Laut-Buchstaben-Zuordnung verfehlt ist. Wortschreibungen des Deutschen wie des Französischen stellen dagegen ein weitgehend regelhaftes System dar, dessen Funktion es ist, Lesern das schnelle Dekodieren eines Textes zu ermöglichen. Expertenleser haben dafür das Wissen über die Zeichenfunktion von Buchstaben und Buchstabengruppen als in Silben strukturierte Abfolgen von Konsonanten und Vokalen erworben (Fayol & Jaffré 2008; Maas 1992; Röber 2009). Darüber hinaus haben sie die orthographischen Strukturen gelernt und automatisiert, die keinen Bezug in der gesprochenen Sprache haben.

Kinder lernen spätestens ab Schulbeginn Schreiben und Lesen in der Schulsprache. Wie schnell der Lernprozess voranschreitet ist individuell verschieden. Allen Kindern hingegen ist gemeinsam, dass sie nicht von Beginn an normativ korrekt schreiben, sondern Lernervarietäten ausbilden. Diese Schreibungen

---

7 Zur Diskussion der Regelhaftigkeit der französischen Orthographie und den Lernervarietäten siehe Catach (1973); Fayol (1997); Fayol & Schneuwly (1987); Jaffré & Bessonnat (1996); Rieben, Fayol & Perfetti (1997). Didaktisch umgesetzt sind diese theoretischen Analysen in Ducard, Honvault & Jaffré (1995a, b).

von Grundschülern spiegeln die Auseinandersetzung zwischen den prosodischen Strukturen der Sprache und deren Repräsentation durch das Schriftsystem sehr deutlich. Ganz kurz soll dies an der Kategorie des Wortes verdeutlicht werden. In Untersuchungen mit Erstklässlern wurde nachgewiesen, dass das Wort als zentrale Einheit der Schrift vorschulischen Kindern zwar ein Begriff ist, dass sie aber noch keinen Zugang zur Identifikation von Wörtern in der Äußerung haben. Röber-Siekmeyer (1997: 128; vgl. Röber 2009: 69–71) zeigte, dass die Kinder kaum Möglichkeiten haben, Wörter in größeren Zusammenhängen auszugliedern. So nehmen Kinder ihren Vor- und Zunamen häufig als „ungegliederte Einheit" wahr und bezeichnen beide als ein Wort. Diese Aussagen der Kinder finden sich in ihren ersten Schreibungen wieder, denn darin nehmen sie zunächst gar keine Wortabtrennung vor. Auch nachdem sie die Konvention der Wortgrenzen entdeckt haben, segmentieren sie die Grapheme weiterhin nach der Struktur der gesprochenen Sprache. Röber-Siekmeyer (1998: 130) beschreibt die ersten Kriterien der Ausgliederung von graphischen Elementen in deutschen Erstschreibungen folgendermaßen:

Offensichtlich orientieren sich die ersten Segmentierungen, die Kinder auf dem Weg vom Ungegliederten zu korrekten Wortabtrennungen vornehmen, an dem Rhythmus der Betonungen im Satz, der mit der silbischen Gliederung verbunden ist. Den Wechsel zwischen Betont und Unbetont, den die Kinder wahrzunehmen scheinen, binden sie an die Einheit Wort: Als Wörter werden nur betonte Elemente wahrgenommen, unbetonte werden wie Silben behandelt und den betonten angehängt [...].

Im Deutschen und Französischen sind die Probleme der Verschriftung ähnlich im Hinblick darauf, dass Schreiblerner sich an der prosodischen Struktur orientieren. Unterschiede ergeben sich durch die prosodischen Unterschiede der beiden Einzelsprachen und die jeweils unterschiedliche orthographische Repräsentation. Die deutsche Orthographie lässt sich im Hinblick auf das trochäische Akzentmuster des Deutschen interpretieren. Die französische Orthographie reflektiert die in Phrasen strukturierten Intonationseinheiten, die durch den Hauptakzent auf der letzten Silbe markiert werden sowie die prosodischen Phänomene von *Liaison, Enchaînement* und *Elision*. Die drei letztgenannten Phänomene beziehen sich alle auf vokalisch anlautende Wörter, die in einer größeren Äußerung den letzten Konsonanten des vorausgehenden Wortes als Anfangsrand erhalten (vgl. Meisenburg & Selig 1998). Beispiele sind *les amis* /le.za.mi/, *une amie* /y.na.mi/ und *l'amie* /la.mi/. Nach der Norm fehlerhafte Zusammenschreibungen entstehen vor allem bei der Verschriftung von Proklitika, deren vokalischer Kern vor einer vokalisch anlautenden Basis getilgt wird. Lautlich verschmilzt in dem Beispiel *viens t'assoir* /vjɛ̃.ta.swaʁ/ (‚setz dich her' komm - 2. Pers. Sing. Pron-2. Pers. Sing. setzen-INF) das Pronomen mit der Basis. Diese prosodische Struktur spiegelt sich auch in der orthographischen Form, da hier das <-e> der vollständigen Form *te* (‚dich') wegfällt. Die enge Verbindung zwischen Klitikon und Basis wird zudem durch das Apostroph – anstatt eines Spatiums – ausgedrückt. In einem Beispiel aus Sabio (2000: 119) schreibt ein Kind die Äußerung als <vient tassoir>. Fehlerhafte Getrenntschreibungen entstehen zudem durch Hyperkorrekturen desselben Phänomens. Hier wird dann der initiale Buchstabe von Wörtern – nach dem Muster von mit der Basis verschmolzenen Proklitika – mit Apostroph vom Wort abgetrennt. Ein Beispiel dafür ist die Kinderschreibung <le loup ne s'avé pas> (*le loup ne savait pas* ‚der Wolf wusste nicht') aus Sabio (2000: 119). Die beiden französischen Beispiele zeigen, dass die Endungen im französischen Schrifterwerb eine weitere Schwierigkeit darstellen (vgl. Guyon 2003).

5. Geschriebene Lernervarietäten des Französischen als Fremdsprache

Der Fremdsprachenunterricht in der Grundschule kann darauf aufbauen, dass die Schüler auf Deutsch schreiben und lesen lernen. Durch das Erlernen von Schriftstrukturen lernen sie, Sprachstrukturen zu reflektieren. Das Wissen über die Strukturierung von Schriftsprache lässt sich schließlich auf andere Sprachen übertragen (Maas & Mehlem 2003). Sprachspezifische schriftstrukturelle Symbolisierungen können Kinder aber nicht erfassen, wenn ihnen – wie in den ersten beiden Jahren des Fremdsprachenunterrichts – orthographische Repräsentationen der Fremdsprache vorenthalten werden (Rymarczyk 2008: 180) und wenn ihnen keine Unterstützung darin geboten wird, die Bezüge zwischen der graphischen und der phonischen Form von Wörtern nachzuvollziehen. Kinder können die orthographische Systematik ebenfalls nicht erfassen, wenn im Unterricht (wie das im Fremdsprachenunterricht häufig der Fall ist) nur mit Wortkarten gearbeitet wird. Diese logographische Darbietung bietet den Kindern nur charakteristische Merkmale des jeweils spezifischen Wortes an, wie die Wortlänge, einzelne Buchstaben und den situativen Kontext. Sie vermittelt ihnen aber keine weitergehende Systematik.

Die Voraussetzungen des Schrifterwerbs in der Fremdsprache unterscheiden sich von dem in der Erstsprache wesentlich dadurch, dass die Schüler schon begonnen haben, schreiben und lesen zu lernen. Sie wissen um die verschiedenen Strukturierungsformen gesprochener und geschriebener Sprache und haben – mit individuellen Unterschieden und Unterschieden in der Didaktik, mit der sie Lesen und Schreiben lernen – ein Wissen über orthographische Repräsentationen des Deutschen. Ein weiterer Unterschied ist die Sprachkompetenz. Anders als Lerner, die in ihrer Erstsprache alphabetisiert werden, müssen Fremdsprachenlerner zugleich zur schriftlichen Repräsentation auch die durch sie dargestellte Sprachstruktur lernen. Darüber hinaus unterscheiden sich die Erwartungen an die Schriftkompetenz in der Schul- und der Fremdsprache. Orthographische Korrektheit hat im Sprachenlernen der nationalen Schulsprache (in Frankreich Französisch, in Deutschland Deutsch) einen anderen Stellenwert als im Fremdsprachenunterricht. Im Fremdsprachenunterricht der Grundschule ist sie noch völlig unerheblich.

Dennoch lesen und schreiben Grundschüler in der Fremdsprache; in Baden-Württemberg ab der dritten Klasse. Entsprechend den Kompetenzbeschreibungen im Bildungsplan von Baden-Württemberg schreiben die Schüler am Ende der 4. Klasse „kurze, bekannte und sehr häufig wiederkehrende Wörter, Wendungen und Sätze so aus dem Gedächtnis [...], dass sie eindeutig erkennbar sind" (MKJS 2004: 78, 92). Was bedeutet aber nun „eindeutig erkennbar"?

6. Erkennbare Schülerschreibungen: die mögliche Rekodierung nach den Systematiken der deutschen und/oder französischen Orthographie und die Entsprechung der phonischen und graphischen Wortstruktur

Im Sommer 2009 begann ich eine noch nicht abgeschlossene Pilotstudie, die die Schreibstrategien von Viertklässlern in sechs Freiburger Grundschulklassen untersucht. Die Erhebung beinhaltet u. a. ein Wortdiktat auf Französisch (selbst erstellt, nicht standardisiert) und ein Wortdiktat auf Deutsch (HSP 4/5)[8], das im Juli 2009 erhoben wurde. Alle beteiligten Schüler (N=96) lernen seit der ersten Klasse Französisch. An dieser Stelle soll nur ein kleiner Teil der Studie vorgestellt werden: die vor der Auswertung zu definierende Frage, wie die nach normativen Gesichtspunkten nicht korrekten Schülerschreibungen interpretiert werden können. Wann erfüllen sie das im Bildungsplan formulierte Kriterium „eindeutig erkennbar" zu sein? Rymarczyk (2008: 175) zeigt in einer Studie über die englischen Schreibungen von Zweitklässlern, dass „einzelne Wörter in den Daten auch nur erkennbar [waren], wenn man sie laut gelesen hat". Zudem konnten etliche Lexeme nur „entziffert werden, weil die Kinder sie (dankenswerterweise!) in semantischen Feldern notiert hatten". Ohne kontextuelle Hilfe blieb aber manches „einfach verschlossen".

Die Erhebung in den Freiburger vierten Klassen zeigte, dass auch hier nur ein kleiner Teil der französischen Schreibungen richtig ist. Welche nach normativer Perspektive nicht korrekten Wörter sind aber „eindeutig erkennbar"? Und nach welchen Kriterien lässt sich „Erkennbarkeit" definieren? Im Folgenden werden

---

8   Es handelt sich um den standardisierten Test der *Hamburger Schreibprobe*. Vgl. May, Malitzky & Vieluf (2001).

für diese Überlegungen an zwei Wortschreibungen von fünf Viertklässlern betrachtet, die diese Wörter (u. a.) im November 2008 und im Juli 2009 geschrieben haben. Ohne didaktische Hinführung haben die Schüler am Ende der Grundschulzeit mit großer Wahrscheinlichkeit noch keine systematischen Bezüge der orthographischen Darstellung und morphologischen oder lexikalischen Strukturen erfasst. Deswegen fokussiert die Analyse der Schülerschreibungen die Repräsentation phonologischer Strukturen. Für die Auswertung wurde festgelegt, dass eindeutig erkennbar geschriebene Wörter 1. der Wortstruktur entsprechen müssen. Sie müssen 2. nach den Systematiken der deutschen und/oder französischen Orthographie rekodiert werden können. Im Folgenden sollen beide Teile dieser heuristischen Setzung erläutert werden.

Die phonologische Struktur von Wörtern lässt sich noch stärker schematisieren, wenn man sie als in Silben gegliederte Abfolge von Konsonanten (C) und Vokalen (V) darstellt. Approximanten werden als (A) symbolisiert (vgl. Ziegler & Ferrand 1998). Die verschiedenen Strukturebenen der beiden hier betrachteten Wörter *garçon* und *fille* (diktiert wurden *le garçon* und *la fille*) sind in Tabelle 1 dargestellt.

Orthograpische Struktur	Wortstruktur	phonologische Struktur
garçon	CVC.CV	/garsɔ̃/
fille	CVA	/fij/

Tabelle 1: Wortstruktur und phonologische Struktur der Wörter „garçon" und „fille".

Die fünf betrachteten Kinder haben in ihren Schreibungen die Wortstruktur der Lexeme unterschiedlich häufig vollständig und korrekt repräsentiert. Die Wortstruktur von *garçon* haben alle Kinder zu beiden Erhebungszeitpunkten richtig wiedergegeben (Tabelle 2).

Schüler/Schülerin	t1, November 2008	t2, Juli 2009
Hayat	garsons	Garson
Kilian	Garco	gârcon
Nicla	garson	garson
Noé	garson	garcon
Nour	garson	garcon

Tabelle 2: Schülerschreibungen von „garçon"

Alle in Tabelle 2 aufgelisteten Schreibungen sind erkenn-, also lesbar. Unerheblich ist bei der Betrachtung der Wortstruktur die graphische Unterscheidung zwischen Oral- und Nasalvokal. Nicht beachtet wird auch die Verschriftung des medialen /-s-/ als <-s-> oder <-c->. Auch unter Gesichtspunkten der phonologischen Struktur ist die Schriftstruktur der Formen – abgesehen von der Majuskelschreibung – in allen Fällen sehr Französisch. Ohne dies im Unterricht gelernt zu haben, schreiben in der ersten Erhebung fast alle und in der zweiten Erhebung alle Kinder den wortfinalen Nasal mit Vokalbuchstaben und Nasalkonsonant. Im Fall des Beispiels *garçon* wählen sie zudem die normativ korrekten Buchstaben <on>. Auch in anderen Wörtern (*magasin, pantalon*) verschrifteten die Kinder einen Großteil der Nasale mit <Vn>. Allerdings variierten in diesen Schreibungen die Vokalbuchstaben zwischen <a, o, i, e>. Hayat versah ihre erste Schreibung von *garçon* mit einem finalen <-s>. Dieses wertete ich nicht als Teil der phonologischen Wortstruktur, sondern als im Französischen häufig auftretende morphologische Form, die in der phonologischen Struktur keine Entsprechung hat.[9] Sie trägt in der Schülerschreibung keine Bedeutung und kann wahrscheinlich als emblematische Form für das französische Erscheinungsbild interpretiert werden. Auf die gleiche Strategie zurückführen lassen sich Buchstabenformen, auf die einige Kinder zum zweiten Erhebungszeitpunkt zurückgreifen. Sie sind stark französisch konnotiert und würden in der deutschen Orthographie nicht in dieser Weise funktionieren. Dazu gehört sowohl die Schreibung mit Zirkumflex <gârcon> als auch die Verschriftung mit <c> anstatt <s> – wenn auch noch ohne Cédille.

Die Verschriftung des Lexems *fille* ist durch die Schwierigkeit des finalen Approximanten uneinheitlicher ausgefallen. Die realisierten Formen sind in Tabelle 3 aufgelistet.

Schüler/Schülerin	t1, November 2008	t2, Juli 2009
Hayat	fie	fie
Kilian	Fihe	fille
Nicla	vil	Fih
Noé	fie	fie
Nour	fiele	fiel

Tabelle 3: Schülerschreibungen von „fille"

---

9   Die Pluralmarkierung <-s> wird nur vor einem folgenden, vokalisch anlautenden Wort, also im Fall von Liaison, als /z/ artikuliert.

Sind auch in Tabelle 3 alle Formen erkennbar? Die Schüler greifen bei den Verschriftungen von *fille* deutlich auf orthographische Muster des Französischen und des Deutschen zurück. Als deutsches Muster des Wortanfangs kann die Majuskelschreibung definiert werden sowie die Verwendung von <v->, das im Deutschen auch als der stimmlose Frikativ /f/ realisiert werden kann. Auffällig sind die häufigen Schreibungen des Vokals als <ie>, welche im Deutschen regelhaft ein langes /iː/ repräsentiert. Die Verwendung von <ie> könnte auf die Schwierigkeit der Perzeption des vorderen Approximanten /j/ zurückgehen, dem der Vokal /i/ zugrunde liegt. Die Schüler hätten somit die diktierte Form als /fiː/ und nicht als /fij/ wahrgenommen. Dafür spricht, dass Noé und Hayat diese Schreibung zu beiden Erhebungszeitpunkten wählen. Die anderen Schüler verwenden nach dem <i> oder <ie> einen Konsonantenbuchstaben. Die Schreibung von <h> oder <l> lässt sich möglicherweise dadurch erklären, dass beide Ähnlichkeiten mit dem Approximanten haben. <l> repräsentiert isoliert den alveolar gebildeten Sonoranten /l/, der in relativer Nähe zu dem palatal gebildeten /j/ liegt. Relativ ähnlich sind beide Artikulationsstellen besonders durch die Koartikulation des vorangehenden /i/ in /fij/. Da die Schüler mir einige Wochen nach dem Diktat ihre geschriebenen Formen vorgelesen haben, ist gesichert, dass die französische Schreibung nicht der deutschen Verbform *fiel* entspricht. <h> symbolisiert den glottal gebildeten Frikativ. Die Engebildung und Reibung der durchströmenden Luft hat /h/ mit dem Approximanten gemein. Zudem zeigen die durch Koartikulation gebildeten unterschiedlichen Artikulationsstellen von /h/ in *Hase, Hose* und *Hüte* die (im Kontext mit dem hohen vorderen Vokal /i/) relative Ähnlichkeit mit dem Approximanten.[10]

Eine Schreibung aus dem kleinen Korpus ist auch nach normativen Kriterien korrekt. Ob diese Korrektschreibung durch die Memorisierung des Wortes erfolgt ist oder ob der Schüler die Systematik der Darstellung von /j/ als <-lle> analysiert hat, kann erst nach der Auswertung des gesamten Korpus der hier vorgestellten Studie beantwortet werden. Die Schreibungen <Fihe> und <file> entsprechen der Wortstruktur von /fij/ dann, wenn man davon ausgeht, dass die Schreibung des finalen <-e> nach französischer Systematik die Funktion hat, den vorausgehenden Konsonanten zu artikulieren. Dies gilt zumindest für <Fihe>. Die Buchstabenfolge <file> entspräche im Französischen dagegen der Lautung /fil/. Möglich ist bei dieser Form der Verschriftung, dass das <-e> nur zur Markierung des Französischen geschrieben worden ist. Weiterhin kann es sein, dass die Schülerin Nour das Wortbild *fille* ganz oder teilweise memorisiert und während des Diktats ein <l> vergessen hat.

---

10 Es handelt sich bei diesen Interpretationen der Schülerschreibungen von <l> und <h> natürlich nur um Vermutungen, die in einem Experiment überprüft werden müssten.

7. Diskussion

Die nicht auflösbaren Interpretationen der obigen Schreibungen zeigen die komplexen orthographischen Bezüge von Schreibanfängern. Anders als einsprachige Schreibanfänger beziehen sich die Schreibungen in der Fremdsprache nicht nur auf die prosodischen Strukturen des Deutschen, sondern auf die prosodischen Strukturen und orthographischen Konventionen des Deutschen und Französischen. Im Fall mehrsprachiger Schüler sind die Bezüge noch komplexer. Eine Analyse von Schülerschreibungen kann deshalb immer nur eine aus Interpretationen geschlossene Annäherung an die Schreibstrategien darstellen. Bei einem großen Datenkorpus lassen sich aber durch quantitative Analyse Tendenzen in den Schreibungen ausmachen und durch die Analyse der Daten im Hinblick auf die gesprochenen Sprachsysteme und deren orthographischen Repräsentationen Strategien der Schüler ableiten.

Ohne eine solche Analyse über die „Erkennbarkeit" von Schreibungen zu entscheiden, ist hochgradig kontextabhängig und unterliegt den orthographischen Kenntnissen des Lesers in den Sprachen, die dem Schreibanfänger als Bezüge dienen können. Ein Problem ist hier, dass die Wortstruktur in den Schreibungen jeweils anders rekodiert wird, wenn man die graphische Form nach orthographischen Mustern des Französischen oder Deutschen liest. Eine weitere Schwierigkeit für die Interpretation sind emblematische Formen, die verwendet werden, um die Zielsprache symbolisch zu verdeutlichen (wie z.B. Diakritika oder finales <-e> im Französischen). Zudem gibt es auch die Möglichkeit, dass Schüler eine ihnen bekannte deutsche Schriftform verwenden und ihr eine Funktion im französischen System zuweisen, wie bei der Schreibung <fiel>.

Schon die wenigen dargestellten Schreibungen der Schüler zeigen, dass sie mit den Schriftstrukturen des Deutschen und Französischen experimentieren. Dazu greifen sie auf ihr Wissen darüber zurück, wie Schrift im Allgemeinen und im System der deutschen Orthographie im Besonderen funktioniert. Darüber hinaus wenden sie einige orthographische Strukturen des Französischen an. Diese haben sie sich (zumindest im schulischen Kontext) nur über Wortbilder einprägen können, deren Schreibweisen sie auf andere Wörter übertragen. Diese „schriftsprachlichen Ressourcen" (Maas & Mehlem 2003) der Kinder können in der Fremdsprachendidaktik nur dann sinnvoll aufgenommen werden, wenn sie erkannt werden.

Beachtet werden muss beim Nachdenken über den Umgang mit Schrift, dass Lesen eine andere Tätigkeit darstellt als Schreiben. Da Orthographie die Strukturen einer Sprache stabil symbolisiert, haben gerade Fremdsprachenlerner beim Lesen die Möglichkeit, in der Schrift Elemente des Französischen zu erkennen, die in ihrer Muttersprache nicht vorhanden sind (Röber 2007). Über die Symbole und ihre orthographische Struktur ermöglicht die graphische Darstellung von Sprache zudem das Kategorisieren und Vergleichen von Elementen und somit eine Reflexion über Sprache. Schreiben hat – vor allem wenn es sich nicht um das Recht-Schreiben handelt – eine andere Funktion. Es bietet den Lernern die Möglichkeit einer Auseinandersetzung mit den Schriftsystemen des Deutschen und Französischen. Die Schreibungen der Schüler nehmen orthographische Elemente auf und bewegen sich in einem „graphematischen Lösungsraum" (Neef 2005), der die möglichen Schreibungen in einer Sprache umfasst und sich eben nicht auf die normativ korrekten Rechtschreibungen beschränkt. Die graphematischen Lösungen entsprechen den Möglichkeiten, die phonologischen und morphologischen Strukturen einer Sprache abzubilden. Auf dieser Definition basiert der hier vorgestellte Ansatz, die im Bildungsplan Baden-Württemberg gewählte Formulierung „Wörter, Wendungen und Sätze so aus dem Gedächtnis [zu] schreiben dass sie eindeutig erkennbar sind" (MKJS 2004: 78, 92) nachzuvollziehen und einen Analyseansatz für das eindeutige Erkennen von Schülerschreibungen vorzuschlagen.

Literatur

Apeltauer, Ernst (2007), Grundlagen vorschulischer Sprachförderung. Flensburg: Universität Flensburg [Flensburger Papiere zur Mehrsprachigkeit und Kulturenvielfalt im Unterricht].

Argod-Dutard, Françoise (1996), *Éléments de phonétique appliquée*. Paris: Armand Colin.

Catach, Nina (1973), Que faut-il entendre par système graphique du français? In: *Langue française* 20, 30–44.

Catach, Nina (1992), *L'Orthographe*. 4. éd. corrigée. Paris: Presses Universitaires de France.

David, Jacques (2006), L'orthographe du français et son apprentissage, historique et perspectives. In : Honvault-Ducrocq, Renée (Hrsg.): *L'orthographe en questions*. Rouen: Publications des Universités de Rouen et du Havre, 169–190.

Ducard, Dominique; Honvault, Renée & Jaffré, Jean-Piere (1995a), *Linguistique, Écriture, et Orthographe. Moniteur d'orthographe du CE1 au CM2*. Paris: Nathan.

Ducard, Dominique; Honvault, Renée & Jaffré, Jean-Piere (1995b), *Le Moniteur d'orthographe. Guide pédagogique*. Paris: Nathan.

Ehlers, Swantje (Hrsg.) (2006), *Sprachförderung und Literalität*. Flensburg: Universität Flensburg [Flensburger Papiere zur Mehrsprachigkeit und Kulturenvielfalt im Unterricht].

Eisenberg, Peter (1995), Die Silbe. In: Drosdowski, Günther (Hrsg.): *Duden. Grammatik der deutschen Gegenwartssprache.* 5., völlig neu bearb. und erw. Aufl. Mannheim: Dudenverlag, 37–46.

Fayol, Michel (1997), *Des idées au texte, psychologie cognitive de la production verbale, orale et écrite.* Paris: Presses universitaire françaises.

Fayol, Michel & Jaffré, Jean-Pierre (2008),. *Orthographier.* Paris: Presses universitaires.

Fayol, Michel & Schneuwly Bernard (1987), La mise en texte et ses problèmes. In: Chiss, Jean-Louis; Laurent, Jean-Paul; Meyer, Jean-Claude; Romain, Hélène & Schneuwly, Bernard (Hrsg.). *Apprendre / enseigner à produire des textes écrits.* Bruxelles: De Boeck.

Grau, Maike & Legutke, Michael K. (2008), Fremdsprachen in der Grundschule. Bestandsaufnahmen, Prinzipien und Perspektiven. In: Grau, Maike & Legutke, Michael K. (Hrsg.). *Fremdsprachen in der Grundschule. Auf dem Weg zu einer neuen Lern- und Leistungskultur.* Frankfurt am Main: Grundschulverband – Arbeitskreis Grundschule, 14–38.

Guyon, Odile (2003), Évolution des procédures d'accord nominal et verbal en français: perspective psycholinguistique. *Les dossiers des Sciences de l'Education* 9, 55–66.

Jaffré, Jean-Pierre & Catherine Brissaud (2006), Homophonie et hétérographie, un point nodal de l'orthographe. In: Honvault-Ducrocq, Renée (Hrsg.). *L'orthographe en questions.* Mont-Saint-Aignan: Publications des Universités de Rouen et du Havre, 145–168.

Jaffré, Jean-Paul & Bessonnat, Daniel (1996), Gestion et acquisition de l'accord. *Faits de Langue* 8, 185–192.

Kierepka, Adelheid; Klein, Eberhard & Krüger, Renate (Hrsg.) (2007), *Fortschritte im frühen Fremdsprachenunterricht. Auf dem Wege zur Mehrsprachigkeit.* Tübingen: Narr.

Maas, Utz (1992), *Grundzüge der deutschen Orthographie.* Tübingen: Niemeyer.

Maas, Utz (2006), *Phonologie: Einführung in die funktionale Phonetik des Deutschen.* Zweite überarbeitete Auflage. Göttingen: Vandenhoeck & Ruprecht.

Maas, Utz & Mehlem, Ulrich (2003), *Schriftkulturelle Ressourcen und Barrieren bei marokkanischen Kindern in Deutschland.* Abschlussbericht des von der Stiftung Volkswagenwerk 1999–2002 am Institut für Migrationsforschung und Interkulturelle Studien (IMIS) der Universität Osnabrück geförderten Forschungsprojekts. Osnabrück: IMIS Universität Osnabrück (Materialien zur Migrationsforschung Band I).

May, Peter; Malitzky, Volkmar. & Vieluf, Ulrich, (2001). Rechtschreibtests im Vergleich: Wie stellt man deren Güte fest und wie besser nicht? Anmerkungen zur Kritik von Tacke, Völker und Lohmüller an der HSP. *Psychologie in Erziehung und Unterricht* 48: 2, 146–152.

McBride-Chang, Catherine (2004), *Children's literacy development*. New York: Arnold.

Meisenburg, Trudel (1996), *Romanische Schriftsysteme im Vergleich*. Tübingen: Narr.

Meisenburg, Trudel & Selig, Maria (1998), *Phonetik und Phonologie des Französischen*. Stuttgart: Klett.

Mertens, Jürgen (2002a), Französisch in der Grundschule – ja! Aber wie? *FMF Rheinland-Pfalz*, Mitteilungsblatt 10, 4–12.

Mertens, Jürgen (2002b), Diskrepanz zwischen Laut und Schrift? Zum Einsatz der Schrift im frühen (Fremd-) Spracherwerb. In: Fitzner, Theo (Hrsg.). *Alphabetisierung und Sprachenlernen*. Stuttgart: Klett, 255–272.

Ministerium für Kultus, Jugend und Sport Baden-Württemberg [MKJS] (2004), *Leitgedanken zum Kompetenzerwerb für Moderne Fremdsprachen. Grundschule, Hauptschule, Realschule, Gymnasium*.
URL: http://www.bildung-staerkt-menschen.de/service/downloads/Bildungsplaene/ Grundschule/Grundschule_Bildungsplan_Gesamt.pdf (10.11.2009)

Neef, Martin (2005), *Die Graphematik des Deutschen*. Tübingen: Niemeyer.

Reich, Hans (2002), Zweisprachig schreiben lernen. *Grundschule : Sprachen* Vol 6, 38–41.

Rieben, Laurence; Fayol, Michel & Perfetti, Charles A. (Hrsg.) (1997), *Des orthographes et leur acquisition*. Lausanne: Delachaux et Niestlé.

Röber-Siekmeyer, Christa (1997), *Die Schriftsprache entdecken. Rechtschreiben im offenen Unterricht*. 3. Auflage. Weinheim, Basel: Beltz.

Röber-Sieckmeyer, Christa (1998), DEN SCHBRISERIN NAS. Was lernen Kinder beim „Spontanschreiben", was lernen sie nicht? In: Weingarten, Rüdiger & Günther, Hartmut (Hrsg.): *Schriftspracherwerb*. Baltmannsweiler: Schneider Hohengehren 1998, S. 116–150.

Röber, Christa (2007), Schrift lehrt Sprechen. Die Heranführung von Deutschlernern an die Artikulation deutscher Wörter und Sätze durch die systematische Nutzung des orthographischen Markierungssystems im Deutschen. *daf. Halbjahresschrift des Zentrums für die Didaktik der dt. Sprache an der Univ. Siena – Arazzo*, 9/10.

Röber, Christa (2009), *Die Leistungen der Kinder beim Lesen- und Schreibenlernen: Grundlagen der Silbenanalytischen Methode. Ein Arbeitsbuch mit Übungsaufgaben*. Hohengehren: Schneider Verlag.

Rymarczyk, Jutta (2008), Früher oder später? Zur Einführung des Schriftbildes in der Grundschule. In: Böttger, Heiner (Hrsg.). *Fortschritte im Frühen Fremdsprachenlernen*. München: Domino Verlag Günter Brinek GmbH, 170–182.

Sabio, Frédéric (2000), Les difficultés de la notion de mot: l'exemple des liaisons graphiques dans les textes d'enfants. *LINX* 42, 119–130.

Siebert-Ott, Gesa (2008), Zweisprachige und mehrsprachige Schulen. In: Ahrenholz, Bernt & Oomen-Welke, Ingelore (Hrsg.). *Deutsch als Zweitsprache.* Baltmannsweiler: Schneider Hohengehren, 493–501

Sprenger-Charolles, Liliane (2004), Linguistic processes in reading and spelling: The case of alphabetic writing systems: English, French, German and Spanish. In: Nunes, Theresa & Bryant, Peter (Hrsg.). *The handbook of children's literacy.* Dordrecht u. a.: Kluwer Academic Publishers, 43–66.

Tannen, Deborah (Hrsg.) (1982), *Spoken and Written Language: Exploring Orality and Literacy.* Norwood: Ablex Publishing Corporation.

Weth, Constanze (2008), *Mehrsprachige Schriftpraktiken in Frankreich. Eine ethnographische und linguistische Untersuchung zum Umgang mehrsprachiger Grundschüler mit Schrift.* Stuttgart: ibidem-Verlag.

Weth, Constanze (im Druck.), Entwicklungen des Lesens- und Schreibenlehrens in anderen Ländern: Frankreich. In: C. Röber (Hrsg.). *Schriftsprach- und Orthographieerwerb: Erstlesen, Erstschreiben.* Band I der Reihe Deutschunterricht in Theorie und Praxis (DTP). Hohengehren: Schneider-Verlag.

Dieter Mindt und Gudrun Wagner

Das Schriftbild im Englischunterricht der Klassen 1 und 2

The article consists of two parts: (1) fundamentals of speech and writing and (2) a new way to attain literacy. (1) Literacy in the mother tongue is compared with literacy in English as a foreign language. The relationship of phonemic and graphemic representations serves as a foundation for looking at analytic and synthetic methods of introducing the written form of English. (2) We start by identifying phonemes and graphemes of English for analytic learning. Learners distinguish their position in words (initial, medial, final). The next step is to utilize a framework of consonants followed by the use of patchwords (words with different representations of graphemes according to their correspondence with phonemes). The final step is the introduction of words in their full graphic form (synthetic learning) for cases with ambiguous correspondences of phonemes and graphemes. The article closes with a summary of systematic steps for building up literacy and fostering insights into the relation of the written form and the grammar of English. This paper is a modified version of the chapter „Das Schriftbild" in Mindt & Wagner (2009).

1. Die Bedeutsamkeit des Schriftbildes in der Muttersprache

Der Schriftspracherwerb gehört zu den größten Bildungserlebnissen der Kinder der Klasse 1. Die Kinder erkennen, dass der Lautstrom der Sprache sich in Wörter gliedert und dass gesprochene Wörter durch eine systematische Aneinanderreihung von Schriftzeichen dargestellt werden können. Jeder Schultag bringt neue Entdeckungen zum Verhältnis gesprochener Laute zu geschriebenen Zeichen.

1.1 Vorzüge des muttersprachlichen Schriftbildes

Die Kinder erfahren, welche enormen Hilfen ihnen das Schriftbild der Muttersprache liefert. Gesprochenes wird von der Bindung an den Augenblick des Sprechens befreit und verliert seine Flüchtigkeit, wenn es durch die Schrift festgehalten wird. Das Schriftbild kann über beliebig lange Zeiträume aufbewahrt werden.

Durch das Schriftbild können Mitteilungen ohne Rücksicht auf Ort und Zeit ausgetauscht werden. Darüber hinaus dienen schriftliche Aufzeichnungen der

Selbstorganisation (Markierung eigener Hefte und Bücher mit dem eigenen Namen). Sie ermöglichen eine selbstständige räumliche Orientierung (z. B. durch Straßenschilder, Bezeichnungen von Bahnhöfen) ohne weitere Rückfragen.

Die Kinder benutzen schriftliche Aufzeichnungen, um ihre Gedanken festzuhalten, Gelerntes zu wiederholen und bei Unsicherheiten nachzuschlagen.

1.2 Selbstständige Wissenserweiterung

Schließlich erkennen die Kinder, dass sie sich durch Lesen von schriftlichen Aufzeichnungen selbstständig neue Erfahrungen und neues Wissen verfügbar machen können. So wird das Schriftbild für die Kinder immer stärker zu einem wichtigen Werkzeug der Erfahrungs- und Wissenserweiterung. Es verschafft ihnen einen nie zuvor erlebten Zuwachs an Selbstständigkeit. Das Schriftbild ist die Voraussetzung für eine zunehmende Selbstorganisation und Mündigkeit.

2. Die Bedeutsamkeit des Schriftbildes in der Fremdsprache

Den enormen Gewinn an Erfahrung und Wissen, den das Schriftbild in der Muttersprache ermöglicht, möchten die Kinder auch beim Lernen der Fremdsprache nutzen.

Durch Schriftbilder in ihrer Umgebung haben die Kinder erkannt, dass auch die englische Sprache in schriftlicher Form vorliegt. Auf elektrischen Geräten sehen sie Schalter mit den Aufschriften *on* und *off*, sie tragen *jeans*, essen *chicken wings* und fahren *mountain bikes*, ältere Geschwister und Freunde lesen *comics*.

2.1 Das Bedürfnis der Kinder nach dem Schriftbild

Eine Methodik, die auf das Schriftbild der Fremdsprache verzichtet, ist lebensfremd und behandelt sechsjährige Schulkinder wie Kleinkinder. Die Lernenden fühlen sich nicht ernst genommen. Um dem dauernden Ausschluss ihrer Bedürfnisse entgegenzuwirken und der damit einhergehenden Demotivation zu entgehen, suchen sie nach Auswegen und erstellen Schriftbilder auf eigene Faust (Hellwig 1995: 76, Schmid-Schönbein 2006: 5, Diehr/Rymarczyk 2008: 7).

Rymarczyk 2008 berichtet von Schriftbildern aus der zweiten Klasse, die die Kinder selbst angefertigt haben, weil sie ihnen im Unterricht vorenthalten wurden. Dazu gehören Schreibungen wie *owensch* für *orange* oder *webid* für *rabbit* sowie *Milg* für *milk* und *Bader* für *butter* oder *Herpi börzder* für *Happy Birthday*.

Diese Schreibungen verfestigen sich schnell (Diehr/Rymarczyk 2008: 7), und die Aufgabe des nachfolgenden Unterrichts besteht darin, die von den Kindern selbst erstellten fehlerhaften Varianten durch die richtigen Schreibweisen zu ersetzen. Dieser Lernprozess ist von unnötigen Umwegen belastet, er ist zeitraubend, und die Ergebnisse sind schwierig zu korrigieren.

2.2 Vorzüge des fremdsprachlichen Schriftbildes

Die Darbietung der Grundlagen des englischen Schriftbildes von Anfang an vermeidet irrtumsbehaftete Umwege, macht es überflüssig, unnötige Fehler nachträglich zu korrigieren, ist zeitsparend und kommt den natürlichen Bedürfnissen der Kinder von Anfang an entgegen.

Die Ausklammerung des Schriftbildes verkennt aber auch, dass das Schriftbild den Kindern enorme Hilfen für das Lernen der neuen Sprache bietet. Die folgenden Bereiche seien beispielhaft genannt:

- Erkennung von Wortgrenzen
- Anzeige von weggefallenen Buchstaben
- Unterscheidung von Formen mit gleicher Aussprache
- Verdeutlichung von syntaktischen Beziehungen
- Frühzeitige Erfassung der Unterschiede des deutschen und englischen Schriftsystems.

2.2.1 Erkennung von Wortgrenzen

Die Lautfolge /əneɪm/ lässt offen, an welcher Stelle sich die Wortgrenze befindet und ob es sich um die Wortfolgen *a name* oder *an aim* handelt. Das Schriftbild schafft die erforderliche Eindeutigkeit.

2.2.2 Anzeige von weggefallenen Buchstaben

Das Schriftbild kann den Ausfall von Buchstaben anzeigen. So steht der Apostroph oft für weggefallene Buchstaben. In *it's* kann der Apostroph für den Ausfall des *i* von *is* stehen. Durch das Schriftbild wird klar, dass *it is* und *it's* dasselbe bedeuten und oft miteinander austauschbar sind (*it is nice* und *it's nice*).

2.2.3 Unterscheidung von Formen mit gleicher Aussprache

Die Bedeutung der Lautfolge /ɪts/ wird erst durch das Schriftbild klar. Durch die Schreibung *it's* wird deutlich, dass der erste Bestandteil das Personalpronomen *it* ist (z. B. *it's nice*). Durch die Schreibung *its* wird dagegen erkennbar, dass es sich hier um ein einziges Wort handelt, das Possessivpronomen *its* (*the snake with its head*). Dasselbe gilt für die Lautfolge /jɔː/, die nur durch das Schriftbild entweder als Possessivpronomen *your* (*your book*) oder als Verbindung des Personalpronomens *you* mit der Kurzform *'re* von *are* (*you're right*) erkennbar wird.

2.2.4 Verdeutlichung von syntaktischen Beziehungen

Durch den Einsatz des Schriftbildes in Form von Wortkarten können syntaktische Beziehungen deutlich gemacht werden. Ein Beispiel ist die Unterscheidung zwischen Aussagesätzen und Fragesätzen. Aussagesätze mit einer Form des Verbs *be* werden durch Umstellung von Subjekt und Verb zu Fragesätzen.

Beispiel: Die Kinder erkennen, dass die Wortfolge *It is* einen Aussagesatz kennzeichnet und dass die Umstellung zu *Is it* die Aussage in eine Frage umwandelt. Dies ist im folgenden Tafelbild (Abb. 1) wiedergegeben.

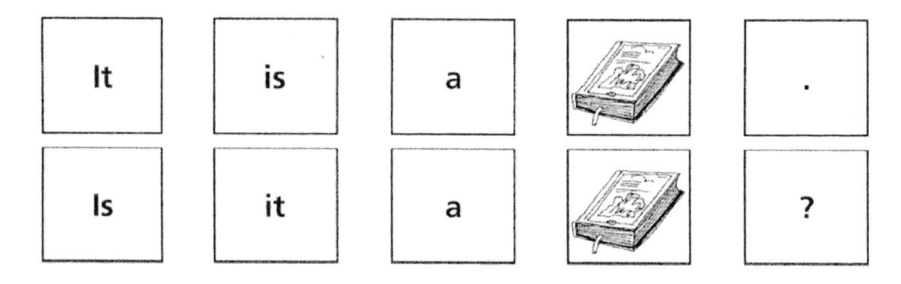

Abb. 1: Wortstellung im Aussagesatz und im Fragesatz

2.2.5 Frühzeitige Erfassung der Unterschiede des deutschen und englischen Schriftsystems

Kinder, denen das englische Schriftbild längere Zeit vorenthalten wird, versuchen, sich am deutschen Schriftbild zu orientieren, wie es an den folgenden von Rymarczyk 2008 gegebenen Beispielen deutlich wird: *Teibel* statt *table*, *Scher* anstelle von *chair*, *swi* statt *three*.

Bei früher Einführung des Schriftbildes wird den Kindern von Anfang an klar, dass das englische Schriftbild anders strukturiert ist als das deutsche und dass Übernahmen aus dem Deutschen oft zu Fehlern im Englischen führen.

3. Das englische Schriftbild und der Unterricht

Ein ausschließlich mündlicher Unterricht erfordert zu jedem Zeitpunkt eine hohe Konzentration und ist äußerst anstrengend. Dies gilt nicht nur für die Lehrkräfte, sondern in besonderem Maße für die Kinder. Das Schriftbild bringt wirksame Abhilfe. Die Flüchtigkeit und Schnelligkeit des Gesprochenen wird durch die Konstanz und Zeitunabhängigkeit des Schriftlichen ergänzt.

3.1 Erleichterung des Verstehens

Das Schriftbild erleichtert das Verstehen durch die zusätzliche visuelle Präsentation des sonst nur Gehörten. Es schafft an vielen Punkten Eindeutigkeit und stärkt das Verstehen, indem es eine Brücke zwischen akustischer und visueller Wahrnehmung herstellt.

3.2 Wechsel der Fertigkeiten

Durch das Schriftbild kann methodisch ein häufiger Wechsel der Fertigkeiten erfolgen. Nachdem das Gehörte sicher verstanden wurde, kann durch die Fertigkeit des Lesens und Verstehens nicht nur die Klärung des zuvor Gehörten geschehen. Der Wechsel der Fertigkeit bedeutet gleichzeitig einen Wechsel der Arbeitsform.

3.3 Einsatz von Medien

Darüber hinaus können zusätzliche Medien eingesetzt werden. Für das Schriftbild kommen in Frage Buchstabenkarten, Wortkarten, Satzkarten, Texte im Schülerbuch und speziell für den Unterricht konzipierte Kurztexte. Alle diese Medien können mit visuellen Elementen (Realgegenständen, Bildern, Illustrationen) verbunden werden.

3.4 Wechsel der Arbeits- und Sozialformen

Der rein mündliche Unterricht vollzieht sich wegen des am Anfang unverzichtbaren Vorbildes durch die Lehrkraft im Wesentlichen als gemeinsamer Unterricht. Durch die Einführung des Schriftbildes kann ein häufiger Wechsel zu Partner-, Gruppen- oder Individualarbeit erfolgen. Die Verwendung des Schriftbildes führt zu einer Vielfalt der Arbeits- und Sozialformen sowie zu einem abwechslungsreicheren und entspannteren Wahrnehmungs- und Lernrhythmus.

3.5 Vorteile für lernschwächere Kinder

Lernschwache Kinder profitieren in ganz besonderem Maß vom Schriftbild. Das Schriftbild bietet nicht nur zusätzliche Verstehenshilfen, sondern ermöglicht den Wechsel von hochkonzentrierten mündlichen Unterrichtsabschnitten zu anderen Arbeitsformen, die ein variables Lerntempo gestatten. In solchen Unterrichtsabschnitten können schneller Lernende die langsameren wirkungsvoll unterstützen. Durch den Einsatz des Schriftbildes wird auf diese Weise auch die Kluft zwischen schneller und langsamer lernenden Kindern wirksam verringert.

3.6 Fazit: Das englische Schriftbild und der Unterricht

Der mit dem Schriftbild verbundene Wechsel von Fertigkeiten, Medien, Arbeits- und Sozialformen macht das Lernen anschaulicher und methodisch abwechslungsreicher. Einzelne Lernschritte können durch das Schriftbild klarer gestaltet werden, Irrtümer und Mehrdeutigkeiten werden verhindert. Die Ergebnisse des Lernens können festgehalten werden, und die Lernenden gewinnen an Sicherheit.

Das Schriftbild dient der Aufrechterhaltung des Interesses der Lernenden und stärkt ihre Motivation. Es ermöglicht den Einsatz von Medien und Arbeitsformen, die einen methodenreichen und anregenden Unterricht zur Folge haben. Das Schriftbild bietet Lernhilfen, die von besonderem Wert für lernschwache Kinder sind. Insgesamt bewirkt das Schriftbild eine erhebliche Erleichterung und Beschleunigung des Lernens der fremden Sprache.

4. Gesprochene Sprache und geschriebene Sprache

Grundlage des deutschen und des englischen Schriftsystems ist das lateinische Alphabet.

4.1 Laute und Buchstaben

Als das westeuropäische Schriftbild entstand, erfand man Buchstaben für Sprachlaute und versuchte zu schreiben, was man hörte. In der lateinischen Sprache wurde z. B. die Stadt Rom mit dem Wort *Roma* bezeichnet. Das Wort besteht aus vier Phonemen, die im Lateinischen durch vier Buchstaben wiedergegeben werden.

Diese einfache Beziehung zwischen Lautbild und Schriftbild des klassischen Lateins ließ sich nicht in allen Punkten auf das Deutsche und das Englische übertragen. Beide Sprachen enthalten Phoneme, die im Lateinischen nicht vorhanden sind.

Für das Deutsche sind hier beispielsweise die Umlaute (*ä, ö, ü*) zu nennen. Für diese Umlaute hat man die vorhandenen Buchstaben <a>, <o>, <u> zu <ä>, <ö>, <ü> abgewandelt. Vorteil: Ein Phonem wird auch hier durch einen einzigen Buchstaben dargestellt. Nachteil: Die Zahl der Buchstaben wird größer als im Lateinischen.

Im Englischen gibt es ebenfalls Phoneme, die im Lateinischen nicht existieren, z. B. /ð/ in *the* und /θ/ in *thing*. Hier hätte man auf das germanische Runenzeichen Þ oder das Altenglische ð zurückgreifen können. Im Englischen blieb man jedoch konsequent beim lateinischen Alphabet. So wurden /ð/ und /θ/ durch die Zeichenfolge <th> ersetzt. Vorteil: Der Umfang des Alphabets wird nicht vergrößert. Nachteil: Die Übereinstimmung von Phonem und Einzelbuchstabe geht verloren. Den Phonemen /ð/ in *the* und /θ/ in *thing* entspricht nicht mehr ein einziger Buchstabe als Graphem, sondern eine Kombination von Buchstaben.

Im Englischen und im Deutschen gibt es gleiche Phoneme, die im Lateinischen nicht existieren. Das Phonem /ʃ/ in *Schiff* oder *ship* wird im Deutschen durch das Graphem <sch> wiedergegeben, im Englischen durch das Graphem <sh>.

4.2 Voraussetzungen der Kinder

Sechsjährige Kinder verfügen über wesentliche Voraussetzungen zum Schriftspracherwerb. Sie sind in der Lage, Phoneme zu erkennen. Sie erkennen den Unterschied zwischen *Haus* und *Maus*, der durch den Austausch von /h/ und /m/ am Beginn des Wortes zustande kommt (Marx 2007: 44).

Diese phonologische Bewusstheit ist die Grundlage des Schriftspracherwerbs in Klasse 1 (Schründer-Lenzen 2007: 33f.). Die phonologische Bewusstheit „wird von den meisten Kindern bereits vor Schuleintritt und ohne Bezug zur Schrift erworben" (Marx 2007: 45). Anders als zwei- bis dreijährige Kleinkinder haben viele Kinder am Beginn der Schulzeit bereits Buchstabenkenntnisse und weiteres Wissen bezüglich der Schrift (Marx 2007: 52).

Diese Voraussetzungen der Kinder gelten nicht nur für den Schriftspracherwerb der Muttersprache, sondern in gleicher Weise auch für die Fremdsprache.

Das gleichzeitige Erlernen des deutschen und des englischen Schriftbildes stellt keine Überforderung der Kinder dar (Diehr/Rymarczyk 2008: 8, so auch Reichart-Wallrabenstein 2004: 559 für Kinder der Klasse 3).

4.3 Das Verhältnis von Aussprache und Schrift

Es gibt Sprachen, die seit der ersten Festlegung der Schrift wenige Lautwandlungen durchlaufen haben. In solchen Sprachen findet man umfangreiche Entsprechungen zwischen Lautbild und Schriftbild. Die Schreibungen sind phonetisch. Das Schriftbild solcher Sprachen ist leicht zu lernen. Die meisten slawischen Sprachen haben eine stark phonetische Schreibung.

Andere Sprachen haben seit der Einführung der Schrift erhebliche Lautwandlungen durchgemacht, die keinen Niederschlag mehr im Schriftbild gefunden haben. Die englische Entsprechung für das deutsche Wort *Licht* hat die ähnliche Schreibung *light*. Um das Jahr 1500 hatten beide Wörter in beiden Sprachen etwa die gleiche Aussprache (ähnlich wie das heutige deutsche Wort *Licht*). Danach hat sich die Aussprache des englischen Wortes stark verändert.

Der Laut /ç/, den wir in den deutschen Wörtern *ich* oder *Licht* finden, verschwand im Englischen (Lass 1999: 116f.). Sein Verschwinden führte zur Längung des kurzen *i* (Horn/Lehnert 1954: 229). Das nunmehr lange *i* wurde nach 1600 zum Diphthong /aɪ/, den wir auch in den Wörtern *I, my, like* antreffen (Lass 1999: 72). Diese Lautwandlungen haben jedoch zu keiner Veränderung der englischen Schreibung geführt. Während die Schreibung von deutsch *Licht* sehr phonetisch ist, gilt dies nicht für das englische Gegenstück *light* /laɪt/.

5. Das Lernen des Schriftbildes

Das Lesenlernen kann auf zwei Weisen erfolgen: (1) analytisch, durch Ermittlung der einzelnen Grapheme eines Wortes und Umsetzung der Grapheme in Phoneme und (2) synthetisch, durch Erfassung des Schriftbildes eines Wortes insgesamt.[1] Der synthetischen Worteinheit wird eine Kette von Phonemen zugeordnet.

---

[1] Diese Verwendung der Begriffe analytisch und synthetisch orientiert sich am Sprachgebrauch der Naturwissenschaften. In der Grundschulpädagogik erfolgt die Benennung gelegentlich in umgekehrter Weise: „analytisch, da vom Wortganzen und seiner Bedeutung ausgegangen wird, synthetisch, da Buchstabenfolgen in einzelne Sprachlautfolgen aufgeteilt und zusammengesetzt werden" (Schründer-Lenzen 2007: 107).

5.1 Lesen durch Analyse

Sprachen, deren Schriftbild überwiegend phonetisch ist, haben eindeutige Beziehungen zwischen Graphemen und Phonemen. Beim Lesen kann jedes Graphem einzeln identifiziert und durch das entsprechende Phonem wiedergegeben werden. Das Lesen eines Wortes vollzieht sich in drei Schritten:

- Analyse des Wortes in Grapheme
- Umsetzung dieser Grapheme in die entsprechenden Phoneme und
- Zusammenfügung der einzelnen Phoneme zur Aussprache eines Wortes.

Dieses analytische Lesen ist stark regelgeleitet und hat alle Vorzüge des regelgeleiteten Lernens (vgl. Mindt & Wagner 2009: 178–189). Es kommt zusätzlich dem Bemühen der Kinder um „eigenständige Regelbildungsversuche" entgegen (Reichart-Wallrabenstein 2004: 561).

5.2 Lesen durch Synthese

Das analytische Lesen funktioniert nicht bei Sprachen, die sich von ihrem ursprünglichen phonetischen Prinzip weit entfernt haben. Die Aussprache der englischen Buchstabenfolge <ea> ist nahezu unvorhersehbar. Sie kann gesprochen werden als /iː/ in *tea*, als /eɪ/ in *steak*, als /e/ in *bread*, als /ɑː/ in *heart*, als /ɜː/ in *learn*, als /ɪə/ in *year*.

In diesen Fällen ergibt sich die Aussprache der Zeichenfolge <ea> nicht durch Analyse der Einzelbuchstaben oder Grapheme, sondern durch das Gesamtbild eines Wortes (der Synthese seiner Buchstaben).

Das Lesen eines Wortes mit dem synthetischen Verfahren vollzieht sich in drei Schritten:

- Erfassung der Gesamtheit aller Buchstaben eines Wortes und Erkennen der Bedeutung des Wortes
- Erinnerung an die Phonemkette, die dieser Buchstabenfolge zugeordnet ist
- Aussprache der Phonemkette.

Beim synthetischen Lesen handelt es sich um arbiträres Lesen. Für nahezu jedes Wort gilt, dass seine Aussprache nur durch die Gesamtheit seiner Buchstaben erschließbar ist. Jede Buchstabenfolge und die ihr zugeordnete Phonemkette müssen unabhängig voneinander gelernt und erinnert werden. Das synthetische Lesen hat alle Nachteile des arbiträren Lernens (vgl. Mindt & Wagner 2009: 178–189).

6. Deutsch und Englisch auf der Skala der Sprachen

Weder das Deutsche noch das Englische verkörpern eines der beiden Extreme der Sprachen (phonetische Schreibung vs. nicht-phonetische Schreibung). Aber beide Sprachen unterscheiden sich deutlich. Das Deutsche liegt eher auf der Seite der Sprachen mit phonetischer Schreibung. Das Englische befindet sich eher auf der Seite der Sprachen mit nicht-phonetischer Schreibung.

Für große Teile des deutschen Schriftbildes kommt daher die analytische Leselernmethode in Frage. Die analytische Methode ist regelgeleitet und führt wegen der Übertragbarkeit in kürzerer Zeit zu schnellen Ergebnissen. Sie muss in kleinen Teilen ergänzt werden durch synthetische Verfahren.

Für große Teile des englischen Schriftbildes kommt nur die synthetische Leselernmethode in Frage. Sie wird gelegentlich auch als Ganzwortmethode bezeichnet. Sie ist lernintensiver und mangels Übertragbarkeit zeitraubender als die analytische Methode. Sie kann in Teilen ergänzt werden durch analytische Verfahren.

Um die Vorteile des analytischen Lesens zu nutzen, müssen die Teile des englischen Schriftbildes ermittelt werden, bei denen eine regelhafte Beziehung zwischen Graphemen und Phonemen besteht.

Generell kann man für das Englische feststellen, dass es für den Bereich bestimmter Konsonanten brauchbare Übereinstimmungen von Phonemen und Graphemen gibt (z. B. *pot, hand*). Im Bereich der Vokale sind solche Übereinstimmungen nur selten zu finden (*h*a*nd* /æ/ vs. *m*a*ke* /eɪ/, *w*a*ter* /ɔː/, *f*a*ther* /ɑː/).

7. Das Schriftbild im Unterricht der Muttersprache

In deutschen Schulen folgt der Schriftspracherwerb der Muttersprache heute überwiegend einer Mischung der beiden genannten Verfahren. Neben analytische Verfahren treten synthetische Verfahren.

7.1 Analytische Verfahren

Am Beginn stützt sich der Unterricht sehr oft auf die Übereinstimmung von gesprochener und geschriebener Sprache. In diesem Fall kann das Gehörte unmittelbar in Grapheme umgesetzt werden. In diesem Fall schreibt man, was man hört.

Man hört die bedeutungsunterscheidenden Laute /m/ und /p/. Die beiden Phoneme treten in den Lautsequenzen /oːma/ und /oːpa/ auf. Der Bedeutungsunterschied beider Wörter entsteht durch den Austausch von /m/ und /p/ in der gleichen

Lautumgebung. Für gehörtes /m/ schreibt man den Buchstaben <m>, für gehörtes /p/ schreibt man den Buchstaben <p>. Die dazugehörigen Wörter schreibt man *Oma* und *Opa*. Mit solchen Übereinstimmungen von Phonemen und Buchstaben beginnen viele Lehrwerke zum Schriftspracherwerb des Deutschen (z. B. Wendelmuth/Stangner 2000: 4).

Ein Buchstabe ist allerdings nicht identisch mit demselben Zeichen. Buchstaben, die im Deutschen am Beginn eines Nomens stehen, werden groß geschrieben. Bei den Wörtern *Mama* und *Papa*, die mit den Phonemen /m/ und /p/ beginnen, treten für dieselben Buchstaben andere Zeichen auf: <M> und <P>.

Dieser einfache Fall (ein Phonem = ein Buchstabe) tritt auch im Deutschen nicht immer auf. Die Kinder haben anfangs gelernt, dass für das Phonem /f/ der Buchstabe <F> oder <f> steht: *Fest, Film, filmen* (Theis-Scholz et al. 2003: 34f.). Aber ein gehörtes /f/ kann nicht überall durch den Buchstaben <F> oder <f> verschriftlicht werden. Für das gesprochene Wort /fɑːtɐ/ oder /foːgl/ muss statt <F> der Buchstabe <V> benutzt werden: *Vater* und *Vogel*. Das Phonem /f/ wird in unterschiedlichen Wörtern durch unterschiedliche Buchstaben wiedergegeben: <F>, <f>; <V>, <v>.

Ein gesprochenes /f/ kann in der Schrift aber auch durch <Ph> (*Photo*) oder <ph> (*graphisch*) abgebildet werden. Das Phonem /f/ wird in der Schrift durch verschiedene Grapheme dargestellt: <F> (*Fall*), <f> (*fallen*); <V> (*Vater*), <v> (*Havel*); <Ph> (*Photo*) oder <F> (*Foto*), <ph> (*graphisch*) oder <f> (*grafisch*).

Diese Beziehung von Phonemen zu Graphemen ist eine wichtige Grundlage für den Erwerb der Schriftsprache. Die Kinder lernen, dass ein Phonem durch mehrere Grapheme dargestellt werden kann: /f/ durch <F>, <f>; <V>, <v>; <Ph>, <ph>. Sie lernen aber auch, dass dasselbe Graphem mehrere Phoneme repräsentieren kann, z. B. wird der Buchstabe <d> einmal als /d/ gesprochen (*leider*), im anderen Fall als /t/ (*Leid*).

7.2 Synthetische Verfahren

Manche Lehrwerke des Deutschen gehen von Anbeginn von synthetischen Verfahren aus. Von Anfang an werden hier ganze Wörter präsentiert (z. B. Bartnitzky/Bunk 2003). Hier wird auf das regelgeleitete Lernen weitgehend verzichtet. Stattdessen wird den Kindern von Anfang an der höhere Lernaufwand des arbiträren Lernens zugemutet. Dies geschieht auch dort, wo regelhafte Phonem-Graphem Beziehungen bestehen und der Rückgriff auf diese Regeln das Lernen erheblich erleichtern könnte.

Üblicherweise werden analytische Verfahren durch synthetische ergänzt. Diese Ergänzung geschieht dann, wenn man schon früh ganze Sätze lesen lassen möchte, ohne dass alle Wörter aus bereits bekannten Buchstaben bestehen. So führen Wendelmuth/Stangner 2000 die nicht durch Bilder darstellbaren Verbformen *ist*, *sind* und *ruft* sehr schnell als ganze nicht zu analysierende Wörter ein. Auch die unterschiedliche Aussprache des Graphems <ch> in i<u>ch</u> /ç/ und a<u>ch</u> /x/ kann nur durch Darbietung ganzer Wörter geleistet werden (z. B. Li<u>ch</u>t und la<u>ch</u>t).

Die meisten Lehrwerke im Deutschunterricht verbinden analytische mit synthetischen Verfahren (Schründer-Lenzen 2007: 107). Der Englischunterricht kann sich bei der Behandlung des Schriftbildes darauf stützen, dass diese Verfahren den Kindern bekannt sind. Neu für die Kinder sind allerdings die Unterschiede zwischen dem deutschen und dem englischen Schriftsystem.

8. Der neue Weg zum englischen Schriftbild

Wir haben gesehen, dass für Sprachen mit phonetischer Schrift das Lesen durch Analyse des Schriftbildes in Frage kommt. Es ist regelgeleitet und führt zu schnellen Ergebnissen. Das Englische ist aber eine Sprache, die in vielen Fällen ein Schriftbild aufweist, das sich von den phonetischen Ursprüngen weit entfernt hat. Deshalb kommen nur Teile des englischen Schriftbildes für analytische Verfahren in Frage.

Um die Vorzüge des Lesens durch Analyse des Schriftbildes so weit wie möglich auch für das Englische zu nutzen, sind zwei Erkundungen notwendig:

1. Welche Bestandteile des Englischen weisen phonetische Schreibungen auf?
2. Gibt es bei diesen Bestandteilen Übereinstimmungen mit dem Deutschen, die für den Unterricht nutzbar gemacht werden können?

9. Phoneme und Grapheme des Englischen

Wir finden eine Reihe von regelmäßigen Entsprechungen von Phonemen und Graphemen (Arnold/Hansen 1998: 128ff. und 102ff.). Abb. 2 nennt die Phoneme (Spalte 2), die Grapheme (Spalte 3) und Beispiele (Spalte 4).

Das Schriftbild im Englischunterricht der Klassen 1 und 2

	Phoneme	Grapheme	Beispiele
1	/m/	m mm	mother, lamp, arm summer
2	/n/	n nn	name, and, begin tennis
3	/p/	p pp	pot, computer, help apple
4	/b/	b bb	ball, number, rib hobby
5	/t/	t tt	tea, hotel, not butter
5	/d/	d dd	dog, garden, bed middle
7	/g/	g	give, begin, dog
8	/h/	h	hand
9	/f/	f ff	finger, left coffee
10	/v/	v	very, seven, five
11	/ʃ/	sh	ship, T-shirt, English
12	/θ/ /ð/	th th	thank, birthday, mouth the, father
13	/l/	l ll	long, cold, camel hello, ball
14	/r/	r rr	room, camera tomorrow
15	/ɪ/	i	in, sit, winter
16	/e/	e	red, end
17	/æ/	a	hat, hand

Abb. 2: Entsprechungen von Phonemen und Graphemen im Englischen

Die in Abb. 2 genannten Phoneme 1 - 8 können mit den zugeordneten Graphemen ohne Probleme für das analytische Lesen verwendet werden. Es gibt regelhafte Entsprechungen von Phonemen und Graphemen. Bei den Phonemen 1 - 8 und den zugehörigen Graphemen können wir auch große Übereinstimmungen mit dem Deutschen feststellen.

9.1 Unterschiede zum Deutschen

Die Unterschiede zum Deutschen beginnen bei 9. Das Phonem /f/ unter 9 kann im Deutschen auch durch das Graphem <v> wiedergegeben werden: *Vater, Havel*. Das Phonem /ʃ/ unter 11 existiert ebenfalls im Deutschen, wird aber durch das Graphem <sch> wiedergegeben (*Schiff, Englisch*). Die Zuordnung von Phonem zu Graphem in den Fällen 9 - 11 ist aber im Englischen eindeutig und regelmäßig.

Bei /θ/ und /ð/ unter 12 gibt es kein phonetisches Gegenstück im Deutschen, aber die Zuordnung von Phonem zu Graphem ist eindeutig und regelmäßig.

Bei den Phonemen /l/ und /r/ unter 13 und 14 finden wir besonders bei /r/ unterschiedliche Aussprachen im Deutschen, aber eine eindeutige und regelmäßige Zuordnung von Phonemen zu Graphemen im Englischen.

9.2 Vokalphoneme

Einschränkungen gibt es bei den Vokalphonemen 15 - 17. Die Verbindung zwischen Phonem und Graphem gilt nur in bestimmten Umgebungen, z. B. muss einem <i> ein einzelner Konsonant am Ende eines Wortes folgen (z. B. *it, begin*) oder dem <i> müssen mehrere Konsonanten folgen (z. B. *film, finger, drink*). In diesen Fällen spricht man von geschlossener Tonsilbe. Leider gibt es viele Ausnahmen (z. B. *girl, right*).

Dasselbe gilt für die Grapheme <e> (regelmäßig: *bed, elbow*, unregelmäßig: *her* und *very*) und <a> (regelmäßig: *cat, apple*, unregelmäßig: *ball* und *class*).

Für das Lesen durch Analyse kommen nur die 14 genannten Konsonantenphoneme mit ihren Graphemen ohne Einschränkung in Frage. Die drei Vokalphoneme /ɪ/, /e/ und /æ/ sind nur begrenzt verwendbar.

Für alle übrigen Phoneme des Englischen muss auf das synthetische Verfahren (Einsatz von Wortkarten) zurückgegriffen werden.

10. Heranführung an das Lesen mit analytischen Verfahren

Die erste Begegnung mit dem Schriftbild des Englischen kann nach etwa sechs Wochen erfolgen. Dies gilt dann, wenn der Englischunterricht zeitgleich mit dem Unterricht der übrigen Lernbereiche am Anfang des Schuljahres beginnt.

In den ersten sechs Wochen nach Schulbeginn haben die Kinder durch den Unterricht in der Muttersprache wichtige Wahrnehmungen über das Verhältnis von Sprache und Schrift gemacht. Im Englischen hat sich ein erster Bestand an bekannten Wörtern gebildet, die nur akustisch bekannt sind.

Für den Fall, dass der Englischunterricht erst zu Beginn des zweiten Halbjahres einsetzt, kann mit dem englischen Schriftbild schon früher begonnen werden. Nach einem halben Jahr des deutschen Schriftspracherwerbs verfügen die Kinder bereits über eine Fülle von Informationen über das Verhältnis von Aussprache und Schreibung des Deutschen.

10.1 Phoneme und Grapheme im Anlaut

Bei der Verwendung analytischer Verfahren im Deutschunterricht wird das Erkennen von Phonemen u. a. so trainiert, dass einem Phonem das entsprechende Graphem (am Anfang ein Einzelbuchstabe) zugeordnet wird. Wie im Deutschen (bei den Anlauttabellen) beginnen wir mit Konsonanten am Beginn eines Wortes, z. B. <t>. Im Englischen sind die folgenden Wörter mit den zugehörigen Bildkarten bekannt: *cat, coffee, dog, milk, table, telephone, tiger, tomato*.

Wir teilen die Tafel in zwei Hälften. Über der linken Hälfte steht der Buchstabe <t>. Die Kinder ordnen Bildkarten für die genannten Wörter in die jeweils richtige Spalte an der Tafel ein. Dies geschieht unter deutlicher Aussprache des Wortes, die durch Chorsprechen verstärkt werden kann. Es entsteht das in Abb. 3 gegebene Tafelbild.

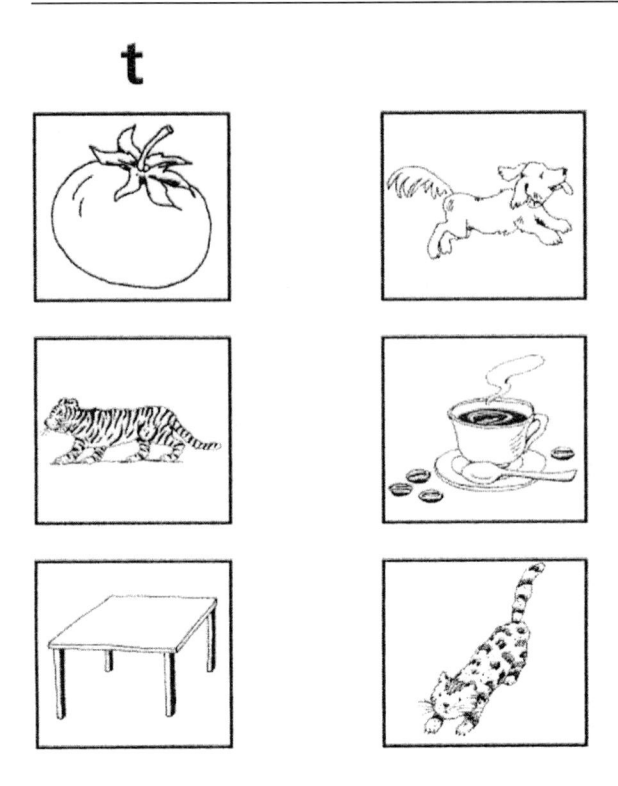

Abb. 3: Phonemerkennung im Anlaut: ein Phonem

Eine Steigerung des Schwierigkeitsgrades besteht in der Kontrastierung zweier Phoneme. Es entsteht das in Abb. 4 gegebene Tafelbild.

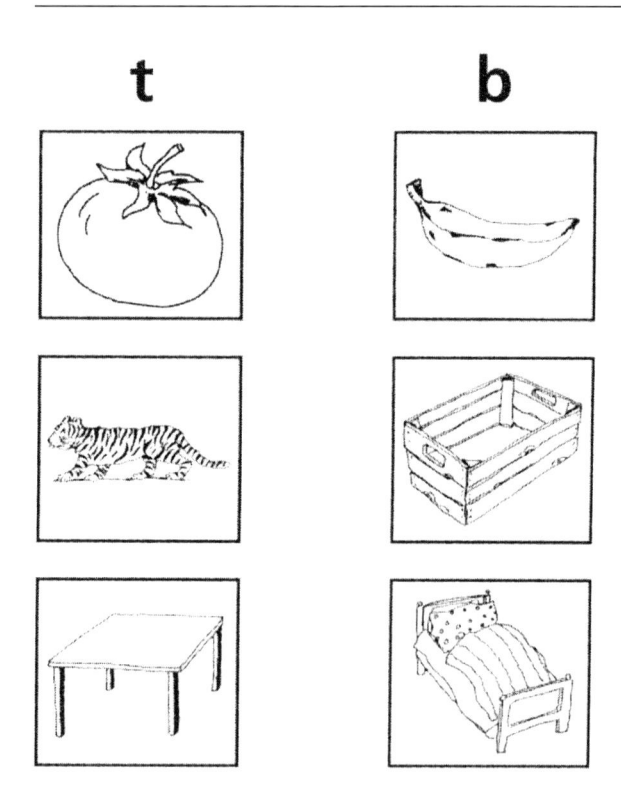

Abb. 4: Phonemerkennung im Anlaut: zwei Phoneme

Für weitere Phoneme kann analog verfahren werden.

10.2 Phoneme und Grapheme im Anlaut, Inlaut und Auslaut

Auch hier können bewährte Verfahren des Lernbereichs Deutsch verwendet werden. Die Kinder erhalten ein Blatt mit Bildkarten und kreuzen an, wo sie ein /n/ hören (Abb. 5).

			x	
				x
	x			

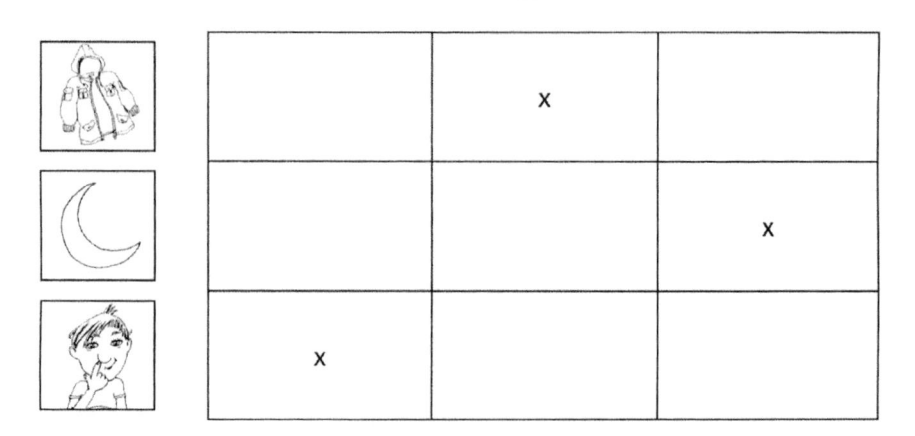

Abb. 5: Phonemerkennung im Anlaut, Inlaut und Auslaut

Durch Wahl anderer Phoneme sowie durch unterschiedliche Erkennung von Phonemen im Anlaut, Inlaut und/oder Auslaut eröffnet sich eine Vielfalt von Übungsmöglichkeiten.

10.3 Verwendung von Einzelbuchstaben

Einzelbuchstaben können sehr früh verwendet werden. Bei der Behandlung des Plurals der Nomen (*finger - fingers*) wird beispielsweise die Buchstabenkarte „-s" verwendet. Dieselbe Buchstabenkarte kommt später bei Verbformen der dritten Person Singular zum Einsatz (z. B. *Susan takes a basket*).

10.4 Aufbau eines Konsonantengerüstes

Ein weiterer Schritt ist der Aufbau eines Konsonantengerüstes auf der Basis der o. g. 14 Konsonantengrapheme. Ein Konsonantengerüst ist keine Erfindung für den Englischunterricht der Klassen 1 und 2. Es geht vielmehr auf eines der ältesten Alphabete der Welt zurück, das hebräische, das anfangs nur Konsonantenzeichen enthielt und bis heute nicht alle Vokale wiedergibt (Kramer/Kowallik 1994: xff.).

Für die Vokale wird der Platzhalter * verwendet. Der Platzhalter steht nicht für einen Vokalbuchstaben, sondern für ein Vokalgraphem, z. B. r*d für r*e*d, r*ea*d, r*oa*d, r*i*d.

Beispiele für Wörter mit Konsonantengerüst sind in Abb. 6 wiedergegeben.

bed	*b*d*	*baby*	*b*b**	*banana*	*b*n*n**
dog	*d*g*	*hello*	*h*ll**	*family*	*f*m*l**
pot	*p*t*	*hotel*	*h*t*l*	*tomato*	*t*m*t**
sun	*s*n*	*bedroom*	*b*dr*m*		
ball	*b*ll*				
tree	*tr**				
good	*g*d*				
hand	*h*nd*				
friend	*fr*nd*				

Abb. 6: *Konsonantengerüst für Wörter*

Wörter mit Konsonantengerüst lassen sich sehr gut für Ratespiele verwenden. Sie bilden einen spielerischen Einstieg in die regelgeleiteten Grundlagen des englischen Schriftsystems.

Die Grenzen des Konsonantengerüstes liegen dort, wo im Lautbild des Englischen Veränderungen stattgefunden haben, die sich nicht konsonantisch ausdrücken lassen, wie das <r> am Ende des Wortes *answer* im britischen Englisch. Dasselbe gilt für Phoneme, die nicht korrekt durch einen Vokalplatzhalter wiedergegeben werden können, wie das für /ə/ stehende <er> am Ende von *daughter*, da das auf /ə/ folgende <r> am Wortende im britischen Englisch nicht gesprochen wird. Auch der frühere Wegfall eines Lautes, der noch im Schriftbild vorhanden ist, wie das <e> am Wortende in *name*, *come*, *home* oder das <k> am Wortanfang in *knee*, machen die Grenzen des Konsonantengerüstes deutlich.

10.5 Die Verwendung von **patchwords**

Die Grenzen des Konsonantengerüstes können durch ein Verfahren überwunden werden, das mit sog. *patchwords* arbeitet (z. B. im Lehrwerk *Sally*). Hier wird die Gesamtschreibung des Wortes gegeben, wobei die Buchstaben in unterschiedlicher Form erscheinen.

Bei *patchwords* handelt es sich um „Wörter, bei denen die in Aussprache und Schrift sich unterscheidenden Stellen zunächst hell wiedergegeben sind." (Bredenbröcker et al. o. J.: 11). Beispiel: brown.

Damit ist gemeint, dass normal gedruckte Buchstaben dort verwendet werden, wo eine eindeutige Beziehung zwischen Phonem und Graphem besteht. Hell gedruckte Buchstaben finden sich dort, wo keine eindeutige Beziehung zwischen Phonem und Graphem besteht.

Wenn ein solches Verfahren sich auf die Trennung der Konsonanten von den Vokalen stützt, befindet es sich im Einklang mit Forschungsergebnissen zum Lesen englischer Texte. Das Lesen englischer Wörter vollzieht sich in zwei Schritten: (1) Erkennung der Konsonanten, (2) Erschließung der Vokalphoneme aus der konsonantischen Umgebung (Berent/Perfetti 1995: 148). Nach diesen Erkenntnissen sollten Konsonanten überwiegend im Normaldruck erscheinen, während Vokale überwiegend hell zu drucken wären.

Die *patchwords* müssten sich daher auf die Ermittlung der phonetischen Schreibungen im Englischen und die Übereinstimmungen mit dem Deutschen (s. o.) stützen und die daraus ableitbare Trennung der Konsonanten von den Vokalen vornehmen. Schon ein kurzer Blick zeigt, dass dies bei den *patchwords* im Lehrwerk *Sally* nicht überall geschehen ist.

Die drei ersten *patchwords* im Lehrwerk *Sally 3* lauten: br*ow*n, wh*ite*, y*ellow*. Bei br*own* und y*ellow* sind die Kennzeichnungen korrekt. Die Aussprache für wh*ite* ist /waɪt/ oder seltener /hwaɪt/. Hier werden die Lernenden durch eine unzutreffende Kennzeichnung des Schriftbildes in die Irre geführt. Dies gilt noch mehr für s*cissors* /ˈsɪzəz/. Das als regelmäßig gekennzeichnete *s* hat in diesem Wort zwei unterschiedliche Aussprachen: stimmlos /s/ am Wortanfang und stimmhaft /z/ am Wortende. Das mittlere *s* wird in diesem Wort stimmhaft gesprochen, obwohl die Schreibweise <ss> im Englischen meist ein stimmloses <s> /s/ anzeigt: ki<u>ss</u>, ki<u>ss</u>es, e<u>ss</u>ay.

Die Verwendung von *patchwords* ist ein psychologisch untermauertes Konzept für die stufenweise Heranführung an das englische Schriftbild. Allerdings müssen dabei die Beziehungen zwischen Phonemen und Graphemen präzise beachtet werden. Geschieht das nicht, so entsteht mehr Schaden als Nutzen durch ein grundsätzlich tragfähiges Konzept.

10.6 Vom Konsonantengerüst zu patchwords

Geht man vom Konsonantengerüst aus, so lässt sich ein bruchloser Übergang zu korrekt gestalteten *patchwords* vornehmen, der für die Kinder leicht nachvollziehbar ist.

Abb. 7 gibt Beispiele für den Übergang vom Konsonantengerüst zu *patchwords*.

b*d	bed	h*ll*	hello	f*m*l*	family	
d*g	dog	b*dr*m	bedroom	t*m*t*	tomato	
b*ll	ball			b*n*n*	banana	
tr*	tree					
g*d	good					
fr*nd	friend					

Abb. 7: *Übergang vom Konsonantengerüst zu* **patchwords**

Wenn die Kinder eine ausreichende Vertrautheit mit den *patchwords* erlangt haben, kann der Übergang zu ganzen Wörtern problemlos vollzogen werden.

10.7 Ganze Wörter, die analytisch lesbar sind

Aus den Entsprechungen von Phonemen und Graphemen in Abb. 2 ergibt sich, dass eine Reihe von Wörtern vollständig durch das analytische Lesen erfasst werden kann. Aus dem Fundamentum des Wortschatzes von Mindt & Wagner 2009 handelt es sich dabei um die Wörter in Abb. 8.

and	end	help	lamp	man	ship	thanks
bed	film	hen	land	milk	sing	that
begin	get	him	left	rat	sit	them
bring	hand	in	let	red	ten	then
	hat	it	lip	sand	thank	thing

Abb. 8: *Wörter des Wortschatzfundamentums von Mindt & Wagner 2009, die vollständig durch analytisches Lesen erfassbar sind*

10.8 Zusammenfassung

Die Heranführung an das Schriftbild mit analytischen Verfahren vollzieht sich in vier Schritten:

- Phonemerkennung im Anlaut, Inlaut und Auslaut
- Konsonantengerüst
- *patchwords*
- ganze Wörter ohne besondere Kennzeichnung einzelner Grapheme

Durch dieses vierschrittige Verfahren ist eine inhaltliche und methodische Anlehnung an den Unterricht der Muttersprache gewährleistet. Auf dieser Grundlage werden die Gesetzmäßigkeiten der englischen Schreibung zum regelgeleiteten Lernen genutzt. Die Schwierigkeiten werden durch eine sorgfältige Abstufung der einzelnen Schritte stark vermindert.

11. Heranführung an das Lesen mit synthetischen Verfahren

Synthetische Verfahren zerlegen die Wörter nicht in einzelne Grapheme, sondern gehen von der Gesamtheit des Schriftbildes eines Wortes aus. Am Beginn des Unterrichts stehen die analytischen Verfahren. Sie werden aber schon sehr früh ergänzt durch die synthetische Darbietung einzelner Wörter.

11.1 Inhaltswörter

Die Schreibung von Inhaltswörtern sollte am Anfang soweit wie möglich analytisch vorbereitet werden. Besonders wenn der Erstleselehrgang in der Muttersprache überwiegend diesem Ansatz folgt, ist damit eine erhebliche Erleichterung des Lernens verbunden.

Wenn bei Inhaltswörtern die analytischen Verfahren ausgeschöpft sind, erfolgt der Übergang zu synthetischen Verfahren. Dies bedeutet aber nicht, dass einzelne wichtige Inhaltswörter nicht schon sehr früh synthetisch eingeführt werden können.

Wenn z.B. aus situativen und gleichzeitigen sprachlichen Gründen das Subjekt *I* und ein Verb, dem ein direktes Objekt folgt (transitives Verb) wie *eat*, erforderlich sind, können beide schon sehr früh als ganze Wörter präsentiert werden. Abb. 9 gibt ein mögliches Tafelbild für das Lesen ganzer Sätze, das zwei Wortkarten (*I* und *eat*) enthält sowie Bildkarten für die Lebensmittel.

Abb. 9: Tafelbild mit Wortkarten *I* und *eat*

11.2 Funktionswörter

Funktionswörter (z. B. *I*) werden früh und überwiegend synthetisch eingeführt. Sie sind weniger zahlreich als die Inhaltswörter und nicht an spezielle Inhalte oder Themen gebunden. Aus diesem Grunde sind sie für elementare Kommunikationsbedürfnisse unverzichtbar.

Zu den Wörtern, die früh synthetisch eingeführt werden, gehören:

- Determinatoren/Artikel: *a/an, the*
- Verneinungspartikel: *not*
- Interjektionen, z. B. *yes, no*
- Konjunktionen, z. B. *and*
- Präpositionen, z. B. *on, for*
- Personalpronomen, z. B. *I, you, he, she*
- Verben, z. B. *is, are, has.*

12. Das Schreiben

Die für das Lesen verwendeten Schritte zur Heranführung an das Schriftbild können auch für das Schreiben genutzt werden. Das Schreiben kann erst stattfinden, wenn zuvor intensiv gelesen wurde.

12.1 Schreiben von Graphemen (Einzelbuchstaben oder Verbindungen von Buchstaben)

Wir präsentieren Bildkarten für Wörter. Die Kinder erhalten den Auftrag, den Buchstaben zu schreiben, den sie am Beginn des Wortes hören (Abb. 10).

Wir präsentieren	Die Kinder schreiben
 (Tomate)	t
 (Hund)	d

Abb. 10: Schreiben von Einzelbuchstaben

Dieses Verfahren kann im Schwierigkeitsgrad verändert werden, indem später Bildkarten für Wörter mit wechselnden unterschiedlichen Anlauten präsentiert werden, z. B. Bildkarten für *baby, finger, hamster, elbow, glass, lamp, mouth, room, sock* etc.

Anstelle von Einzelbuchstaben können auch Verbindungen von Buchstaben geschrieben werden. Auf diese Weise werden die Kinder vom Buchstaben zum Graphem geführt (Abb. 11).

Wir präsentieren	Die Kinder schreiben
 (Schiff)	sh
 (Theater)	th

Abb. 11: Schreiben von mehreren Graphemen

Dasselbe kann mit inlautenden und auslautenden Graphemen erfolgen.

12.2 Schreiben von Konsonanten im Konsonantengerüst

Wir präsentieren Bildkarten für Wörter. Diesmal erhalten die Kinder den Auftrag, das Konsonantengerüst auszufüllen (Abb. 12).

Wir präsentieren	Vorgabe	Die Kinder schreiben
 (Bett)	☐ * ☐	b * d
 (Baum)	☐☐ *	t r *
 (Hand)	☐ * ☐☐	h * n d

Abb. 12: Ausfüllung eines Konsonantengerüstes

Abb. 12 zeigt, dass der Schwierigkeitsgrad durch Veränderung der Struktur des Konsonantengerüstes im Verlauf solcher Übungen verändert werden kann. Durch Weglassung der Bildkarten und Beschränkung auf die Vorgabe kann eine weitere Steigerung der Schwierigkeiten vorgenommen werden.

12.3 Schreiben von Graphemen für Vokale

Wir geben *patchwords* mit hell gedruckten Vokalen vor. Die Kinder schreiben ganze Wörter unter Einschluss der in der Vorgabe hell gedruckten Vokalgrapheme (Abb. 13).

Vorgabe	Die Kinder schreiben
pot	pot
baby	baby
tomato	tomato

*Abb. 13: Schreiben von Vokalgraphemen mit Vorgabe von **patchwords***

12.4 Schreiben von Wörtern mit Vorgabe der Anzahl der auszufüllenden Buchstaben

Wir präsentieren Bildkarten für Wörter. Die Kinder erhalten ferner eine Vorgabe, die für jeden zu schreibenden Buchstaben einen Rahmen vorgibt (Abb. 14).

Wir präsentieren	Vorgabe	Die Kinder schreiben
 [Bild]	☐☐☐	l i p
 [Bild]	☐☐☐☐	f i l m

Abb. 14: Schreiben von Wörtern mit Vorgabe der Anzahl der auszufüllenden Buchstaben

Das Beispiel in Abb. 14 bezieht sich auf Wörter, die analytisch im Englischen erarbeitet werden können. Nach der Einführung synthetischer Ganzwörter kann das Verfahren auch für diese Wörter übernommen werden. Durch Weglassung der Bildkarten kann später eine Steigerung der Schwierigkeiten vorgenommen werden.

12.5 Schreiben von Wörtern ohne Vorgabe der Anzahl der auszufüllenden Buchstaben

Eine Variation dieses Verfahrens besteht darin, dass bei Verwendung der Bildkarten auf die Vorgabe der Anzahl der auszufüllenden Buchstaben verzichtet wird.

In einem späteren Stadium kann zusätzlich auf die Bildkarten verzichtet werden. Die Kinder hören das Wort und schreiben es. Hierbei handelt es sich um die erste einfache Diktatform mit der Umsetzung der akustischen Wahrnehmung eines Wortes in die Schriftform.

13. Analytische und synthetische Verfahren in den Klassen 1 und 2

Von Beginn an werden analytische und synthetische Verfahren nebeneinander verwendet. Durch den anfänglich stärkeren Rückgriff auf analytische Verfahren erschließen sich wichtige Teile der englischen Rechtschreibung auf regelhafte Weise und in Analogie zur Muttersprache.

Die analytischen Verfahren haben ihren Schwerpunkt in Klasse 1. Sie können eingeschränkt noch am Beginn von Klasse 2 fortgesetzt werden. In Klasse 1 werden analytische Verfahren von Beginn an durch die o. g. synthetischen Wortbilder ergänzt.

Wenn die analytischen Verfahren ausgeschöpft sind, erfolgt der Übergang zur synthetischen Darbietung des Schriftbildes ganzer Wörter. In Klasse 2 sind die wichtigsten Grundlagen der Alphabetisierung in der Muttersprache erreicht. Im Englischunterricht liegt der Schwerpunkt jetzt bei den synthetischen Wortbildern.

14. Das Verhältnis von Lesen und Schreiben

Wir beginnen mit dem Lesen nach ca. sechs Wochen. Wenn der Englischunterricht erst im zweiten Halbjahr von Klasse 1 beginnt, können erste Schritte des Lesens schon früher erfolgen. Jeder Schritt des Schreibens folgt zeitversetzt der vorherigen Stufe des Lesens. So ergibt sich für das analytische Verfahren die in Abb. 15 wiedergegebene Reihenfolge der Stufen des Lesens und Schreibens.

Lesen	Schreiben
Grapheme (Einzelbuchstaben und Verbindungen von Buchstaben)	
	Grapheme (Einzelbuchstaben und Verbindungen von Buchstaben)
Grapheme im Konsonantengerüst	
	Grapheme im Konsonantengerüst
Grapheme in *patchwords*	
	Grapheme in *patchwords*
Einzelwörter	
	Einzelwörter

Abb. 15: Stufen des Lesens und Schreibens

Für das synthetische Verfahren, das neben dem analytischen früh beginnt, gilt der Grundsatz „Lesen vor Schreiben" in gleicher Weise.

15. Das Schriftbild als Hilfe zur Erschließung anderer Sprachebenen

Ein grammatisches Problem am Beginn von Klasse 1 besteht in der Verwendung der Formen *a* und *an* für den unbestimmten Artikel (Determinator). Hier kann der frühe Einsatz von Wortkarten eine wirksame Lern- und Erinnerungshilfe darstellen. Ein Beispiel für ein Tafelbild mit diesen Wortkarten findet sich in Abb. 16.

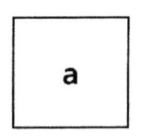

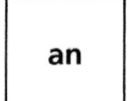

Abb. 16: Wortkarten für den unbestimmten Artikel

Ein anderes grammatisches Problem ist die Beziehung zwischen Vollformen und Kurzformen von Verben. Das Verb *be* hat in der dritten Person Singular die Vollform *is* und die Kurzform *'s*. Der Unterricht muss deutlich machen, dass zwischen der Langform *is* und der Kurzform *'s* kein Bedeutungsunterschied besteht. Er geht dabei von der Langform aus. In einem zweiten Schritt folgt die Kurzform *'s*.

Dazu dienen drei Wortkarten zur Erstellung der Wortgruppe *It is a ...* . Diese Wortgruppe wird mit Bildkarten von Nomen verbunden (z. B. *dog, tiger, elephant*). Später kann die Wortgruppe *It is a ...* durch die Wortgruppe *It's a ...* ersetzt werden (Abb. 17). Durch die Gegenüberstellung von *It is a ...* und *It's a ...* erkennen die Kinder, dass zwischen der Langform *is* und der Kurzform *'s* kein Bedeutungsunterschied besteht. Auf diese Weise können die Kinder zunehmend an den Gebrauch der Kurzform herangeführt werden. Durch das Schriftbild erkennen sie, dass es sich bei *'s* um eine Variante der Langform *is* handelt.

| It | is | a | Bildkarte |
| It | 's | a | Bildkarte |

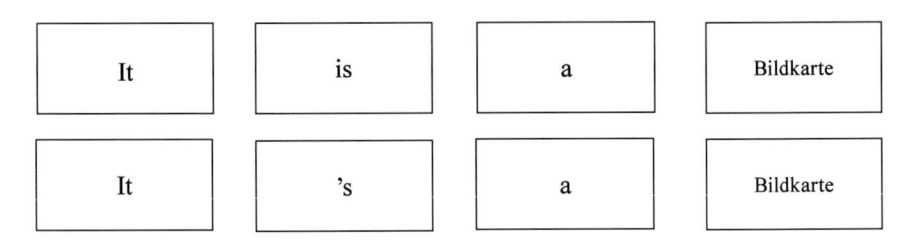

*Abb. 17: Gegenüberstellung der Formen **is** und **'s***

Literaturverzeichnis

Arnold, Roland & Hansen, Klaus (1998), *Englische Phonetik*. 11. Aufl. Leipzig u. a.: Langenscheidt Enzyklopädie.

Bartnitzky, Horst & Bunk, Hans-Dieter (2003), *Kunterbunt Fibel*. Leipzig: Ernst Klett.

Berent, Iris & Perfetti, Charles A. (1995), A Rose Is a REEZ: The Two Cycles Model of Phonology Assembly in Reading English. *Psychological Review* 102/1, 146–184.

Böttger, Heiner (Hrsg.) (2008), *Fortschritte im Frühen Fremdsprachenlernen: Ausgewählte Tagungsbeiträge - Nürnberg 2007*. München: Domino Verlag.

Bredenbröcker, Martina, Elsner, Daniela, Gleixner-Weyrauch, Stefanie, Gutwerk, Simone, Lugauer, Marion & Spangenberg, Anke (o.J.), *Sally 3: Lehrermaterialien*. München: Oldenbourg.

Diehr, Bärbel & Rymarczyk, Jutta (2008), Zur Basis von Lese- und Schreibversuchen in Klasse 1 und 2: ‚Ich weiß es, weil ich es so spreche'. *Grundschulmagazin Englisch* 1, 6–8.

Hellwig, Karlheinz (1995), *Fremdsprachen an Grundschulen als Spielen und Lernen: Dargestellt am Beispiel Englisch*. Ismaning: Hueber.

Horn, Wilhelm & Lehnert, Martin (1954), *Laut und Leben: Englische Lautgeschichte der neueren Zeit (1400–1950)*. Berlin: Deutscher Verlag der Wissenschaften.

Kramer, Johannes & Kowallik, Sabine (1994), *Einführung in die hebräische Schrift*. Hamburg: Buske.

Lass, Roger (1999), Phonology and Morphology. In: Hogg, Richard M. (Hrsg.) (1999), *The Cambridge History of the English Language: Vol. III: 1476–1776*. Cambridge: Cambridge University Press.

Marx, Peter (2007), *Lese- und Rechtschreiberwerb*. Paderborn: Schöningh.

Mindt, Dieter & Wagner, Gudrun (2009), *Innovativer Englischunterricht für die Klassen 1 und 2*. Braunschweig: Westermann.

Reichart-Wallrabenstein, Maike (2004), *Kinder und Schrift im Englischunterricht der Grundschule: Eine theorie- und empiriegeleitete Studie zur Diskussion um die Integration von Schriftlichkeit*. Teil 1. Berlin: dissertation.de.

Rymarczyk, Jutta (2008), Früher oder später? Zur Einführung des Schriftbildes in der Grundschule. In: Böttger, Heiner (Hrsg.) (2008), 170–182.

Schmid-Schönbein, Gisela (2006), Vom Lesen zum Schreiben: Der Weg zum kommunikativen Gebrauch des Englischen. *Primary English* 4, 3–5.

Schründer-Lenzen, Agi (2007), *Schriftspracherwerb und Unterricht: Bausteine professionellen Handlungswissens*. 2. Aufl. Wiesbaden: VS Verlag für Sozialwissenschaften.

Theis-Scholz, Margit, Thümmel, Ingeborg & Hasert, Jürgen (2003), *Die Luna-Fibel*. Leipzig: Ernst Klett Grundschulverlag.

Wendelmuth, Edmund & Stangner, Isolde (2000), *Meine Fibel*. Berlin: Volk und Wissen.

Authors

Prof. Dr. Petra Burmeister
Pädagogische Hochschule Weingarten
Abt. Englisch
Kirchplatz 2
88250 Weingarten
Germany
burmeister@ph-weingarten.de

Prof. Dr. Bärbel Diehr
Bergische Universität Wuppertal
Fachbereich A: Anglistik/Amerikanistik
Gaußstraße 20
42119 Wuppertal
Germany
diehr@uni-wuppertal.de

Leanne Fried
Edith Cowan University
Fogarty Learning Centre
Faculty of Education and Arts
270 Joondalup Drive
Joondalup WA 6027
Australia
l.fried@ecu.edu.au

Stefanie Frisch (M.A.)
Bergische Universität Wuppertal
Fachbereich A: Anglistik/Amerikanistik
Gaußstr. 20
42119 Wuppertal
Germany
frisch@uni-wuppertal.de

Dr. Deslea Konza
Associate Professor: Language and Literacy
Edith Cowan University
Fogarty Learning Centre
Faculty of Education and Arts
270 Joondalup Drive
Joondalup WA 6027
Australia
d.konza@ecu.edu.au

Maureen Michael
Edith Cowan University
Fogarty Learning Centre
Faculty of Education and Arts
270 Joondalup Drive
Joondalup WA 6027
Australia
m.michael@ecu.edu.au

Dr. Amparo Lázaro Ibarrola
Universidad Pública de Navarra
Departamento de Filología y Didáctica de la Lengua y la Literatura
Edificio Los Magnolios
Campus de Arrosadía
31006 Pamplona
Spain
amparo.lazaro@unavarra.es

Prof. em. Dr. Dieter Mindt
Freie Universität Berlin
Institut für englische Philologie
Habelschwerdter Allee 45
14195 Berlin
Germany
mindt@zedat.fu-berlin.de

Annika Musall (M.A.)
Pädagogische Hochschule Heidelberg
Institut für Fremdsprachen und ihre Didaktik
Abteilung Englisch

Im Neuenheimer Feld 561
69120 Heidelberg
Germany
musall@ph-heidelberg.de

Prof. Dr. phil. Thorsten Piske
Pädagogische Hochschule Schwäbisch Gmünd
Institut für Sprache und Literatur
Englisch
Oberbettringer Straße 200
73525 Schwäbisch Gmünd
Germany
thorsten.piske@ph-gmuend.de

Prof. Dr. Jutta Rymarczyk
Pädagogische Hochschule Heidelberg
Institut für Fremdsprachen und ihre Didaktik
Abteilung Englisch
Im Neuenheimer Feld 561
69120 Heidelberg
Germany
rymarczy@ph-heidelberg.de

Gudrun Wagner
Grundschule im Moselviertel
Brodenbacher Weg 31
13088 Berlin
Germany
gudrun.wagner22@t-online.de

Dr. Constanze Weth
Pädagogische Hochschule Freiburg
Institut für Fremdsprachen
Französisch
Kunzenweg 21
79117 Freiburg
Germany
constanze.weth@ph-freiburg.de

Inquiries in Language Learning
Forschungen zu Psycholinguistik und Fremdsprachendidaktik

Edited by / herausgegeben von Christiane Bongartz / Jutta Rymarczyk

Vol. / Bd. 1 Bärbel Diehr / Jutta Rymarczyk (eds. / Hrsg.): Researching Literacy in a Foreign Language among Primary School Learners. Forschung zum Schrifterwerb in der Fremdsprache bei Grundschülern. 2010.

www.peterlang.de